It's Time

Change Your Thinking, Change Your Life,
Change The World

EWAN MOCHRIE

ISBN: 9781795634861

For Beth, James and Joshua

CONTENTS

ACKNOWLEDGMENTS

Nothing is achieved alone

This book would not have been possible without the work of many other people who have influenced me by their example or their endeavours. There is a bibliography at the back with a full list of the sources I have used. I owe thanks to every one of the people listed therein. To quote philosopher Arthur Schopenhauer: *"Reading is the equivalent of thinking with someone else's head instead of one's own."* Without the huge benefit of being able to see the world from other people's perspective, my efforts would have amounted to nothing more than a thin gruel.

There are more people who have influenced me than those listed at the back too. I am reluctant to produce a list at the risk of omitting someone significant. Nevertheless, special thanks to: Tim Freke, The Monroe Institute, Tad and Adriana James, all my training delegates since teaching is a two-way learning process, Darryl Anka, and Bashar.

Supporters

"Being deeply loved by someone gives you strength, while loving someone deeply gives you courage." – Lao Tzu.

Special thanks to my family for loving me unconditionally. And to my business partner Joanne Binks, without whom I would still be working as an accountant. During the last year, Joanne has been assimilating a breast cancer diagnosis into her life and enduring the associated treatment. My heartfelt appreciation to her husband Nick, and her daughters Lauren and Jenna for being with her through this unwelcome challenge.

This book has been a long time in gestation and has taken over two years to write. Natalie Debrabandere listened to my first conceptions, read early drafts, made suggestions, provided constant encouragement, and corrected my English even though she is French. This book would not have happened without her support. Thanks Nat.

Thanks also to Steve and Jane Shergold, James Segal, and my brother for reading drafts and for providing helpful comments. And to my nephew Daniel Ashton for spending two days of his work experience writing up the bibliography.

Music

This book was written to the musical accompaniment of *Pink Floyd's* albums *Animals*, *Atom Heart Mother*, *The Dark Side Of The Moon*, *The Wall*, and *Wish You Were Here*.

Through this book I act as a mirror to reflect the light of others.

INTRODUCTION

"I feel it is the duty of one who goes his own way to inform society of what he finds on his voyage of discovery." - Carl Jung.

Reality Check

Very early on in my life, I got a sense that something was wrong with our understanding of existence. Much like how it feels when you get a stone stuck in your shoe. You can move your foot and the slight irritation will go away for a while, only to return some time later, letting you know it was still there.

I was brought up by Christian parents, relaxed Church of England types who would attend religious services on Sundays, but not people who would force their ideas upon their children. Instead, we were allowed to develop our own opinions, whilst at the same time being presented with Christianity as a sort of 'take-it-or-leave-it' option. At home, we never talked much about God, Jesus, or the *Bible*. We just went to church and Sunday school and were expected to 'pick-it-up' by a process of osmosis. At Sunday school, I listened to various *Bible* stories, and I must admit that even then, I thought that some of them were a little farfetched. I mean, an ark with two of every type of animal? How did Noah and his family stop the animals eating each other? I could hardly imagine rationalising with a lion about why she could not eat the zebra straight away, as we only had two of them... And the idea of Jonah being swallowed whole by a big fish, did not seem to match with the information about big fish I saw on the television either. But despite this early sense of disquiet, I kept going to church, which eventually led to confirmation classes when I was about eleven years old.

But the more I learned, the more my doubts about the literal truth of what I was being taught grew. Eating bread and drinking wine to represent the body and the blood of Jesus seemed to me to be a rather unusual and somewhat morbid ritual. I was introduced to the idea of the Holy Trinity; the Father, Son, and Holy Ghost. I had a father, a mother, a sister, and a brother; the feminine aspect definitely existed in my family. Yet in

Christianity women appeared to be peripheral and distant. On top of that, I had previously been told that ghosts did not exist either. Despite asking many people about the meaning of the Holy Trinity, that concept remained about as transparent as the very walls of the church itself. I was also taught that the basis of Christian doctrine was the idea of the Original Sin of Adam and Eve. Adam and Eve ate from the Tree of Knowledge in defiance of God's express instructions, and then, in the Christian tradition at least, we have all inherited their sin. That seemed a bit unfair. Whenever I did read bits of the *Bible*, I found it a little heavy-going too. It did not say much to me about my life, nor was the *Bible* easy to pull clear messages from. Though to be fair there were some parts I could understand, such as: *"Whatever you wish that others would do to you, do also to them."* Now, that makes a lot of sense. Looking back today, I guess my parents just wanted their children to grow up with a sense of community; with the identity, the values, and the assurance that their faith gave to them. But my young, curious, enquiring mind was not going to believe things that did not make sense.

Regular school was a better match for me. I learned history, geography, French, maths, and science. History was my absolute favourite, although I soon discovered I was actually best at maths and science. I still think that the history we learn at school leaves out the most interesting parts. I loved the ancient tales, and the epic conflicts from the past. The Romans, the Celts, the Greeks, the Egyptians, and the Persians. But at school, the curriculum was skewed towards the industrial revolution. This was a period of massive change, for sure. But I did not find the story of James Watt and his steam engine very gripping…

So, it was maths, physics, and chemistry for me. All subjects that are fairly logical. Well, most of the time, anyway. Newton's laws of motion seemed like a good rational platform to build on. But then science started to get just a little bit weird too. For example, Einstein gave us his theory of relativity, in which time and space were not two separate things, as they appeared to me, but one thing. This new understanding was rather clumsily described by simply putting the two words together and calling it space-time. Relativity is good for large scales, and when studying physics and chemistry at school, I also became familiar with smaller scales, studying the stuff that everything is made of. You, the chair you are sitting on, and everything else in the world is made of atoms. And if you drill down into what atoms are made of, what you find is they are actually made of almost nothing at all, being 99.99% empty space. That seriously did not match with my experience either. Yet, there was more! The things that atoms are made of, like electrons, protons, and neutrons, behave in the most bizarre ways you can imagine. This is the world described by quantum physics. In the Alice in Wonderland world of quantum physics, light and electrons behave as both a wave and a particle; one cannot say anything about sub-atomic particles unless one is observing them; and two particles can become 'entangled' together, somehow retaining a 'memory' of their past liaison. By that point, science had stopped describing my experience and was getting just about as weird as religion. Nevertheless, on balance, the path to follow in life seemed to be further into the logical and the rational rather than the mystical and philosophical.

Maybe it was my love of history, or maybe it was growing up through the late 1960s to early 1980s that motivated me to seek sponsorship from the army to go through university. The world seemed to be a dangerous place, locked in endless conflicts; Vietnam, the Middle East, the Falklands, and of course, the enduring Cold War. The army suggested that I study Civil Engineering. But just before I was about to go to Sheffield to start my studies, the army rejected my application. This came as a real shock, because when I was growing up, joining the army was the only thing I thought I was going to do with my life. Despite still feeling a little confused about this turn of events, I went to university and immersed myself in structures, concrete, surveying, fluid dynamics, and more maths. But I had never really wanted to be an engineer. And so, two years into my studies, at the age of 20, I sat down one night and asked myself the big question: *"What should I do with my life?"* The only idea that emerged into my awareness was to be a teacher. Now, this is an honourable profession, but my conscious mind was a little disappointed with that answer. After all, what could I teach? The only thing I thought I was any good at was maths. And to be honest, I did not think that teaching would earn me lots of money either. I can still remember this moment in my life very well. It was then that I made the conscious decision to learn the language of business. I would become an accountant, and put off till later what I was really going to do with my life. So, I got my Civil Engineering degree, became a Chartered Accountant, got married, and had children. I was normal. I had a mortgage, I paid my taxes, and I had a cat.

Awakening

One morning as I lay in bed, I can remember being gently roused from sleep by my five-year-old daughter talking quietly to her mother on the far side of the bed. As I became aware of them talking, it also dawned on me that I was gently falling too. I remember thinking, *"This is a bit odd"*. But I stayed with the experience, just to see what would happen. Many people describe falling sensations in dreams, and I had had them before, though this one did seem a little different; but in no way scary or unnatural. The thought even crossed my mind that I was going to be under the bed when I woke up, rather than in it. Then I started to become aware of physical sensations: my body against the bed, and the dryness of my mouth. I was very pleased to discover I was in bed, and not under it after all. This was not the first time that something strange had happened to me, and I had seen other people on television discussing psychic or paranormal-type experiences too; even people who claimed to have seen UFOs. But it is easy to dismiss all of these as fanciful, misguided, or in some way explainable by science. And when only the occasional odd thing happens to you, it is easy to dismiss that as well.

My grandmother died when I was at university. I knew she was ill and I had promised to call regularly to see how she was. This was in the 1980s, well before the days of mobile phones. The room that I stayed in was in a residential complex. There were pay phones, but they were far away from my room; down several flights of stairs, along multiple corridors, and through numerous fire doors. She died at my parents' house one afternoon. Later that evening, I was working in my room. I had meant to call earlier in the day, but I had forgotten. Suddenly, I was startled by the sound of a ringing phone. But, as I said, it was impossible for me to hear a telephone ringing from where I was. Immediately, this reminded me to phone home, and when I did, I found out that my grandmother had passed away. For me at the time, this was a weird experience. It really stood out, but in isolation it was easy to dismiss. Science, I was sure, would have an explanation;

like my unconscious mind reminding me to call and using the apparent sound of an external phone ringing to do that.

For Christmas one year, my brother bought me a book written by someone who used psychic abilities to spy for US military intelligence. The book was packed with strange things I had only vaguely heard of before, like remote viewing. This involves accessing information about distant places and events, using only your mind. The world described in that book seemed to have a physical aspect I was familiar with, and a non-physical one which I was not. And since all this was supposedly being used by the US military, I thought that surely some form of psychic ability must be real, and that 'they' were just not telling us the truth. Then again, maybe the guy who wrote the book was a little mad too… How could I know for sure? In any case, my curiosity was being roused from the unnatural slumber that my normal life had placed it in.

Not long after this, I bought a book by William Buhlman, who claimed to have transferred the centre of his consciousness outside of his physical body. This is called astral projection, otherwise known as having an out-of-body experience (OBE). Again, I think the content would have been easy to dismiss, and I could have allowed the routine of daily life to once more anaesthetise me from the reality of reality. However, in this book there were directions on how to train yourself to have an OBE. This, I had to try! Because obviously, if it did not work, I could forget about ideas of the non-physical and get back to important things like earning money, the children's education, a bigger house, and a faster car. The instructions were simple. As you went to sleep at night, you set your intention to go out of your body, and then you imagined, in as much detail as possible, exploring another part of your house or someone else's house that you knew well. So, that night, I had a go. I was not expecting anything to happen, but straight away I got a little bit more than I bargained for! As I lay in bed, imagining walking around the dining room, I heard a sort of click in my head, went out of consciousness, and then back into it again. At that point, I was aware of someone breathing behind me, which I now think was my physical body. My awareness, my consciousness if you will, was more heightened than it had ever been before; and my whole body was vibrating strongly, as if I had an electric current running through me. This lasted only for a few seconds and I remember thinking, *"This is so easy."* But then, I could feel myself getting tired, and I lost consciousness altogether. When I woke the next morning, I still needed to get ready for work, the children still needed breakfast, and the cat's litter tray still needed emptying. Reality remained as it had always been, but my understanding of reality had been turned upside down and inside out. Through my own personal experience, I was now able to consider some of the things other people had written about could be part of my reality too. The stone in my shoe now felt more like a boulder, so I decided it was now time to have a serious look at this problem.

It's Time

From that moment on, I made it my personal goal to understand the reality of reality, and to share that understanding with others. I put aside my accountant's pencil and took several trainings with personal development and spiritual teachers. Since 2006, I have been a trainer of Neuro Linguistic Programming (NLP), Time Line Therapy™, Coaching, and Hypnosis. During this time, I have worked with hundreds of people to help them to create more of what they want in their lives, and less of what they do not want. I have also continued to study the nature of reality. This book is about what I discovered. I have organised it into three parts.

Part I – Change Your Thinking

Over the course of our history we have created many ways to understand what reality is and how it works. We have labelled these as religion, philosophy, and science. In their own way, all these disciplines have accessed elements of the 'truth'. In *Part I*, I will explore relevant aspects of these various models and then present my case for the idea that time is an illusion, and physical reality is a projection of consciousness. *"So what?"*, you may well ask. You could have lived your life very well indeed so far without this knowledge, so what difference does it make?

It is true that you can achieve a lot in life without fully understanding how things work. For instance, do you really know how your car works? As you drive along, do you think about how the power is being converted in the engine from the liquid hydrocarbons stored in the fuel tank? How that energy turns into the rotational motion of the wheels, which are using friction to grip the road to propel you forward? Probably not. However, if you do know how things work, then you can have a more expansive and fulfilling experience. Racing car drivers have a much better understanding of how their cars function than I do about mine. If I want to become a high-performance driver, or simply to get the most out of my car, then I need to know more about how it works.

Part II – Change Your Life

As you begin to change your thinking, through this new conception presented in *Part I*, you start getting the sense that you are not actually who you previously thought you were. The idea of physical reality being a projection of consciousness can shift from being a reasoned philosophical or scientific argument to an experiential fact. In *Part II*, I explore Near-Death Experiences, Out-of-Body Experiences, and Reincarnation, so that you can start to appreciate your current earthly existence from a new perspective. As you do, you can ensure the choices you make in this life are aligned with who you really are. *Part II* contains guidance for living a physical life in a non-physical multiverse. It is focused on you and your life.

Part III – Change the World

Homo sapiens (wise man) first graced the planet about three-hundred-thousand years ago. This upright walking ape-man currently dominates the surface of the planet. Our technologies have brought comfort and prosperity to many, but not all. We have visited our own satellite, the moon; we have sent probes around and even beyond the solar system. Our achievements are immense. Our sciences allow us to look out deep into space, and deep down into the secrets of atoms. We can travel great distances with ease, we can cure many diseases, and we could feed, clothe, and house all seven billion of us if we chose to do so. We entertain ourselves with sports, the arts, and music. We have much to be proud of, and yet, we are at a crossroads in our development. We can continue to use the power of the grey spongey stuff between our ears to grow and evolve into more of who we are. Or we can use it to destroy ourselves and the planet, simply because we have failed to realise just how powerful we are. As a collective today, we do face a rather stark choice: do we continue to evolve, or do we go extinct?

For The Journey

We all have our own model of the world, which is our idea about the structure and the meaning of our reality, and what we think our capabilities are. These models have been formed by our life experiences, our values, beliefs, and memories. This book is fundamentally the introduction to a new model of the world. I am not presenting this to you as fact, but I am asking you to consider and explore it. I know that your consideration of it will be affected by how you perceive the world currently, based on your prior experiences, amongst other things. I am not invested in you believing it either. It works for me, and I think that it can work for you too, but that will be up to you, not me. Ultimately, the 'truth-out-there' can be considered to be like a sphere, because it matters not which direction you approach it from: it will always look the same.

This journey we are about to embark on is going to challenge what you understand about time, space, and consciousness. It can allow you to expand into more of who you are, because no matter who you think you are right now, you are actually much more than that. As you might imagine, a quest through time, space, and consciousness can be confusing and dangerous for the ill-prepared. So, as you get ready for this adventure, let me share a little of what you will need. Make sure that you bring with you the sword of a rational enquiring mind, to cut through unsound thinking; and like any lover, you will need to know exactly when to put that down and just go with the experience. You will also need bags of patience as you gather all the pieces of this puzzle. The puzzle that this book is addressing is not entirely new, but at this time, we are bringing more and more of the pieces into our awareness.

I believe the way for all of us to grow is to change how we understand existence itself, because through that we can connect more consciously with the limitless power that we already possess. But this change in thinking is nothing short of a revolution. Are you ready for that?

PART I

Change Your Thinking

1. I PERCEIVE THEREFORE I AM

"Today you are You, that is truer than true. There is NO ONE ALIVE who is Youer than You!" - Dr Seuss.

Everything Starts With Awareness

It was René Descartes, 17th century French philosopher and mathematician, who famously said: *"Cogito ergo sum"*, *"I think therefore I am"*. To you reading this now, that might sound rather obvious, but sometimes the obvious escapes us, and sometimes what we think is obvious is just not so. Descartes used a thought experiment to help him come to this conclusion. He imagined that even if he was just a brain stored in a vat, and was being deceived about his outside experiences by an evil demon, he could still think, and that proved he existed. Simply being able to read this sentence now means you must have perception; you are aware, you are conscious, and therefore you exist. But what are you conscious of? The words that you see, the letters on the page. These are, of course, just patches of light and dark arranged into shapes. Shapes which you were taught to understand as letters, which when grouped together in certain ways form words, which you learnt to ascribe meaning to. As you read the words, you see them, and you might sound them out in your thinking mind too. Even as your eyes trace over these words, you can probably also see other things in your field of vision; you can hear sounds around you; and you can feel your body, your clothes, and the sensations of your breathing.

We perceive the world through our senses, which are seeing, feeling, smelling, and tasting, plus our thinking sense, to make six senses. To broaden Descartes' idea slightly, you perceive therefore you are, and this perception is centred inside your head. You look out through your eyes, and you can see your hands and this book; you can feel the book too, so you know it exists. You can pick it up and put it down, so you know that you are not the book, it is separate from you. If you can see other people from where you are, then it is likely that they are moving independently of you through the space around you. Though you are reading this now, you are aware that there was a time before now when you were doing something else, and you expect there will be a time in the future when you will be doing something completely different too. So, if we just pause for a moment and reflect; there is you, other people, things, space, time, and you are aware. I hope this is not news to you. These are all familiar everyday experiences, all I am doing is pointing them out to you. The thing is, as we move through this book we are going to go deeper and deeper. I will point out other things to you, some of which may be familiar and some of which may not be. I am going to ask you to think about your experience and your life in new ways, because I believe many of the things in this world that we take for granted are not actually what we think they are.

But before we go any deeper, a little exploration of how we perceive, and what we are perceiving with is required. So we must start with a discussion about perception, brains, and consciousness.

Doors To Perception

As humans, we use our senses to take in information about the world around us. We then talk to ourselves about that in our heads. But we do not perceive the whole spectrum of information available to us through our senses. Infrared and ultraviolet light are invisible to humans, but snakes can sense (if not see) infrared. Many animals can see ultraviolet, including insects, fish, reptiles, and even some mammals. Humans do not hear in the full range of available sounds either. Dogs are well known for hearing in higher pitches, and elephants can hear in lower ones than us. So, even before we think about what we do with the information coming into our neurology, we have to recognise that we do not take in everything that is potentially 'out there' anyway. Therefore, human experience is different when compared to every other animal on the planet. Bats use echolocation to find their way around. This is much like radar. Due to this alone, without even considering what they like to eat, the world experienced by bats must be very different to our own.

As external information reaches the ninety billion neurons that make up human brains, it is processed into what we experience. But this experience is not simply a photograph, or a tape recording of what is being perceived. Incoming information is assessed within the context it is being experienced in, and in association with similar prior experiences. This is why when we see something in the distance, or something out of place, or incongruous, we may not initially recognise it for what it really is. But then, as we take a little longer to assess it, we perceive it 'properly'.

Though we do have to rely on our senses, it is understood they can be confused sometimes too. There are many famous optical illusions, like Escherian stairs in fig 1 (page 15), which start at the end and end at the beginning. The Necker Cube in fig 2 (page16), which appears to be either recessed into the page or extending out from the page at you, even though it is just a set of two-dimensional lines. And the old woman, young woman illusion in fig 3 (page16). Can you see both of these ladies? These are fun, and included here to highlight the fact that not everything is always easy to perceive the way it is.

Even putting illusions aside, our senses do not give us an objective view of the world in the way that we assume they do. This is because we are perceiving inside of our own neurology, which has been affected by our unique past experiences. I have worked with a number of people who have had phobias of dogs, cats, spiders, wasps, moths, buttons, heights, and even metal coat hangers, to name a few. By definition, these are irrational fears. Unusual phobias will cause amusement in people who do not suffer from them, and absolute terror in those who do. I worked with someone who was phobic of cotton wool. His young children found it amusing to chase him around the house with it. This man saw cotton wool as you would, but the meaning of the cotton wool was very different for him than for his children. Some people also have a degree of sensory impairment, commonly in vision or hearing, whilst others are colour-blind or have synaesthesia, where one way of perceiving can overlap with another – so that some people actually smell colour.

Words can carry different meanings for people too. The word love can mean a myriad of things, ranging from a look, a touch, a rose, security, connection, to a wet lick on the face from your dog. Love is a word that has many meanings, whereas other words like doorbell or credit card have fewer meanings. This is just part of the natural structure of thinking and language. We also have other ways to filter our experience. These include beliefs, things which are true for us, something like, *"I can easily learn and understand new ideas"*; or values, which are things which are important to us, like trust, results, or commitment. We also have innate preferences which filter our experiences too, such as being introverted or extroverted, or whether we prefer detailed information or big-picture ideas. And we have memories of past experiences which could carry emotional content for us too.

All of these things together, our past experiences, beliefs, values, innate preferences, our own interpretation of words, and the way that our neurology selects, interprets, and processes information contribute to the creation of our unique perception of reality. In fact, we can say that our experience is our brain's best guess at what is happening on the 'outside', and what that means to us. Or to put it another way, we do not perceive the world the way that it is, instead we perceive it the way that *we* are. What this means is *your* own perspective is totally unique and valid. No one else can or will have your unique perspective and experience.

The Brain and Consciousness

Our principal organ of perception is the brain, and it is this that sets us humans apart from other species. We have a larger brain, measured by brain-volume to body-weight ratio, than just about anything else on the planet. From an evolutionary perspective, the human lineage split from chimps and bonobos about six to eight million years ago. Our ancestors learned to walk upright four million years ago. But hominid brains did not start to grow that much until about three million years ago. At this time, brain size went from three-hundred-and-fifty grams in *Australopithecus* to double that, one-million years later, in *Homo erectus*. Today, our brains are about one-thousand-three-hundred grams, and we have evolved large frontal lobes which are associated with 'higher-level' thinking functions.

When at rest, the brain consumes a fifth of the oxygen and most of the glucose being carried in the blood. And although energy consumption is much reduced when we sleep, if we are dreaming, the brain works twice as hard as when we are awake. The idea that the two brain hemispheres do, to a degree, perform slightly different functions has entered our everyday lexicon. In the vast majority of right-handed people, the left hemisphere of the brain is associated with logic and verbal skills. Whilst the right hemisphere tends to perform in a more artistic manner, and is associated with intuition and pattern recognition. However, in everyday language we usually refer to the mind and not the brain, because we have a better sense of direct access to our mind, than we have to the underlying brain structures. Our mind is represented by our experience, our memories, thoughts, beliefs, and values.

We also use terms like the conscious and the unconscious mind. If you have awareness of something through your senses, then you are conscious. This consciousness can include self-reflecting, reporting of mental states, and the sense of 'I' as opposed to 'other'. Basically, the unconscious mind, or if you prefer unconscious processing, accounts for everything outside of your awareness. In fact, most of our brain activity is unconscious; much of what we do is instinctive, habitual, automatic, and already built into our makeup. What we think of as our conscious choices are influenced by many things outside of our conscious awareness, something that all advertising executives know to be true.

As I write this, I am conscious, and I assume that you are too, because you are reading these words. We naturally impute consciousness upon others because they look, sound, feel, act, and think as we do. It would be unnatural to assume I was conscious but that no one else was. We also impute consciousness onto animals by observing their behaviour and by putting them through cognitive tests. Most dog and cat owners would assume their pets are independently conscious, and few people would consider dolphins and chimps not to be conscious either. But no sane person would impute consciousness onto a rock, because it does not seem to display anything that we would consider to be part of our conscious experience. It is even difficult to imagine some vertebrates, and especially invertebrates as being conscious, as their general morphology, neurology, and behaviour appear to be so alien to our own humanness. I cannot imagine a snail thinking about what it is about to do next, and even less so with plants and trees. It seems probable that there is a gradation of conscious experience, from our own down through the animal kingdom, but even just understanding our own consciousness seems hard enough.

The Hard Problem

Australian philosopher David Chalmers opens his book *The Conscious Mind - In Search of a Fundamental Theory*, with a quote from *The International Dictionary of Psychology* by Stuart Sutherland: *"Consciousness is a fascinating but elusive phenomenon: it is impossible to specify what it is, what it does, or why it evolved. Nothing worth reading has been written on it."* According to Chalmers, there are easy problems of consciousness which science can address. Things like how we focus our attention from moment to moment; our ability to display conscious control over our behaviour; the feel of emotional or mental states that we can report; the ability to discriminate, categorise, and react to sensory stimulus in our environment; and the determination of wakefulness and sleep. The principle point that Chalmers is making is that regardless of how well we have solved, or are solving these 'easy' problems of consciousness, what remains is the as yet unresolved 'hard' problem of consciousness. To quote Chalmers, *"Why is all of this processing accompanied by an experience of an inner life?"* Or why are we conscious at all? And what actually is consciousness anyway?

The current mainstream scientific working hypothesis is that consciousness is related to the nervous system and the brain in particular. And that consciousness arose through evolutionary processes. This is a reasonable working assumption, which has brought a wealth of understanding about how the brain functions.

If consciousness is produced in the brain through evolution, then this must have happened because being conscious was useful in some way and gave our ancestors an edge. From this evolutionary perspective, consciousness must have evolved a long time ago, or perhaps evolved independently several times. Some birds do seem to display elements of human-like consciousness. Magpies can pass the mirror test for visual self-recognition, a test that a human infant will fail prior to being about eighteen months old. Western scrub jays, who are part of the same crow family as magpies, have been shown to plan ahead. This was something previously considered the domain of humans, chimps, and dolphins. Jays have been observed watching other birds cache their food before stealing it for themselves. Then, just before the jay caches its own food, it checks to see if it is being watched. They have also been observed calling for other jays to come so that they can screech together, for up to half an hour, over the body of a dead jay. These things together seem to suggest that jays have a sense of self and others. Much of the mammalian brain is given over to the processing of information about the perceptual world. If you cannot perceive friend from foe, or tasty berries from poisonous ones, then evolution will treat you rather harshly. So, if evolution did cause consciousness to arise, at what point during evolution did that occur? When the nervous system first started to evolve, about five-hundred-million years ago? Or does consciousness require a certain 'critical mass' of nerve connections to arise? If so, where is the cut-off point? And what was the specific purpose for the evolution of consciousness?

Another hypothesis is that being conscious is simply a free added bonus of having a brain in the first place. This hypothesis classifies consciousness as an epiphenomenon, like the whistle on a steam engine. It is not the primary function of a steam engine, but you get the whistle for free just because you have the steam. This conception suggests that the consciousness we love so much, is just a handy side effect of having a brain for perception and survival in the first place.

Today, it is still fair to say that science has not yet provided an adequate explanation of what consciousness is or how it arises. However, mapping electrical brain activity has been a fruitful area for neuroscientific research. This work has produced ideas about consciousness being correlated to the level and complexity of brain activity. It has been found that greater complexity and interconnectivity of the electrical firing across the brain is associated with higher states of consciousness. Such as being consciously aware and active, as opposed to being in a coma. These electrical patterns of activity show that many different parts of the brain connect together and interact. No one part of the brain seems to be essential. Of course, some are more important than others – the loss of the brainstem inevitably leads to death. And when parts of the brain are unable to communicate effectively with each other, consciousness breaks down. But does this work explain what consciousness is, how the electrical brain activity creates consciousness, or what a conscious experience is like? No, probably not; or not yet, anyway. This work is important because it helps us to understand various neurological conditions, and may even contribute to the development of artificial intelligence. However, is what we are seeing here simply the simultaneous appearance of two non-causal events? The presence of consciousness, and at the same time, the presence of complex, integrated communication between different brain structures? Does consciousness cause complex electrical activity? Does complex electrical activity cause consciousness? Or does something else altogether cause both? Perhaps electrical brain activity is simply the passing footprints of consciousness as it walks through the wet sand of the brain.

What is it Like to Be You

What experience is like is also something that consciousness scientists like to debate. Is my experience of blue, red, or purple the same as yours? And what makes your experience of red feel the way it does? To stimulate debate, thought experiments have been proposed. Here are two to get your neurons firing. The first one concerns modern philosopher Frank Jackson's idea of Mary: she is brought up in a world where she can only experience black and white, and has no experience of colours at all. In this monochromatic world, she studies to become the world's leading expert in the brain structures that produce colour vision. Eventually, she knows everything about how colour experience is created. At this point, she is then allowed out of her black and white world into one of colour. The question is, does she learn anything new when she then experiences the colour red for the first time?

The second of these thought experiments is from another modern philosopher, Thomas Nagle: imagine you are a neuroscientist who has studied the neurological structure of a bat to such an extent that you know everything there is to know about bat neurology, and how bats create their experience. Would your knowledge then mean that you could accurately imagine what it is actually like to be a bat?

What these thought experiments are asking you to consider is whether you believe that science can answer the question of consciousness from studying brains, or is there something about experience that is individual, unique, and not reducible by scientific enquiry? In the final analysis, is 'what-it-is-like-to-be-you' forever beyond the reach of science?

How Do You Know?

What the thought experiments above also highlight is the philosophical question about how we know what we know. Do we use reason (our own thinking sense), do we rely on our experience (all our other senses), or should we use both?

We use our experiences of the world and our reasoning about it to create ideas about what is going on in our reality, and how that reality works. We all have our own unconscious hierarchy, which attributes significance and authority to different sources of information. Be that friends, family, TV, the internet, government, books, or films. For most people, the highest authority is usually reserved for direct personal experience. The example I like to use to illustrate this is the assassination of John F. Kennedy on 22nd November 1963. You will doubtless have an opinion about what happened on that day in Dallas, but what is your opinion based on? I have an opinion, but I was not there. I was not even born then. My opinion is based on reading Jim Marrs' book *Crossfire*; listening to half a dozen radio interviews; watching the Zapruder film (the video of the assassination filmed by a bystander), the Oliver Stone movie starring Kevin Costner, at least four or five documentaries; and discussing the event with family and friends. All this external information has also been filtered by my pre-existing beliefs about what I consider to be possible or not. Such as, do I believe governments lie to their electorate? But I am not a doctor or a ballistics expert. I have not interviewed any witnesses. I have only read one book about the assassination out of the hundreds available on the market, and I have not read any of the eight-hundred-and-eighty-nine-page official US Government Warren commission report, nor its twenty-six volumes of supporting documents. None of this stops me from forming an opinion, and neither should it. But we all need to be honest with ourselves about what our opinions and beliefs are based on.

This idea also includes people who have opinions very different to our own. What is their opinion based on, and what makes it any more or less valid than ours? After all, someone who disagrees with you is really doing you a favour, by giving you the opportunity to assess your own views against the background of a contrasting one. Accept that people may have views and opinions that are perhaps different to yours. Choose to see the value in others, even if it is just as an example of how not to be. Remember this when considering information from people who claim to have had experiences that are strongly at variance with your own experiences or beliefs. These include religious, spiritual, and psychic experiences, or even people who claim to have encountered extra-terrestrial craft or entities. Just because we may not have had these experiences, or because they do not conform to our model of the world, does not mean that those people are wrong and that we are right. Explore and consider the evidence, and be open-minded enough to expand your horizons… But of course, not so open-minded that your brain falls out.

Also, notice that both experience and reason occur inside your mind. Your whole sensory experience is happening in your mind, and your reasoning is, by definition, in your mind too. But if everything is in your mind, then the idea of there being an objective 'truth-out-there' to study starts to become a little shaky. Nevertheless, this apparent lack of objectivity should not prevent us from moving our understanding forward either.

Paradigm Shift

Ideas about what we know and how we know what we know have been explored by humans ever since we had time enough to think about them. Today, we tend to generalised these into the conceptions of religion, philosophy, and science. We will turn to these three subjects in the next two chapters. What then follows in *Chapter 4* is a new conception of reality, a new model of the world.

It was science historian Thomas Kuhn who popularised the now overused term 'paradigm shift' with his book *The Structure of Scientific Revolutions*. Although Kuhn was only talking about science, what he says also resonates with other established models of the world from philosophy and religion. Generally speaking, at any given time, there exists a paradigm which is broadly accepted by the scientific community. Normal science, according to Kuhn, is work conducted within this generally accepted paradigm. He adds that most of what is undertaken in science is normal science, the fleshing out of details within an already accepted model. He does not say that this is a problem as such, but reflects that discoveries and change in science tend to be rather less linear in reality, than the way they are presented in science books and in schools. When a new paradigm eventually emerges, that process only happens against the contrasting background of an existing paradigm. Anomalies tend to arise from the normal science being conducted within the existing paradigm. That does not mean that a new model becomes accepted immediately of course, there is invariably resistance. After all, scientists are humans too, and many may well have spent years working within, and even teaching a particular paradigm. To admit it is in some way wrong can be seen as a failure too big for some of them to accept. This creates what is known in psychology as cognitive dissonance. All of us humans, no matter how well educated, can behave in irrational ways when we are presented with information that contradicts our existing beliefs or values. The more highly-prized the belief, or the more we have invested in it, the greater the dissonance will be. This 'investment' could be by making public pronouncements about our beliefs, because we draw a sense of personal identity from them, or even the amount of money we have spent demonstrating our beliefs. One behavioural approach commonly adopted when faced with cognitive dissonance is to simply ignore information that conflicts with our existing beliefs. And, let us not be coy, all human belief systems are guilty of this. There is an old joke which illustrates this point –

A man was travelling through Vienna when he came across a gentleman sat outside a café, drinking coffee. The man also had a banana sticking out of each ear. The traveller stopped and said to the man outside the café, "You have bananas stuck in your ears." *The man just looked at the traveller, shrugged his shoulders, and carried on drinking his coffee. The traveller had another go, but a little louder this time.* "You have bananas stuck in your ears!" *Again, the other man just shrugged and carried on drinking his coffee. Becoming a little exasperated, the traveller tried once more, but even louder.* "YOU HAVE BANANAS STUCK IN YOUR EARS!" *The man sitting outside the café looked at the traveller and said,* "I AM SORRY, I CANNOT HEAR WHAT YOU ARE SAYING. I HAVE BANANAS STUCK IN MY EARS."

Sometimes, it is the very things we believe that stop us from seeing that it is what we believe that is the problem. And shouting at each other seldom moves us forward. Therefore, all I ask of you as you progress through this book is to be open to the idea that there is something more for you to learn here.

To quote Kuhn –

"In science...novelty emerges only with difficulty, manifested by resistance, against a background provided by expectation...even resistance to change has a use...ensuring the paradigm will not be too easily surrendered..."

Or to quote German physicist Max Planck, who was at the leading edge of the quantum physics revolution at the start of the 20th century –

"A scientific truth does not triumph by convincing its opponents and making them see the light, but rather because its opponents eventually die and a new generation grows up that is familiar with it."

Science, it would seem, progresses funeral by funeral. And although new models are never accepted by some, for others the realisation can be sudden. What was seen before as the old woman (in fig 3) is now seen as the young woman instead, and people are left scratching their heads as to why they did not see it before. As I said, this does apply to religion and philosophy too; sometimes the light of new ideas can only be considered against the background of ideas which already exist. It is much easier to see a single candle in the dark than it is to see the same candle set within a thousand other candles. The sudden, paradigm-shattering change of view is much more accepted in a religious sense – it is that 'road-to-Damascusmoment'. But whether it happens in science, religion, or philosophy, we are talking about the same thing: a change in our model of the world.

Summary

You perceive; therefore, you exist. But you do not perceive the world as it is, you perceive the world the way you are. You and your perspective are individual and unique.

The current mainstream scientific model is that consciousness is produced by and in the brain. But is it? The thing about consciousness is that when you are conscious you are always aware of something, and this something is your experience. If you were conscious but aware of absolutely nothing, how would you know that you were conscious at all? Even if you said to yourself, *"I'm aware of nothing"*, then you would no longer be aware of nothing; you would then be aware of yourself saying, *"I'm aware of nothing"*. If you did experience something and yet had no awareness of that, then how would you know that you were having an experience at all? Awareness and experience go together, *always*.

Science, religion, and philosophy are really all arguing about the same things: how do we know what we know, what is it that we think we do know, and what causes what to happen? All these questions are important, and the last one particularly so. This is because if you know what causes what to happen, you know what the control levers in your life are. You can then create a sense of how to conduct your life, so that you can have more of what you want and less of what you do not want.

Before we consider changing our thinking, we need to know what the current model of the world is. To do so we must enter the temples of religion and the academies of philosophy in *Chapter 2*, before we don a white coat and enter the laboratories of modern science in *Chapter 3*.

What have we covered:

- You exist.
- You do not perceive the world as it is, you perceive it the way that you are.
- Your experience is unique to you; and you are unique.
- Awareness is always present with experience, and experience is not accessible without awareness.

What remains to be explored:

- Does mind create matter or does matter create mind?
- Why do you exist?
- What does your experience mean?

Fig 1

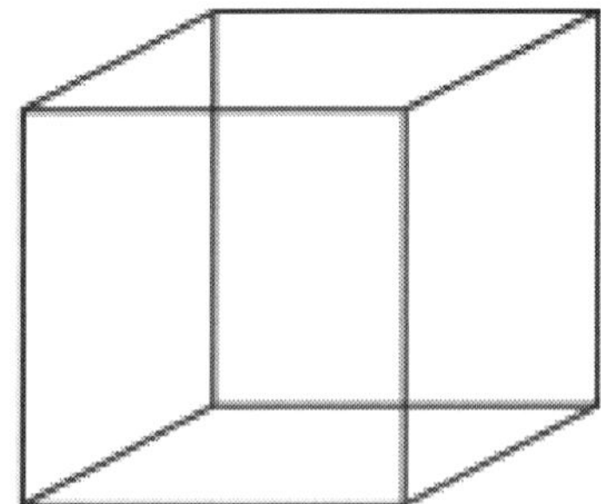

Fig 2

Fig 3

2. MAPPA MUNDI

"The map is not the territory it represents, but if correct, it has a similar structure to the territory, which accounts for its usefulness." –
Alfred Korzybski.

In Hereford Cathedral, England, there is a *Mappa Mundi*, Cloth of the World. It dates back to the thirteenth century, it is circular, about fifty-two inches in diameter, and Jerusalem is at its centre. What lies east of Jerusalem is positioned at the top. This would be north in our concept of map making. One would struggle to use this map as a navigational aide, but that was not its purpose. It was a teaching tool. As well as giving a sense of geography, it aimed to depict the perfection of God's creation. It is not the oldest map in the world either. There are examples of maps from Roman and Greek times, as well as from early China, and some which go way back into prehistory. It has even been suggested that the earliest maps of all are painted on cave walls in Lascaux, France; these are over fifteen thousand years old. They do not even represent the earth, they are instead maps of the stars.

We create mental maps of the way the world is so that we can navigate our way through life. We make generalisations about these maps, and label them as religion, philosophy, or science.

Religion

For millions of people throughout the world, their religious belief system is very important to them. It provides a sense of meaning and purpose to their life on Earth. The rhythm of the year is marked out by festivals and celebrations. One's religion has the authority to provide moral guidance, to tell you what is right or wrong, good or bad. It gives instructions about what to think, and how to act in certain situations. Particularly about sex and sexuality, as well as rules about what women can and cannot do. There are also rules about what to eat and how to kill what you eat. All religious belief systems share the idea of the supernatural being real, be that through deities, abilities, or places existing somewhere beyond the reach of our five senses. And all of them include the idea of 'revelations' being presented to prophets, usually whilst they are up a mountain or under a tree. These revelations come either directly from a deity or simply as a profound personal realisation. The prophets then teach the information that they received. At some point the teachings are written down by a close circle of followers. This happens either whilst the prophet is still alive or just after they have died. Eventually, the teaching of the prophet's ideas coalesces around a priesthood, who then perpetuate them. However, this is seldom in one indisputable complete form. Varying interpretations of the prophet's ideas exist, and over time there are splits and schisms within the religion.

One of the benefits that a religion provides is a sense of identity. This allows you into the club with thousands, even millions of others who believe and act the same as you. Another advantage is the security of knowing that death is not something to be feared. As a follower of a religion you imagine that you are part of something larger, and ultimately mysterious. Religious belief and devotion are incredibly strong and powerful in some people. This moves them to express the depth of their conviction and connection with God through beautiful art, poetry, and song. The sincerity and passion of devotees is not to be doubted. And at the same time, throughout human history, ideological wars have left a red stain on the vestments of religion. Although one could argue that many of these wars were really rooted in power politics, and religion was only used as an easy way to motivate people to action. Today, religion still exercises significant power by its ability to influence its followers, and because of its integration within the state, even in the more secular Western world.

Western Religions

The principal Western religions are Judaism, Christianity, and Islam. All these monotheistic religions share the idea of the one God who created the world. From time to time He likes to get involved in people's lives. This is either by sharing information with them or by rewarding good and punishing bad behaviour. Like most religions today, Western monotheistic religions are book-based. The holy books are considered to be the word of God and are inalienable and unalterable.

Judaism

Judaism is an early monotheistic religion, and within it there is the idea that the Jewish people are a special people, chosen by God. Its history spans three thousand years, although its practice during that time has evolved and changed. Prophets like Abraham, Jacob, Moses, and Samuel are important in Judaism. In antiquity, the Kingdoms of Israel and Judah (largely today's State of Israel) were stuck between many powerful neighbours. As a result, they were often either vassal states of bigger powers, or were totally conquered. In 586 BCE, many of the Jewish people began over sixty years of exile in Babylon, after being defeated by King Nebuchadnezzar. It was during this time that much of the *Torah* (*Genesis, Exodus, Leviticus, Numbers, and Deuteronomy*) was first written down. Historically, the Temple in Jerusalem was the focus of religious practice. But in a revolt against Roman rule in the first century of the common era this was destroyed and the Jewish state dissolved.

Christianity

Christianity emerged out of Judaism with Jesus. Christians believe Jesus was born of a virgin, was the Son of God, died on the cross, and was physically resurrected before ascending to heaven. Various teachings of this new testament were then written down, and a new religion emerged over the next few centuries. Initially this was through the efforts of Paul, who lived just after Jesus. Christianity was adopted by Roman Emperor Constantine in 313 CE, and became established as the religion of Rome ten years later. The books that make up the New Testament were decided at the Council of Nicaea in 325 CE, presided over by Constantine. The Jesus that we know today only comes from these approved Gospels. But as we will see shortly, these are not the only representation of his teachings. There are also some awkward problems within the canonical New Testament itself. Mathew's and Luke's gospels contain two very different genealogies for Jesus' lineage. They are attempting to establish his familial connection through his father, Joseph, to the historic Jewish King, David. However, they are totally different. They even disagree on who was Jesus' grandfather! But of course, Joseph was not even Jesus' father anyway. The holy spirit was responsible for that conception.

Islam

Islam, like Judaism and Christianity, is an Abrahamic religion. Muslims do revere some Judaic and Christian prophets such as Abraham, Moses, and Jesus. But they regard the work of their prophet, Muhammad, to supersede and correct the work of these earlier prophets. The *Quran*, which literally means 'recitation', was written down between 610 and 632 CE. It is considered the literal word of God, transmitted by Him through the archangel Gabriel, spoken by Muhammad, and then written down by Muhammad's followers. The *Quran* contains one-hundred-and-fourteen chapters and is organised in accordance with chapter length. The shortest chapters are at the end and the longest at the beginning. Not surprisingly, the *Quran* is then best understood by reference to Hadiths, traditions that were supposed to have been approved of or followed by Muhammad. Most of the rules of Sharia Law come from Hadiths, not the *Quran*. After Muhammad's death, Islam was spread by trade and by the sword, through North Africa and east into Persia (modern Iran).

Eastern Religions

The easiest way to divide the East and the West is the eastern border of Iran. The dominant civilisations of the East arose in India and China. In one way or another Indian ideas about religion and philosophy have influenced the whole of the East. The roots of these ideas stretch way back into prehistory, but today we refer to them in the West as Hinduism.

Hinduism

Hinduism is the world's third largest religion and it has no founder as such. It is also probably the oldest religion still practiced today. The holy texts of Hinduism are the *Vedas*, written in Sanskrit. These include the *Upanishads* and the *Mahabharata*, which itself includes the *Bhagavad Gita*. The *Bhagavad Gita* is largely a discourse between prince Arjuna and his charioteer Krishna, who is an incarnation of the god Vishnu. Krishna provides teachings and guidance. The traditional term for the Hindu religion is *Sanatana Dharma*, Sanskrit for 'the eternal law'. Karma is a key concept in Hinduism; it means action, work, or deed. Basically, good deeds lead to good karma, and bad deeds lead to bad karma. Karma is linked to the idea of reincarnation (*Samsara*), which is also central to Hinduism. This is a cycle of aimless wandering and drifting that can be terminated by attaining *Moksha*, which is liberation from this cycle of rebirth. Hinduism is polytheistic, because it encompasses many gods. Prime among them is Brahman, who is the creator god.

Buddhism

Buddhism was born in India against the backdrop of Hindu beliefs and then travelled east into China and Japan. Buddhism was started by Siddhartha Gautama in the 5th century BCE. After years of contemplation, Gautama attained a sense of enlightenment. Henceforth, he was called the Buddha, or the 'awakened one'. Buddhism shares many of the facets of Hinduism, such as karma and reincarnation. The Buddha rejected the idea of a supreme God altogether, and considered life on Earth to be suffering. The primary aim of Buddhism is liberation from this suffering. This is done by cultivating a sense of non-attachment to earthly things, be that pain or pleasure. By doing so, one can achieve Nirvana, similar to the

Hindu idea of *Moksha*. Zen is Buddhism under the influence of Daoism.

Daoism

Daoism, or if you prefer Taoism, means 'The Way'. It is more of a Chinese philosophical approach than a religion as such. The most revered person in Daoism is Lao-Tzu, which literally means 'Old Master'. He is credited with being the author of the *Daode Jing*, which means *The Scripture of the Way and its Power*. The Way is not something encoded within human society or thinking. Rather, the Way is intrinsic to the natural world, which includes us. One can follow the Way by practicing the paradoxical art of *Wu-wei* (action without intent). The essence of which is to be in balance with the natural way that things happen. Paddle with the flow of the river, rather than against the current. Daoism also teaches that there can be no black without white, no good without bad. You can only know what black is because you know what white is. So, there must be both, and to make a trinity, there is also balancing on the razor's edge between them.

Melting Pot

As you can see, we have an abundance of different (but in some ways related) religious ideas on the planet. If you wanted to choose one to follow, it would almost take you a lifetime to read all the sacred texts before you could make your choice. In fact, you cannot actually choose some of them. In *The God Book*, Michael Arnheim draws a distinction between creed and communal religions. Christianity and Islam are creed religions, because they are based on a set of beliefs. Judaism and Hinduism are communal religions, because you inherit them by dint of your ethnicity. Arnheim makes the point that all early religions were in effect communal religions, which is probably why the Greeks did not even have a name for 'religion'. But today, the creed religions act like communal ones, in that we tend to inherit our religious persuasion from our parents.

These days, we do like to categorise things and to have nice tidy labels for them. But in the world of religious thought, there has been plenty of cross pollination of ideas. It seems likely that ancient Persian Zoroastrian and Hindu Vedic texts were both influenced by a common source. And that Zoroastrian and Egyptian beliefs both influenced Judaism. Today, there is only a small enclave of followers of the prophet Zoroaster. This is because his ideas were almost wiped out by the conquering armies of Islam, as they marched through Persia. Zoroastrianism pre-dates Judaism, and it too was monotheistic. Its God was Ahura-Mazda, Lord of Wisdom. Lord was masculine and Wisdom feminine. In Zoroastrianism, people are considered to have freewill, and they are individually responsible for their actions. But there was a continuous battle between good and evil happening within their minds.

No one follows the Egyptian belief system today. Nevertheless, there are striking similarities between the biblical Ten Commandments and Egyptian beliefs. A newly dead soul had to utter forty-two statements as their heart was weighed against a feather in front of Ma'at, the Egyptian goddess of truth, balance, and judgement. Statements like, *"I have not committed sin"*, *"I have not stolen"*, *"I have not committed adultery"*. There are also similarities between the flood story in *The Epic of Gilgamesh* and the story of Noah in *Genesis*. In fact, they are so similar it is difficult not to see the *Genesis* account as a direct copy. *The Epic of Gilgamesh* is Sumerian (modern Iraq) and dates from about 1,800 BCE. It was written in cuneiform script, wedge-shaped indentations made on clay tablets. Which is probably why it has survived for so long.

Many Greek scholars, such as Pythagoras, stated that they had been instructed by priests in Egypt. Rome used much of the Greek pantheon for its own gods. Also popular in the Roman military from the first to the fourth centuries CE were the Mysteries of Mithras. This included seven stages of initiation, a communal meal, and a form of baptism. In fact, the similarities between Jesus and Mithra made the adoption of Christianity easier for many Romans. Mithra was originally a Persian dying and resurrecting sun god. There are also references to 'Mitra' in the Hindu Vedas, so it is likely that they are talking about the same deity or concept.

What survives in all religions today, from all parts of the world, is incomplete and steeped in the cultural clothing from whence it came. Some of the information is clearly anachronistic, and some of it is conveyed metaphorically. Much of the problem with old religious written records is that you can find some things that you like, and some that you do not.

Mysteries and Secrets

Interwoven within religion there has been a tradition, particularly in the West, of running a parallel secret, oral, esoteric (hidden), set of teachings. As well as the written, exoteric (open to all) teachings. These secrets were usually only taught to selected individuals. Disclosure of the teachings and practices was punishable by death. If the content of secret knowledge was communicated, it was obscured from the uninitiated through symbols. This way any message would only be understood by those who were 'in-the-know'. As you might imagine, we are left a little bereft of direct and easily accessible information about the teachings of these secret 'mystery' schools. They were officially closed in the late third century CE, by Roman Emperor Theodosius. Prior to that, there were the Eleusinian Mysteries in Greece, the Mysteries of Mithras, which I mentioned above, and from Egypt, the Mysteries of Isis and Osiris. According to Jonathan Black, author of *The Secret History of the World*, some of their practices included dance, drama, sensory deprivation, hallucinogens, and altered states of consciousness. Black said,

"Almost by definition the operations of secret societies leave scant traces. If they are successful, they leave little to go on. Yet the claims are very grand indeed: that these societies are representatives of an ancient and universal philosophy, that this is a coherent, consistent philosophy that explains the universe more adequately than any other, and that many if not most of the great men and women of history are guided by it."

He goes on to cite historical figures such as Plato, Alexander the Great, Cicero, Newton, Washington, and Gandhi, who, if not fully initiated, knew at least some of these secret teachings. I have not been initiated into any of the organisations that today lay claim to secret knowledge. Nevertheless, my instinct is that what I will present through the remainder of this book is aligned with their teachings.

The closest that one can get to these secret teachings, from a purely religious sense, is through the more mystical interpretations of religion rather than the literal versions. In Judaism, Kabbalah is an example of a secret oral tradition. The Zohar, first presented in Spain in the 13th century CE, is a written version of Kabbalah. Even early Christianity contained a mystical branch with esoteric teachings. They were known as the Gnostics, from the Greek word for 'knowing'. But it was the Roman Catholic version of Christianity that emerged as the 'winner', during the first few centuries following the death of Jesus. The Gnostics lost, and the early Church then attempted (almost successfully), to eradicate their ideas. Some of these ideas did persist and some have come to light only more recently. In 1945, in Nag Hammadi, Egypt, a collection of buried Gnostic Gospels was unearthed. To give you a sense of the message of this competing branch of Christianity, here is a quote from Elaine Pagels' book *The Gnostic Gospels*,

"Orthodox Jews and Christians insist that a chasm separates humanity from its creator: God is wholly other. But some of the Gnostics who wrote these gospels contradict this: self-knowledge is knowledge of God; the self and the divine are identical... The 'living Jesus' of these texts speaks of illusion and enlightenment, not of sin and repentance like the Jesus of the New Testament."

In the Islamic tradition, esoteric mystical interpretation and practices are known as Sufism. From the outside, people like to imagine Sufism as a separate branch of Islam, like Sunni and Shia. But Sufism is an inward-facing philosophy that is supported by the outward-facing exoteric practices known as Sharia. Some scholars attribute the rise of a more literal, and at times radical interpretation of Islam to the decline of Sufism. Probably the most famous Sufi scholar was the 13th century Sunni mystic Rumi.

All these mystical interpretations of the Western monotheistic religions have a great deal more in common with each other, and with Hindu beliefs, than they do with the more literal, rule-based, dogmatic, mainstream interpretations of their own religion.

Following a religious belief system can mean that you do not have to think for yourself, not too much anyway – the book interpreted by the priests will do that for you. Thinking for yourself rather than having a prophet or deity doing it for you is what philosophy is.

Philosophical Roots

Philosophy is man's own attempts to understand the natural world and to guide people's actions. In the ancient world, philosophy was what passed for science, and it is in effect the midwife of modern science. It does address some of the same questions that religion claims to answer, concerning God and life after death. In the East, philosophy is more closely intertwined with religious thought than in the West.

The Greeks

Early Western philosophy was dominated by the Greeks. There were many Greek philosophers, but the three stars of the show were Socrates, his student Plato, and Plato's student Aristotle. As with religion, it is not easy to say who thought what first, nor is it really important. All we can do is work with what has survived. Plato acknowledges the influence of Parmenides, who is thought to have been forty years Socrates' senior. Parmenides is credited with stating that everything was one single thing, eternal and unchanging. Because nothing cannot become something, and something cannot become nothing. We know of Socrates principally through the writings of Plato, as nothing written by Socrates has survived. What has is the idea of the Socratic Method, which consists of breaking down a problem by a series of questions. This is considered the basis of the scientific method. It is thought that all Plato's work has survived intact since his death two-thousand-four-hundred years ago. Most of his books are written as dialogues between Socrates and other Athenians. Plato was exploring themes by using the discussions of others rather than saying definitively what he thought. Nevertheless, mathematician and philosopher Alfred North Whitehead said, *"The safest general characterisation of the European philosophical tradition is that it consists of a series of footnotes to Plato."*

Aristotle's work provided a substantial intellectual framework, upon which Islamic scholars would first build. Later, the scientists of the late Middle Ages in the Christian world would begin to construct modern science from these earlier efforts. Aristotle is credited with making contributions to logic, geology, linguistics, politics, and zoology, just to name a few. One of his works was called *Physics*, from the ancient Greek word for 'nature', which, although it does not bear much resemblance to modern physics, is still where the term comes from. He was also the tutor of Alexander the Great.

Some of the themes that Plato explored were about the organisation of society, the acquisition of knowledge, and questions of life after death. Plato's book *The Republic* finishes with a story about a near-death experience and reincarnation.

The Cave

Also included in The Republic is the Allegory of the Cave. As it was originally written as a dialogue, I have paraphrased it below:

"Imagine people who have been imprisoned since childhood in a cave, where they are chained and unable even to turn their heads away from the opposite wall of the cave. Behind them is another wall, and behind that and higher up is a fire. People walk behind the wall, holding up various objects and statues of people or animals, such that they project a shadow onto the wall that the prisoners can see. Some of the people speak, as they walk holding the objects and statues. The prisoners would believe that the shadows presented their 'reality', and they would assume that the voices were the shadows speaking. Now, imagine that one of the prisoners is freed. At first, as he sees the fire, which is the source of light in the cave, he would be dazzled. Then, as his eyes become accustomed to the power of the light, he would be able to see the real objects that were casting the shadows which were once his reality. To begin with, the adjustment to the new reality would be difficult and the shadows would still look real. But eventually, the freed prisoner is allowed out of the cave altogether. The sun replaces the fire in the cave as the source of light, and the whole

process of adjustment to reality is repeated once more. He will then become convinced that it is the sun that gives rise to the seasons and the years, and is the guardian of all that is visible in the world. Now imagine that, feeling for his erstwhile companions who are still imprisoned, he returned to the cave to tell them of his ascension. And attempted to convince them of the unreality of the 'reality' of the shadows in front of them. If they could, the prisoners would surely attempt to apprehend him and kill him."

Story is a very powerful communication tool. It can be used to help people understand what is not known by using what is known. With this allegory about the cave, is Plato attempting to direct our attention to something deeper and more mysterious about the human condition?

The Light of Reason

Through much of the 16th and 17th centuries, philosophy and science were equal partners in the quest for truth. It is important to remember that, certainly in the West, the Catholic Church attempted to keep a tight rein on thinking in a way that people today seldom imagine. Not believing in God was heresy. The last person to burn at the stake for heresy in England was executed in 1612, and the last execution for blasphemy took place in 1697. Eventually, science began to challenge the primacy of Church doctrine, and it was Descartes' ideas of a mind-body dualism that created the philosophical construct that allowed science to flourish independently of religion. Descartes' idea was that one has both a body, which works much like a machine does, and a mind (or soul), which largely controlled the body. Descartes' idea of soul was that it 'connected' to the body through the pineal gland in the brain. The effect of these ideas was to allow science to study the material nature of the world more thoroughly, whilst still retaining at least a fig leaf of religious observance. Philosophy has produced many great thinkers right up to the present day. Though increasingly through the last five-hundred years, it is science that has taken the dominant role in society. Nevertheless, there are some philosophers who still warrant a mention before we explore modern science more thoroughly in the next chapter.

Spinoza

Baruch Spinoza was a 17th century Dutch philosopher of Portuguese-Jewish descent. He disagreed with Descartes' mind-body dualism. Spinoza asserted that mind and body are the same thing, just appearing to be two things. Controversially for the time, he equated God with nature, rather than some sort of transcendental being who influenced humanity's fortunes. Spinoza regarded everything to be one thing; God is not outside the world or in the world, God is the world. Not surprisingly, his work was banned by the Catholic Church. It was from Spinoza's ideas that Einstein drew when asked whether he believed in God; *"I believe in Spinoza's God, who reveals Himself in the lawful harmony of the world, not in a God who concerns Himself with the fate and the doings of mankind."*

Hume

David Hume was an 18th century British philosopher. He maintained that knowing can only be arrived at through experience, and that reasoning and ideas about causal relationships do not have any meaning. If a billiard ball struck another one and that other moved, we only believe that there is a causal relationship present, because we have seen it happen many times before. Hume argued that all that exists are 'constant conjunctions' of events, from which we infer that there is an underlying causal relationship. Whereas, in reality we do not know that there is one at all. Just because all you have ever seen are black crows, does that therefore mean that all crows are black? This is an issue for both scientific formulations and for mystical experiences. Can we really draw scientific conclusions from a handful of observations and a few mathematical calculations? If you get a pill from the doctor and you get better, how do you know that it was really the pill that made you better? Also, just because someone thinks that they have had a mystical experience does not empower them to assume everyone can, or that they have accessed an underlying universal truth… Does it? Hume even challenged our belief about there being a world which exists outside of our sensory experience of it. From his book *A Treatise of*

Human Nature, "Why we attribute a continued existence to objects even when they are not present to the senses; and why we suppose them to have an existence distinct from the mind and perception?"

The German Golden Age

After Hume, from the 1780s to the 1880s, Germany enjoyed a Golden Age of philosophy. One of the first of these German philosophers was Immanuel Kant. He considered both experience and reasoning to be important in the quest to understand reality. He said that in effect, human experience is filtered through reasoning (thinking), but that reason without experience would only lead to hollow theories. Kant's view was that we cannot know the world itself directly as it is. Instead, we only ever experience the world through our senses, and experience is filtered by the concepts of time, space, and causality. One of Kant's successors, Arthur Schopenhauer, basically said that it is *us*, the subject of experience, that imposes these ideas of time, space, and causality onto the world. And it is us that classifies and separates an otherwise indivisible reality into separate things. Kant also said that if God is transcendent (not of this world), then we cannot know anything about Him from our perspective, other than the idea that God transcends our experience. Basically, Kant was saying that you cannot prove or disprove the existence of God.

In today's world we have access to so much information instantaneously, that it can be difficult for us to think about living in a world without that. We can look at, or at least purchase modern translations of ancient texts at will. But Eastern philosophy was actually only introduced into modern Western thinking in a meaningful way in the 1820s. When Schopenhauer was presented with Hindu ideas, he was astonished to discover that they were basically saying the same thing that he was. The only difference being that Hindu authors had arrived at those conclusions whilst travelling down a completely different path.

Summary

Ever since our basic survival needs were easily met we have been asking questions about what this experience is all about. Who am I? Why am I here? What is death and what happens after death? How do we know what we know, and what is it that we do know? Should I rely on my thinking and my experience, or what other people say? How was the universe created? Who created it? Is there a God, and if there is, where is He or She? Some people claim to have ideas or revelations which answer these questions, and feel that they need to inform everyone else about what they know… Whilst others just throw their hands in the air and say, *"So what; who cares?"*, and just get on with their lives. I think this final position would be perfectly acceptable. Except for the fact that by not taking some of these deeper questions more seriously, we are in danger of sleepwalking ourselves into a great big mess.

Historically, religion and philosophy have been answering the fundamental questions about life for us. And they have produced what seem to be many, many competing ideas. But we can boil all these down to just one question. Is my conscious experience of the material world created in the material world, or does my consciousness create the experience of a material world?

In the West, because of the way Catholicism dominated society, the scientific approach emerged slowly, and became predominately focused on the physical world. The guiding scientific philosophy was, and still is, reductionist materialism. This is the idea that we can understand higher level systems by breaking them down into their constituent physical parts. Hume's philosophical musings about the 'constant conjunctions' of events were set aside, and physics forged ahead to describe the cause and effect of the natural world in terms of forces, energy, mass, time, space, electricity, magnetism, and particles. All wrapped up in the hard logic of mathematical laws.

Humanity has been using its power of reasoning, through science, to explore the universe for almost five-hundred years, and it has achieved a lot. But what I have observed, through teaching personal development courses over the last twelve years, is that most people do not have a good grasp of what modern science is actually saying about reality. To be fair,

I think many scientists are also struggling to explain what the science is saying. Any good scientific theory should be explainable to an eight-year old, and many of the current models fail this test. If we want to understand how existence works, then we need to understand what science has been doing for the last five-hundred years. Are you sitting comfortably? Because science class is about to begin…

What have we covered:

- There are a plethora of religious ideas to explain existence and to tell people what to do.
- Most religions do not ask you to think for yourself.
- Philosophy is thinking for yourself.
- In the West, philosophy has been an alternative to religion to answer deep questions about existence.
- In the East, philosophy and religion have been more intertwined.

What remains to be explored:

- What is it about reality that secret societies claim to know?
- What has science discovered in the last five-hundred years?

3. THE EDGE OF REASON

"The public has a distorted view of science because children are taught in school that science is a collection of firmly established truths. In fact, science is not a collection of truths. It is a continuing exploration of mysteries." - Freeman Dyson.

Science is doubting, science is reasoning, science is thinking for yourself. Today, the majority of our society regards science as the principle tool to uncover how the universe functions. Science is a process, which is encapsulated within the scientific method. Broadly speaking, this is about making observations of the natural world, developing hypotheses, testing them, gathering data, creating laws or theories, and then cycling through that process once more. This scientific approach to understanding the material world produced results that challenged the authority of the Catholic Church. This started with the publication in 1543 of Nicolaus Copernicus' theories, which placed the sun and not the earth at the centre of everything. An idea that was in direct opposition with the view of the Catholic Church. In the years that followed, Johannes Kepler and Galileo Galilei supported and expanded upon Copernicus' ideas, with the aid of telescopes. Galileo was tried by the Inquisition in 1633 for his heresy, he was forced to recant, and it was not really until Descartes' assertions of mind-body dualism that science began to flourish separately from religion.

Clockwork Universe

In 1687, Newton published *The Mathematical Principles of Natural Philosophy*, setting out his laws of motion. Even today these laws work very well for large bodies, providing that they are not approaching the speed of light or are in a large gravitational field. His first law states that objects remain at rest, or moving in a constant velocity, unless acted upon by a force. If I look at the mug on my desk, it has not moved since I last touched it. I would be somewhat surprised if it did, because it has never moved before without a force of some description acting upon it. Newton's laws give us the impression of a clockwork universe; where there is absolute space, in which things exist and interact in accordance with the laws of motion, over absolute time. In his book, Newton also presented his ideas about gravity, his inverse square law. Basically, he said that all matter in the universe exerts a force on all other matter. This force is proportional to their masses multiplied together, divided by the square of the distance between them. This was derived by observation and deduction. Throw a ball in the air, and it comes back down again, due to gravity.

Initially, Newton was not without his critics, who asked, "*How is this gravitational force exerted over large distances?*" Newton did not say. Nevertheless, his ideas and his new mathematics of calculus proved remarkably successful, and with it came the sense of a clockwork universe. If we know the initial conditions of a system, through the laws of physics, we can make predictions about how that system will behave in the future. This is what became labelled as a deterministic world view. God establishes His universe, and everything then plays out in an entirely predictable manner. All this progress arose by following the scientific method, and steadily but surely breaking the natural world down into smaller and smaller things, which interacted in accordance with Newtonian principles. So the universe was made of things such as planets, stars, tables and chairs, and they all existed in absolute limitless space, evolving in a deterministic manner through universal, absolute, never-ending time. One could imagine the universe to be inside an invisible (though limitless) box, with a big clock running on the outside.

Over the next two-hundred years, these laws helped other scientists and engineers to drive the industrial revolution. This has provided the relative material comfort that many of us enjoy today.

Relatively Speaking

However, one or two scientific anomalies still remained. One of these was the failure to detect aether, through which science had assumed electromagnetic waves, such as light and x-rays, propagated. Contemplating this puzzle led a young Albert Einstein to publish a theory called Special Relativity in 1905, about moving bodies without gravity, and then another in 1915 about moving bodies with gravity, called General Relativity. This is the idea that motion is measured relative to something else. If you are sitting down now, you might think you are motionless. Relative to your chair, you probably are; but relative to the sun, you are moving, and relative to the centre of the galaxy, you are again moving, but at a different speed than you are when compared to the sun. The cornerstone of Einstein's thinking is that the speed of light in a vacuum is fixed, regardless of the motion of the observer, or of what was being observed. Not only is the speed of light fixed, but it is also the upper limit for how fast anything can move. Though technically anything with mass cannot actually attain the speed of light because it would require infinite energy to accelerate something with mass to the speed of light. However, photons of light are massless, and they do move at the speed of light. Interestingly, if you were somehow able to put a clock on a photon of light, you would observe that for the photon, no time passes at all, and relative to everything else, there would appear to be no separation in space either.

A slightly counter-intuitive effect of relativity is that space and time are not fixed, but they are relative for the observer too. This means that time is not simultaneous across the universe. Instead of there being one clock on the 'outside' of the universe, we all now have our own clocks which we 'carry around' with us. And why had no one realised this before? Well, probably because we all live our lives in the same gravitational field, because we all live on Earth; and because we move at speeds which are a tiny fraction of the speed of light, which in a vacuum is one-hundred-and-eighty-six-thousand miles per second. Newtonian physics, which works very well for everyday life, can be considered to be a special case of Einstein's theory. The special case being moving at a slow speed, as compared with light, and being in a consistent gravitational field.

Like any good scientific theory, relativity makes many predictions which have been borne out experimentally. Such as the fact that at speeds close to the speed of light, measuring rods (and everything else) get shorter, and clocks run slower. An illustration of this is the twin paradox, though there is nothing paradoxical about it – it is just relativity. Imagine that one twin travels into space on a super-fast rocket and then returns to Earth, whilst the other twin stays on Earth throughout the journey. When the travelling twin returns, they will find their stay-at-home twin has aged considerably more than they have. In effect, the travelling twin 'used up' more space, and the stay-at-home twin 'used up' more time. This is because another effect of relativity is that space and time are not two separate things. They are one unified thing called space-time. Time is in effect another dimension of space. All this is well supported experimentally, and today we need to adjust the time on GPS satellites to account for the time dilation effects of relativity.

Relativity was not done yet either. Einstein's formulations included the idea of an expanding universe. Admittedly, this was not an idea that he was comfortable with, and initially he inserted a cosmological constant to keep the universe in a steady state. He had to remove it later when the universe was indeed shown to be expanding.

The Big Bang

The evidence that proved the idea of an expanding universe was gathered by American astronomer Edwin Hubble, in 1929. Hubble measured what is known as the red shift of galaxies, and found that they were moving apart. Red shift is the Doppler effect in light, this is familiar to us in everyday life with sound. If you hear a police car with its siren on, it sounds different as it approaches, passes, and then disappears into the distance. That is because the sound waves are compressed as they come towards you, and then extend as they recede. Similarly, the wavelength of light is compressed by a luminous object moving towards you, known as blue shift, and extended if a luminous object is moving away from you, which is red shift.

The Big Bang theory is accepted today by physicists to explain the existence of the universe. This is largely because the theory fits with relativity, and because it made predictions which have been successfully observed. Predictions like cosmic microwave background radiation. This is the remaining signature of the massive heat that was present at the time of the Big Bang. The theory arises from the backwards extrapolation of currently observable phenomenon, using the mathematics of relativity. From this, physicists tell us that the universe started 13.7 billion years ago from a singularity; a point of infinite density and infinite temperature. From this singularity, and for reasons unknown, the universe then exploded outwards. Well, more specifically, space started to expand, and as time and space are in effect the same thing, time started to expand too. It is not the case that galaxies are moving away from each other, it is actually that the space between them is expanding, and in fact, that expansion is accelerating too.

So, space and time started to increase 13.7 billion years ago from a super-dense, super-hot point, for reasons unknown.

Quantum Leap

Newtonian and Einsteinian physics tend to be labelled as classical theories, to distinguish them from quantum theories. In a classical system, things exist in space and time. You perceive things around you; you move through space; and you experience the passing of one moment into another. Classical physics works well for big things like you and me, tables, chairs, planets, and stars. But all these things are made up of tiny little atoms, which are themselves made up of a collection of sub-atomic particles like protons, neutrons, electrons, leptons, bosons, etc. When one gets down into the very fine detail of what exists, and how what exists interacts, classical formulations do not work anymore. This is where quantum physics steps in.

The components of quantum physics came together over a number of years and included the work of many people. The person who first coined the term 'quantum' was German physicist Max Planck in 1900. He used it to account for how electromagnetic radiation only appeared in discrete amounts, or quanta. Quantum theory then developed with significant contributions from Albert Einstein, Niels Bohr, Werner Heisenberg, Louis de Broglie, and Erwin Schrödinger. The theory is also very well supported experimentally, but it does introduce some tricky philosophical questions. Quantum physics suggests that a sub-atomic particle is a wave function of possibilities until it is measured, and only then does it become something classically real. The wave function includes all possible outcomes for the particle simultaneously, it then somehow 'chooses' to be one of these outcomes specifically when it is measured. This seems to suggest that the future is determined by probability rather than the mechanisms of classical cause and effect. It also introduces the idea that one cannot know the location and momentum of a particle unless and until it is measured. This is known as the Heisenberg uncertainty principle. The uncertainty inherent within quantum physics is not caused by a limit of our technology, or about disturbing the system by making a measurement. No uncertainty is a fundamental property of the quantum wave function; all possibilities exist at once, until a measurement is made.

There are three experiments from quantum physics which illustrate the nature of what tends to be described as 'quantum weirdness'. The first one is a real experiment called the double-slit experiment, originally performed with light (though you can do it with electrons and other things too); the second one is a thought experiment called Schrödinger's Cat; and the third one is known as the EPR paradox, named after Einstein and two collaborators, Boris Podolsky and Nathan Rosen.

The Double-Slit Experiment

At the start of the 19th century, Thomas Young, a British polymath who assisted in the deciphering of the Rosetta Stone, first conducted the double-slit experiment with light. The structure of the experiment was devised to determine whether or not light was a wave. The experiment is set up as shown in fig 4 (page 50).

A single light source is shone through two narrow slits onto a screen. The idea being that if light is a wave, the two beams of light emanating from the two slits will interfere with each other and create a pattern of light and dark bands on the screen. As an analogy, it is the same sort of thing that would happen if you dropped two stones into a flat pond simultaneously, a small distance apart. Both stones would create circular patterns of ripples which would propagate outwards from the point of impact. As they spread, they would then encounter ripples created by the other stone. Where peaks from each wave meet, you would see a peak of double intensity, and where a peak from one wave and a trough from the other meet, they would cancel each other out. When Young conducted the double-slit experiment with light, the expected interference pattern was observed, so everyone was happy that light was a wave.

However, problems with the conclusion that light was indeed a wave began to emerge some years later, as no one could detect what the light was travelling through. On top of this, Planck found that electromagnetic waves only existed in discrete amounts, which he labelled as quanta. As light is also an electromagnetic wave, it behaves in the same way. Quanta of light are called photons. So, the theory that light was a wave was breaking down because no one knew what the light was 'waving' through, and light was also found to have particle-like properties.

The obvious step was to conduct the double-slit experiment again, but this time to release individual photons of light one at a time, and then to see what happened. The strange thing about the double-slit experiment is that once you do release the photons one at a time, over a set period, you still end up with the same bands of light and dark on the screen. What that means is the individual photons are acting as if they were still a wave. The only conclusion reached to date is that light is both a wave and a particle. But this still begs the question of what exactly each individually released photon of light is actually interfering with in the first place. As it travels towards the screen it is the only photon in the experiment. So what else is it actually interfering with? Well, let us turn to Paul Dirac, erstwhile Lucasian Professor of Mathematics at Cambridge, and ask him. According to Dirac, *"Each photon...interferes only with itself"*. Well, at least that is clear then. Each photon that you release seems to 'know' what your experimental set up is. The standard quantum physics interpretation of this is that light remains as a wave until it is observed, and then behaves as if it were a particle. The act of measurement is the observation of the photons on the screen. This is what is meant by saying that the ‘wave function collapses’. This sense of observation is a central theme of quantum physics.

If you design this double-slit experiment in such a manner as to attempt to discover which slit the photon goes through before hitting the screen, then this measurement/observation collapses the wave function at that point, and the interference pattern is no longer produced on the screen. This means that *it is the whole setup of the experiment which matters*. Prior to observation, quantum systems are a wave, and only after they are measured/observed do they become classically physical. Whilst in the wave form, the wave represents all possible outcomes together, and only on observation does the wave collapse into one of these outcomes to become matter. This wave form of all possible outcomes is known as superposition.

Now, although quantum physics works perfectly well for really small things such as electrons, it surely does not work for big things like you and me, tables, chairs, planets, or stars…does it? In 1924, De Broglie proposed that all matter can display wave-like behaviour. Since then, the double-slit experiment has been performed with molecules containing eight-hundred-and-ten atoms, and a five-thousand atom molecule has also been seen to display wave-like properties. Does this then mean that all reality is a wave of potentiality until it is observed?

Schrödinger’s Cat

It was Schrödinger who developed the wave equations for quantum mechanics, and he also devised the famous ‘cat-in-a-box’ thought experiment. He developed this in correspondence with Einstein, as they were both uncomfortable with the probabilistic nature of quantum physics. One of Einstein’s famous quotes is, *"God does not play dice with the universe"*. This was his way of attacking the inherent randomness of quantum theory, rather than a statement about him being a believer in a religious deity. This apparently random property of quantum systems is illustrated by radioactive decay. Radioactive decay happens when unstable isotopes release energy in the form of protons, neutrons, electrons, or gamma rays, and through this process become more stable isotopes. For example, carbon-14 is a radioactive isotope of carbon. Carbon-14 decays (releases energy) to become stable nitrogen-14. One cannot say which carbon-14 atom will decay at any particular time, all that can be said with certainty is that half of any given amount of carbon-14 will become nitrogen-14 in 5,730 years. This is what is known as 'half-life'. It is this property of carbon-14 that is utilised in radiocarbon-dating of organic material by archaeologists.

The setup of Schrödinger's 'cat-in-a-box' thought experiment is like this: imagine you place a cat in a sealed box. Inside the box is an amount of radioactive material. If the radioactive material decays over a certain period, it will release energy that will in turn activate a Geiger counter. Due to the experimental setup, a hammer will then be released which breaks a vial of poison in the box, and kills the cat, as shown in fig 5 (page 50). As radioactive decay is determined according to the principles of quantum theory, we can only say that there is a certain probability of something happening over a given period of time. If we use a radioactive material with a half-life of an hour, and then return an hour later and open the box, we will find that the cat is either dead or alive, and there will be an equal chance of each result.

According to quantum theory, once the experiment has been started and before we open the box, the cat exists in a state of being both simultaneously dead and alive (assuming that the cat does not qualify as an observer). When we open the box to observe what has happened, it is only at that point that the cat becomes either dead or alive. To put that in quantum terminology, we have collapsed the wave equation for the cat in the box from all possible outcomes, to one where the cat is either dead or alive. This seems somewhat strange to us, as we do not think about our experience in this manner. If my daughter is in her bedroom, getting ready to go out, does she exist in a state of superposition of being both ready and not ready at the same time, only to become either ready or not ready when her boyfriend opens the door? Assuming that she does not qualify as an observer, of course. This was the reason for the thought experiment in the first place, because it illustrates how sub-atomic particles behave, and how that behaviour seems very much unlike our experience.

The EPR Paradox

Einstein was philosophically uncomfortable with the apparent lack of determinism inherent within quantum physics. Along with his colleagues Podolsky and Rosen, he proposed an experiment which he thought would disprove the Heisenberg uncertainty principle. It is possible to create two particles in such a way that they become 'entangled' together, and can be regarded as one quantum system. If the two particles are made to travel in opposite directions, and if the properties of one of them is measured, that measurement collapses the wave function and it will determine the properties of the second, as yet unmeasured particle. For that to happen, some form of communication must be required between the two particles, but that rate of communication would need to happen faster than the speed of light – which, according to relativity, is impossible. Einstein claimed that this showed that quantum physics, as a theory, was incomplete. He believed that the measurement of one of the particles would not actually determine the property of the second one. He was also convinced that conditions in the universe were locally determined, and he did not like the idea of 'spooky action at a distance'. The EPR Paradox started life in 1935 as a thought experiment. However, real experiments first performed by Alain Aspect in the 1980s, and then again by others more recently, have confirmed that measuring one particle does indeed determine the properties of the second one. The two particles remain entangled and information seems to be transferred faster than light. There is no paradox, quantum physics is just weird.

Quantum Weirdness

The double-slit experiment, Schrödinger's cat, and the EPR paradox, highlight some of the weirdness inherent in quantum theory. At the same time, quantum theory has been described by science writer Michael Brooks "[as the]*...most successful theory of physics. There is not one shred of experimental evidence that doesn't fit with its predictions*".

Despite its undisputed success, quantum physics describes a counter-intuitive world. Physicists have at least eleven interpretations of how quantum theory works and what it says about reality. The standard one is known as the Copenhagen interpretation, named after the 'spirit' of thinking developed by Bohr and Heisenberg whilst they worked together in Copenhagen. In this interpretation, light, and everything else for that matter, is a wave whilst not being observed and a particle when being observed. The act of measurement/observation 'collapses the wave', making it present itself in a more classical manner as a particle. It is not possible to know the position and momentum of a particle at the same time, and future outcomes associated with quantum systems are determined by probability. The Copenhagen interpretation of quantum theory is often referred to by physicists as, the 'shut-up-and-calculate' interpretation. Because it works mathematically and scientifically, but do not ask any tricky philosophical questions about what it means for how reality works.

However, the world of sub-atomic particles is not the only place where there is a degree of scientific weirdness going on.

What Are The Chances?

Parapsychology is the scientific study of a collection of apparently psychic phenomenon. It has been placed by mainstream science right at the very edge of acceptable topics to be studied, even disparagingly labelled by vocal sceptics as pseudoscience. It has not been easy for researchers to obtain funding, or to get experimental results published in serious journals. Many 'proper' scientists have poured scorn on the whole field, even though they may not have taken the trouble to consider the experimental protocols or the results. This is because psychic functioning definitely does not fit within a classical, materialistic world view. There is no acceptable mechanism for it to happen, and therefore, *a priori*, it cannot exist.

However, some brave, professional, dedicated scientists have dared to work in this field. J.B. Rhine was one of the early trailblazers of parapsychological studies. Rhine pioneered the use of Zener cards (which display one of five different motifs) to study telepathy, and dice-rolling experiments to investigate mind over matter, known as psychokinesis. Rhine published results which seemed to suggest that he had studied subjects who were able to achieve card predictions well above pure chance expectations. Rhine also documented what is now known in parapsychology as 'the decline effect'. This is where subjects perform above chance to begin with, and then, as the testing becomes boring or the subject loses interest, the results fall back to chance expectations. Rhine found that the phenomenon being observed was subtle and often elusive. It also seemed to depend on the attitude towards the phenomenon that the test subject had, and the relationship between the subject and the experimenter.

Where Rhine had gone, others followed. One of these was Charles Honorton, who set out to explore telepathy by working on the assumption that if there really is a 'transfer' of information amounting to a sixth sense, maybe its signal gets overwhelmed by the cacophonous input of our regular five senses. Honorton was instrumental in developing Ganzfeld (German for whole field) telepathy experiments. In ganzfeld experiments, the receiver has their eyes covered in halved ping pong balls whilst a red light is shone onto them. This creates the sense of seeing a soft shade of red in all directions. At the same time, white noise, a bit like a waterfall, is played into their ears. The ganzfeld experimental setup significantly dampens the usual, familiar sensory input, allowing the receiver to focus on the psychic channel instead. Meanwhile, the sender attempts to telepathically send them information about a picture on a computer screen, which has been randomly selected for them to send. The receiver verbally describes the impressions that form in their mind. At the end of the experiment, the receiver then chooses the picture that they thought was being 'sent' to them, from a selection of four pictures. If the receiver was simply guessing which picture was being sent, then the experimental results would show a one in four, or twenty-five per cent success rate. In his book *Entangled Minds*, parapsychologist Dean Radin reports that between 1974 and 2004, eighty-eight separate ganzfeld experiments reported 1,008 hits in 3,145 trials. This is a thirty-two per cent success rate, which itself is twenty-eight percent better than chance expectations. If the overall results of these eighty-eight experiments were themselves simply due to chance, that could only happen once if you ran these eighty-eight experiments twenty-nine-million-trillion times. What this means in layman's terms is that there is a real effect here, this is not a chance occurrence. The apparent telepathic effect may be smallish, but it is real nevertheless.

Card guessing, dice rolling, and ganzfeld are not the only parapsychological experiments that have been performed either. The influencing of random number generators, dream telepathy, conscious and unconscious detection of being stared at, precognition, and animal telepathy experiments have all been performed. The cumulative effect of all this work, using good experimental protocols, has shown results of psychic functioning above chance expectations. Any study which demonstrates that consciousness is not limited to the confines of the skull, totally undermines the idea that the brain creates conscious experience. This is because in a materialistic model of the world, it is not possible for brain-created consciousness to extend or perceive outside the body, except through the usual five senses. What would the mechanism for this 'transference', or 'effect' be anyway? There are no acceptable materialistic answers that match the parapsychological experimental results, so the questions they raise go unanswered by mainstream science.

Remote Viewing

Remote viewing (RV) is the practical application of psychic abilities similar to ganzfeld. In 1995, the US government declassified the fact that, for twenty years, it had been using RV for intelligence gathering work. The backstory of project STARGATE, as it was latterly known, has been told before by those involved. Basically, it started with two curious Stanford Research Institute (SRI) scientists, Harold Puthoff and Russell Targ, a psychic artist named Ingo Swann, and the CIA. But what is RV? According to Puthoff and Targ, it is *"a human's perceptual ability to access, by mental means alone, information blocked from normal perception by distance, shielding, or time."*

With RV, all the sensory experience can be there, but the input channel is not through the body's usual sensory organs. Instead, it seems to come directly into the mind. The viewing experience is subtle. Joe McMoneagle worked for the US Army at Fort Meade on the STARGATE project for a number of years, and was designated viewer #001. He describes his experience with RV as being *"...like that of a feather brushing across my mind. The softest and lightest touch of information."* Though both left and right brain functions are present, the initial perception tends to be driven more by the pattern and shape recognition functions of the right hemisphere. In fact, too much left brain 'naming' of what is being observed can disrupt the viewer's perception. In RV, this kind of left brain activity is called Analytical Overlay (AOL). Sketching and drawing of what is being perceived is useful to connect with the process and to solidify perceptions. If one is viewing a round red ball, it is best to simply describe the structure of it: *"It seems to be red and round"*. If you then think, *"It must be an apple"*, then an apple is what you will perceive, and other apple-related associations may come to mind too, meaning that accurate information relating to the target is lost.

In August 1987, the Fort Meade viewers were tasked with viewing America's then highly classified stealth programme, to test what the Soviets might be able to detect using their own remote viewers. All the Fort Meade viewers were given were random coordinates assigned to the target, and a date. They were not told they would be observing an aircraft. The viewers produced very passable drawings of the stealth aircraft, even though it was unknown to them at that time. They described that the aircraft was being developed in a hot, arid environment, characterised by hard ground and a lack of vegetation. The stealth aircraft was developed at Groom Lake, Nevada, also known as Area 51, which is indeed a hot, arid environment with minimal vegetation. They described the aircraft skin as being composite and having a matte finish. They also mentioned it contained 'light tubes', which the viewers did not understand the meaning of. The aircraft actually used fibre optics instead of pneumatics to control the steering mechanisms. What this illustrates is that very accurate information can be perceived by the remote viewer, even though they might not fully understand what it is they are seeing. Though the existence of the RV programme was declassified in 1995, the vast majority of its viewing work still remains classified.

The ability to do RV is a skill that we all possess. Some of us are better at it than others. Cheerful, bright, extroverted people tend to do well, and a degree of artistic ability is helpful. As with most human skills, some people will take to it better than others, though we can all do it to some degree.

How does it work? The viewers say that they tune into the 'signal line' of the target, a sort of address frequency in the Matrix. A word that they were using long before the iconic 1999 film by the same name. To quote from the remote viewing manual published in 1986, which was developed by the SRI scientists and Swann: *"The Matrix has been described as a huge, nonmaterial, highly structured, mentally accessible 'framework' of information containing all data pertaining to everything in both the physical and the nonphysical universe. It is this informational framework from which the data encoded on the signal line originates."* Basically, it is being suggested that time and space are illusions, that everything exists now in the form of 'information', and that human consciousness can access it.

Does this mean RV is one-hundred per cent reliable and infallible? No, it does not. McMoneagle says that RV is only about sixty-five per cent reliable, because sometimes, for reasons unknown, the viewer does not pick up the signal line of the target; and sometimes, the information obtained is accurate but not useful, or simply wrong due to AOL or other unknown reasons. Future or precognitive viewing is possible, but was not found to be as reliable as viewing the present. Of course, the other thing this tells us is that perhaps consciousness does not originate in the brain after all. Or in the words of Paul Smith, another Fort Meade viewer, from his book *Reading the Enemy's Mind*: *"...that human consciousness is not locked within the narrow confines of our physical bodies, that it* [does] *not stop at the edge of our skins, but that within certain limits a human consciousness can roam virtually at will across the face of the planet."*

So, if remote viewing is so great, why then did the US Government stop using it? According to Smith, what happened was that in the later years of the STARGATE programme, the operational protocols and the general management of the viewers deteriorated. Therefore, so did the quality of the viewing output they produced. The Cold War was over, and running a government programme that looks to the outside world like psychic spying can be, shall we say, politically awkward. So, in 1995, the CIA asked the American Institute for Research (AIR) to assess the effectiveness of the RV programme. There are very good discussions of the AIR report in Stephan Schwartz's book *Opening to the Infinite*, Dean Radin's *The Conscious Universe*, and Joe McMoneagle's *Mind Trek*.

Through reading these, it seems to me that the fate of the programme was sealed prior to the AIR review taking place. Whatever the truth may be, the bottom line is that the CIA used the report to close down the government-sponsored RV effort. However, I will leave the last word on this to STARGATE viewer Paul Smith: *"It died because bureaucrats went out of their way to avoid risk... But it wasn't just risk, it was also skepticism that defeated government remote viewing. People with influence didn't want it to be true."*

Summary

In our everyday lives, the universe seems to be classically Newtonian. This 'normal' model of the world does seem to work for most of us, most of the time. In this universe, there are separate objects in space interacting over time. Within materialistic, reductionist philosophy, consciousness is produced by and in the brain. This philosophical approach has been spectacularly successful for five-hundred years. One of its crowning achievements is quantum physics. Through this discipline, science has brought humanity to the very edge of reason, but we are left a little baffled by what we see. Quantum physics remains a little weird, yet as far as we can tell, it is totally correct.

The statistical proof of psychic functioning, which has been available for at least forty years, should have sent shockwaves through the materialistic, reductionist world of science. But it has not. It is so revolutionary that the shockwaves themselves should have totally demolished the house of materialism. Yet the structure still stands and is enthusiastically supported by mainstream science. If you have a strongly held model of the world in which you have invested much of your being, a significant degree of cognitive dissonance is created by this accumulation of data. Quite simply, if you do not believe in the potential for psychic effects, nothing anyone can say and no amount of mind-bending statistics will, in any way, convince you to change your mind. And if you are already convinced, then you do not need the statistics anyway.

Through five-hundred years of achievement, science has operated as a dispassionate third-party observer, working on the assumption that there is an objective reality 'out-there'. The working assumption has been that we can uncover how cause and effect works through natural knowable forces. But as Max Planck said, *"Science cannot solve the ultimate mystery of Nature. And it is because in the last analysis we ourselves are part of the mystery we are trying to solve"*. There is no objective world 'out-there', because it exists within our own consciousness. It is in the 'in-here' that we are attempting to understand the 'out-there'. Consciousness, your consciousness, remains part of this mystery.

There are different ways of looking at all this data. Some philosophers and scientists have looked, and then recoiled from what a potential new interpretation of this data means, but others have not. In order to move forward, we do need to radically change our thinking. Through that process, much unlearning of old concepts will be required to make space in our minds for new ones. I think we are on the edge of a complete revolution in science. But this is not Paris in 1789, nor is it Petrograd in 1917; we are not heading to the Bastille or the Winter Palace. No, this revolution is about time and consciousness. You can join this revolution from the comfort of your armchair… But the Revolution is here, and you are at the centre of it.

What have we covered:

- In physics, the idea of an observer is built in.
- The future is represented as a wave function of all possible outcomes.
- Consciousness is not bounded by space and time.

What remains to be explored:

- What is consciousness?
- What is time?
- What are the laws of cause and effect?

Fig 4

Fig 5

4. THE SUPER-NOW

"You never change things by fighting the existing reality. To change something, build a new model that makes the existing model obsolete." - Buckminster Fuller.

When a horse is running, do all four of its hooves leave the ground at once? This is an easy question to answer today, but prior to 1872, it was a much-debated issue in horse racing circles. A running horse was simply moving too fast for a definitive view to be made with the human eye. However, in that year, Eadweard Muybridge finally settled the dispute by producing a series of twelve still consecutive frames of a running horse. One of the frames showed that all of the horse's hooves were indeed off the ground at once. This was the birth of moving pictures. When you go to the cinema and watch a film, twenty-four separate motionless frames are flashed on the screen, one after the other, every second. Your consciousness is not granular enough to see each static frame separately. Instead, what you perceive is movement, whereas in reality there is none at all.

The Puzzle

The world that we live in seems simple enough. You exist, so do other people, and other things. Everything happens in space, over time, and in a mathematically predictable manner. Einstein did adjust this model by giving us all our own clocks and by fusing together the concepts of space and time. But in everyday life, Einstein's adjustments to classical Newtonian physics affect us very little. However, this simple, easy-to-understand clockwork representation of the world is not really how everything works. The most successful scientific theory ever, quantum physics, tells us that the future exists as a wave function of potentiality, and it is our consciousness that converts it into something that appears to be material. At the same time, science is also having a tough time telling us what our consciousness really is. And even aside from this, parapsychology, a peripheral branch of science, is saying that the reach of consciousness is not limited to what we perceive through our five regular senses.

Nevertheless, you might still be tempted to ask, *"So what?"* It may be true that science does not yet fully understand some things, but really, what is all the fuss about? Well, I believe that we have some of the puzzle pieces jammed together in the wrong way, in a vain attempt to hold up the materialistic model of the world. We have assumed that physical reality, space, and time, are fundamental to existence, when they are not. What is fundamental instead is consciousness and change. If we now rearrange our model of the world with this in mind, an abundance of new possibilities will open up for us. And the key to unlocking the whole conundrum is our understanding of time.

Time To Change

"Time is nothing but change. Change is the measure of time and not time is the measure of change." - Julian Barbour.

Time is such an ever-present feature of our lives that one would seem somewhat foolish to even question its existence. But by challenging our current ideas about time we can unlock our understanding of consciousness and physical reality. By doing that, rather paradoxically, we can open the door to a better future. The constant backdrop to our lives, the thing persistent and ever-present in our experience is not time, instead it is change. Time is an illusion. We measure the change of things, and then we call that time. We interpret the changing positions of the hands of a clock as measuring the passage of time. The vibration of particles in an atomic clock, measured with wonderful precision, is again a measure of the change of things, and not of time. The turning of the planet, which brings day and night, the seasons, the waxing and waning of the moon, and the 25,920-year procession of the equinoxes, all of these are the measurement of changes in things, which we call time.

The quote above comes from physicist Julian Barbour, author of *The End of Time*. In his book, Barbour sets out the science behind his case for the illusion of time. He also notes that the question of what time is has been raised before, as long ago as two-and-a-half thousand years, by Greek philosopher Zeno of Elea, a student of Parmenides. Zeno proposed many paradoxes which challenge our ideas of motion, and by extension our ideas of time. One of them includes Achilles and a tortoise. Achilles is going to race a tortoise, but as Achilles is a fair-minded sort of chap, he is going to give it a sporting chance and allow it to have a head start. As soon as Achilles starts to chase after the tortoise, he will need to cover half the distance between himself and the tortoise, and as he does so, the tortoise will have moved on another small amount. Again, as Achilles progresses, he will need to once more move half the distance from himself to the tortoise, by which time our intrepid tortoise will have moved on a little further. And so, this dance of Achilles edging ever closer and closer but never actually catching up with the tortoise continues. The paradox is, of course, that Achilles sprints past our poor, ponderous reptile in no time at all.

But why does it make any difference if change is what remains constant, and what we call time is simply our measure of the change of things? Well, it could not be more significant. If time is an illusion then now is all there is. So, let me ask you this: do you exist right now? Let us presume, for the sake of this discussion, that you said yes. If now is all there is, and if you exist now, then you cannot ever not exist, *period.* Your consciousness can transform, for sure, but you will never not exist. From this perspective, death is simply a transition from one form of consciousness to another. The 'you' which you think you are transforms and continues. And do not confuse amnesia with not existing. You do have a degree of amnesia when you sleep, but as you may well know, your partner still existed whilst they slept, and so do you. I have induced a state of amnesia in others with hypnotic trance, and rest assured, my hypnotic subjects still existed during the parts of the session that they could not remember. Some surgical anaesthetics even allow for both awareness and pain to occur during surgery, but thankfully, create amnesia to prevent the subsequent recall of the pain.

Why do we think that time does exist in the first place? One of the things that tells us that there is time is our memories of the past, and our ideas about what we might do in the future. However, the concepts of the past and the future only exist in our minds. It is easy enough for us to imagine that the future is not real, and that when we think about our future plans, it is only in our imagination. We think that the past was real when it happened, but now, as we think about the past, its reality is expressed in our mind as memories. As I sit typing right now, some of the things I can see are my PC, an empty glass, and a bowl of fruit. I can remember a moment about fifteen minutes earlier when my glass was full of water. I can remember countless times when I have sat in front of my PC, in various different locations, and I can remember buying the fruit. I quickly get the sense of the passing of time simply by remembering that I filled the glass with water and then drank it. The memories I have are supported by the evidence of the empty glass, which is also in the now. There is a *consistency* in my experience, both in the memories and in the perception of what I am experiencing in the now. These things together provide a coherent narrative for my conscious mind, something which I can accept as real, and the construct that completes the narrative for me is that time must have passed.

Although I did not build the PC, I believe someone did, because I can see that it is made of separate parts. In fact, the room where I am sitting in this rented apartment is like a time capsule, a concept that Barbour utilises in his book. By implication, at some time prior to now, someone built the building and furnished the room. The stone used as part of the building material, I intellectually understand formed millions of years ago, through natural planetary processes, that I learned about at university. The wood in some of the furnishings contains evidence of past tree growth, which I have seen on television as a means of dating trees. The metals must have been mined and smelted, because I learned at school that that is how metal is formed into things useable by man. All this implies the passage of time.

Even my body implies the passage of time. I have a small scar on the middle finger of my left hand. I can still remember the woodworking incident at school that caused it. And I am balding. I can remember times when I had much more hair, and I have the pictures to prove it. Our memories and the evidence in this now both imply the passing of time. But what we are actually doing is imputing the idea, indeed the illusion of time, based on the information which is all present in the now.

The most direct way to appreciate this illusion is in the moment. If you stop and pause, you will realise that all of your life happens in the now. All of it, all of the time, happens now. Your life is not happening yesterday. Yes, you might remember yesterday, but your life is happening now, even if that means that you are spending now remembering yesterday. The same can be said of the future. All your life happens now, because now is all there is. The ever-present law of nature is not time, it is change. If nothing at all in your experience changed, how would you know that time had indeed passed?

What Exists?

The concept about what 'things' are has also exercised philosophers over the years. Here is an old version of a commonly used paradox. To paraphrase Plutarch, *"The ship in which Theseus* [of Minotaur slaying fame] *returned to Athens from Crete was preserved by the Athenians over many hundreds of years by replacing rotten planks with new ones. Such that after many, many years the philosophers of Athens wondered whether or not it was the same ship anymore."* If I change a tyre on my car, is it the same car? How many parts of my car can I change, and still believe that it is the same car?

To understand what time is, we need to re-examine what actually exists in the first place. When you get right down into the detail, my body, the PC, my empty glass, and the fruit bowl are not even things in the way that our consciousness perceives them to be. These 'things' are actually made of billions of atoms that are not static either, but are in a constant state of flux. Although the atoms that constitute our physical bodies are constantly interacting and changing, our gross physical features do remain broadly the same moment by moment. Nevertheless, as measured by the arrangement of my atoms, I am not the same person now as I was when I sat down to type half an hour ago. This is because the atoms within my muscles, sinews, and bones have moved about inside me all by themselves. The molecules within me have interacted as I drank the water, and the information I have been perceiving and processing has changed me. I am a different me now than I was then.

To understand what really exists, we need to return briefly to quantum theory. Before a measurement is made of a quantum system, it exists as a wave function, as described by Schrödinger's equations. This wave represents the superposition of all possible outcomes for that system. An observation then forces the wave to collapse, and just one of all the potential outcomes is observed. To quote Barbour, *"Contrary to the impression given in many books, quantum mechanics is not about particles in space: it is about systems being in configurations..."* The wave function is describing the potential configurations of the whole system. When an observation is made, one configuration is observed; one configuration of the whole thing. And in a physics experiment, that means the whole experimental setup. This then is asking us to change our perspective about what we are defining as being real. As you do, what you notice is that what exists is not actually 'things-in-space'. Instead, it is frozen, static *configurations*. Or to put it another way, things-in-space over time do not exist, what exists instead are Nows. These Nows consist of *information* about *configurations* of what *appear* to be things-in-space.

Nows are analogous to the static frames of a film. If you looked at the contents of an individual film frame, what you would see are different coloured patterns, which you can interpret as representing things-in-space. But they are not separate things-in-space. They are patterns of information about how, what appear to be things are arranged, and it is the whole arrangement that exists together, as one thing – as the frame. What exists are Nows, huge, vast slices of information about the arrangement of what we perceive to be things-in-space. By this understanding, the empty glass on my desk is not the same glass that I previously drank from. Each Now contains a version of the glass. So, I drank from an extremely similar glass in a different Now, in what I consider to be fifteen minutes ago. I measure this quantity of time by the different position of the hands on the clock in this Now, as compared to their position in the previous Now, which I am still connecting to by what we call memory.

By changing our understanding of what exists into Nows, instead of things, our experience of time then becomes the observation of our consciousness moving between Nows. All of which have slightly different arrangements of what appear to be things in them. In reality, each Now that you move through is what fundamentally exists, not the separate things that we have heretofore considered to exist.

This is a radical way to think, which is probably why we have never noticed it before. Except of course for Zeno, with his analogy of Achilles and the tortoise. What happens here is that there exists a sequence of Nows containing arrangements of Achilles and the tortoise, and then eventually, we run out of Nows in which Achilles is behind the tortoise. In the next Now, they are side by side, and in the next one, Achilles is just ever so slightly in front. Just like if you filmed their race in slow-motion and then laid out the thousands of individual frames on the floor in sequence. What this means is that existence is discontinuous, like frames of a movie. And all the frames of existence exist now. Before you go to the cinema to see a film, all the frames of that film exist. You simply perceive them one at a time. What happens in our lives is that we traverse through frames, very quickly in sequence. And it is the process of doing that which makes us believe in time. In reality, all the frames exist right now, and we are simply accessing them in consciousness one at a time.

We can certainly have the experience of time by moving sequentially through Nows, but time is not a fundamental property of existence. *Everything that can exist exists now.* Time is an experience *within* our existence, but our existence is not subject to time. This is a revolution in thinking that requires us to totally reconsider who we are, how cause and effect works, and what we can achieve. This revolution of thinking will change everything. This is what a paradigm shift looks like. When you woke up this morning, you were literally a different person than when you went to bed! You are a different person now than you were when you started reading this chapter. More than that, the you that you want to be exists now in an as yet unexperienced Now. But it *does* exist now. The question is, how do you get into it?

Shine A light

When we take this concept of separate Nows back into quantum physics, and re-examine quantum weirdness, what we find is that it all stops being quite so weird. The weirdness is instead shifted into our understanding of consciousness, cause and effect, and who we are. And it only seems weird there because it is different from how we have been used to thinking about ourselves.

The whole concept of information about configurations contained in separate Nows explains how a photon in the double-slit experiment seems to 'know' what the experimental setup is. This is because it is not actually the separate photon, screen, and slits arranged in space which exist. Instead, it is the arrangement of them all together in the Now that actually exists. What is generally implied from this experiment is that everything is connected to everything else. A new way to appreciate this 'connection' is to recognise that it is the total arrangement of everything in the moment that counts, and it is all one thing, a Now. In one Now, the entire universe, every galaxy, star, planet, rock, animal, person, atom, and sub-atomic particle is arranged in a particular way. It is not that the photon of light in the experiment 'knows' what the setup of the experiment is. Instead, the photon is part of the whole arrangement, and it seems to act the way it does, because it is the whole arrangement that matters. Not the appearance of individual things within the arrangement. In the EPR paradox, particles that appear to be entangled are not entangled over time, they are present in the same Now. The 'communication' between them appears to be instantaneous, faster than the speed of light. This is because the Now that contains the information about the measured property of one particle is the *same* Now that contains the information about its partner. In the Schrödinger's cat-in-a-box experiment, what is happening is that all possible outcomes already exist. There is no wave collapsing. Both outcomes, dead cat and living cat exist in separate Nows. We simply perceive one of them, which of course begs the question, what is it that determines which Now we experience?

The Super-Now

Without time, there was no creation of what exists. What exists just exists. It is uncreated, and its principal property is simply to exist; it always has, and always will, now. There was nothing before, and there will be nothing after, because now is all there is. This could not be a more significantly different way to think. It means that it is not the apparently material world you perceive that is eternal, it is *you*.

If we think about our own universe, the Now containing what we imagine to be the Big Bang is just one Now that exists now, as does the Now that we currently occupy. This Now is acting like a time capsule. It contains information that we can extrapolate backwards from, to imagine a whole series of Nows. We can then measure the change of information within those Nows, impute the illusory concept of time, and even measure that illusion. But all the Nows within that sequence exist right now. So, how many Nows are there? How big is now? This is part of the mystery for us to explore. Even though the number is likely to be extremely large, there is probably a finite number of Nows which contain expressions of you or me. However, I see no reason not to imagine that there is an infinite number of Nows within the whole of existence.

If time does not exist, then neither does space. *Everything is here and now.* This is why in remote viewing, information is accessible without limitation through space and time. Which is all well and good, but how do we even start imagining what this is like? Any metaphor that you are likely to think of will be one that contains a sense of space. Thinking from our space-time experience is difficult without doing so. Nevertheless, we must do the best we can with what we have. You could imagine each Now as the frame of a film, where all frames exist now; or as an infinitely-faceted crystal, or as the early Hindu metaphor of Indra's net, an infinite net of jewels in which each jewel contains the reflection of every other one. Another metaphor to work with is white light. White light contains all possible wavelengths of light. It is one thing which has the potential to appear to be many different things, many different colours. In an echo of Parmenides, it seems to me that however we want to imagine existence to be, without time and space it is one single thing, eternal, and unchanging;

we could call it the One, All-That-Is, or the Super-Now. But if there is just one thing, how do we then account for our experience of consciousness?

Mirror, Mirror

"Reality resembles a mirror. Every deed we perform, each emotion we display and every word we speak is reflected back to our lives in equal measure." - The Zohar.

Everything starts with awareness. What you are aware of and what it means to you is your experience. No awareness, no consciousness, no experience; and if you had consciousness and were aware of absolutely nothing, then how would you know that you were conscious at all? Consciousness appears to be dualistic. When you are conscious, you are always conscious of something. There is always subject and object. But if all that exist is just one thing, the Super-Now, then how can you be conscious of anything at all?

If there is nothing outside of what exists, what is it that perceives what exists? In this conception without time where everything exists now, consciousness must be an aspect within the Super-Now itself. It must be a fundamental quality of existence. The way that I imagine this is that consciousness is the experience of self-reflection. You are both what you perceive and the awareness of perceiving it. Another way of imagining this is by comparison to a dream. When you dream, you perceive yourself to be in the dream. You are invariably aware of a landscape, other people, and things within the dream. Yet, the whole dream is happening within you; you are the dreamer and the thing of which you dream. As with a dream, so too with consciousness. There is nothing outside of you. You are the consciousness and the content of your conscious experience. You are both at the same time.

Returning to the analogy of a film, what exists are informational Nows, and your consciousness is the ability to reflect those Nows. Your consciousness is like the projector light that shines through the film, frame by frame, so fast that you do not notice that each frame is separate and individually motionless. You are both the film frames and the projector light that illuminates them. By this understanding, the physical world is a projection of your consciousness. Everyone and everything in the physical world is you. You are watching the film of your life. Once you have finished watching this film, you will simply leave the cinema and do something else, before perhaps watching another film of your choosing.

Using another similar analogy, your experience is like virtual reality. If you had a virtual reality headset and a full body suit, you could replicate your experience, and it would seem just as real as life does to you now. You could even 'die' in virtual reality, and think you were dead, until you took off the virtual reality suit, and remembered who you really are. Does that mean that the other people you think you are interacting with in your life are simply just projections of your own consciousness? Is your partner just a reflection of you? Is your boss a reflection of you? Is the smelly man next to you on the bus just a reflection of you? Well, yes and no. Imagine that each individual has their own projector light, and that we are all shining our lights through the same film frame, but through different aspects of it. I shine my light through the film frame that we share from my perspective, and you do it from yours. We are sharing an experience with other aspects of the Oneness, by projecting the same information through a different perspective of the One. I imagine it is very much like playing a video game online. You are playing against other real people, but you perceive what you perceive on your PC. Others take the same information that you perceive, and they view that on their PC. Ultimately though, at some other 'higher' level, we are all still one. In the same way that white light is one thing, which can also appear to be many different things. The totality of what exists is the One, and we are aspects of that oneness appearing to be many different things. This means that what you are is not a material body in a material world, with a consciousness created in that material world. It is not even the dualistic idea that you have a soul and a material body. You are consciousness, and the material world is a projection of your consciousness, contained within your consciousness. You are all mind.

Everything that you experience is then a reflection of what you are, a reflection of your mind. Is this then why all religions contain The Golden Rule, *"Do to others what you would have them do to you"*? Though it does appear in slightly different forms, for instance as Karma in Eastern religions, nevertheless it is a common feature of religious thought. If everything 'out there' is you, how you treat others comes back to you in some way, somehow. This is why Ghandi said, *"There is no path to peace. Peace is the path."* Fighting for peace is an oxymoron. To experience peace, you need to *be* peace.

"Because of time's existence, we mistakenly believe that goodness goes unrewarded while wickedness goes unpunished." – Yehuda Berg.

What Now?

If things-in-space over time do not exist, if it is Nows which exist instead, and if my experience is a reflective projection of information in a Now, what is it that determines which Now I experience? When time and space cease to be fundamental properties of existence, what happens to cause and effect?

Science is the study of causes and effects in the material world. If our experience of the material world has become a projection in consciousness of information contained in a Now, what has become of all the causes and effects that science has successfully studied, and that I experience? If I drop my now empty glass of water onto the tiled floor, I fully expect it will fall and break, which will then cause me to have a 'pan-and-brush-type' experience. Philosopher David Hume considered our experience to be the constant conjunctions of events, not necessarily linked by cause and effect in the way that we thought they were. Just because every time that I dropped a glass onto a hard floor and it broke does not mean that there is a fundamental law of physics at play…does it? Working on the assumption that there are fundamental laws is what has brought us to the edge of realising that if there are, they might not be the ones that we thought they were from the outset.

I am suggesting that what is fundamental is consciousness, therefore it must be both your conscious and unconscious mind that determines what you experience. This is taking us back to the very core of the debate between science and religion. Has our science really just been the study of conjunctions of Nows? Is the cause and effect of things-on-things as much of an illusion as the things are themselves? If this is what we think, then surely, we are throwing out centuries of science in an off-handed manner, and this itself will cause us to usher in an era of woolly-headed, superstitious 'positive thinking'. Well, again I think the answer is both yes and no. What we need to start comprehending is that it is the information in the Nows that distinguishes one Now from another. White light contains superimposed information about all the colours of the rainbow. We perceive these based on their different frequencies. In a similar way we differentiate Nows based on their informational content, or you could say their signature frequencies. We need to look at our world with new eyes, eyes that do not see things-in-space interacting with other things-in-space, but instead we need to start exploring the ideas of frequency and resonance.

One of the reasons we do not tend to question the ideas of scientific cause and effect, is because we have experiences that are consistent and sequential frame by frame. If you had an experience where there was an apparent discontinuity from one frame to the next, such as money appearing in your empty pocket just at the moment that you needed it, or a scientifically unexplainable disease remission, then understanding experience as a reflection of consciousness would not be such a big step.

It is because we are 'creating' the experience of continuity that we have scientific 'laws' of cause and effect. Think about it this way. In 1543, the year of Nicolaus Copernicus' death, I could have travelled from where I live in Bolton to London. This is a journey that would have taken me some considerable time, and no small amount of effort. The quickest method would have been by horse. My conscious mind would have been more than a little surprised if I had been sitting in my hovel in Bolton, thought about being in London, and then suddenly found myself by the edge of the Thames. I would have proclaimed it to be a miracle. In fact, if it happened today, I would still think that it was somewhat miraculous.

Today, my conscious mind can accept the idea of the internal combustion engine, cars, motorways, trains, and planes. Therefore, I can accept the idea of getting from Bolton to London in under four hours, and perhaps as fast as two hours. One way of thinking about this is of course through the advances of science. Another way of thinking about it is that my conscious mind is able to accept that I can physically locate the vibrational frequency of London from Bolton today, in a sequence of intermediate steps that takes no more than four hours. Whereas the intermediate steps that my mind would have accepted in 1543 would have been many, many more. If my mind could accept the idea of instantaneously being physically in London from Bolton, then I would be. Point-to-point travel is possible once we change our mind-set about what exists. Of course, as we do, we are still likely to label that change of mind-set as being the scientific advance of teleportation. Remember that remote viewing tells us that accessing London in your mind, whilst sitting in Bolton really is not such an issue. Admittedly, knowing that you can physically move there instantaneously is still difficult for our minds to accept, unless there was a technology that permitted us to believe that it was possible.

What I am saying is that all technology actually does for us, is that it allows us to believe something that is inherently possible within the structure of existence in the first place. Some of the evidence for this is how synchronicities appear in our lives. They defy the scientific laws of cause and effect. We need to start paying attention to them, and to how our thinking on the 'inside', as well as our behaviour, is reflected back to us on the 'outside'. This way, we can start to realise that we are not limited by the physicality that we have convinced ourselves we inhabit. Cause and effect is what you believe cause and effect to be – your mind is everything.

Keeping It Simple

"All ideas we form of the outer world are ultimately only reflections of our own perceptions. Can we logically set up against our self-consciousness a 'Nature' independent of it? Are not all so-called natural laws really nothing more or less than expedient rules with which we associate the run of our perceptions as exactly and conveniently as possible?" – Max Planck.

As the quote from Planck above indicates, our scientific laws are generalisations about how we are interpreting the reflection of existence back to ourselves in this Now. In this model, where time is an illusion and consciousness is self-reflection, what is it that remains fundamental?

1. You Exist: As Descartes pointed out to us, you exist. When you stop and think about it for a moment, the only thing that you *know* for sure right now is that you are having an experience, that is all. And the fact that you are having an experience means that you exist. This idea, coupled with the understanding that time is an illusion and that now is all there is, means that you will never, ever not exist. And you are not just having an experience, *you* are creating it!

2. All is One: The whole of existence is one thing, the Super-Now, appearing to be many different things. What we call physical reality is a projection of consciousness in consciousness. Each Now represents a different perspective of the One. Everything simply exists. Nothing was created, nothing is destroyed, and everything exists now.

3. Everything is here and now: As an extension of all being one and time being an illusion, is the idea that space is also an illusion. The only way we perceive any separation is by selectively tuning into different frequencies, much like tuning a radio or television. Just because you are paying attention to one channel does not mean all the other channels are non-existent. All it means is you are not tuned into the other channels. In our lives, we do experience a world of time and space, this is true. But time and space are not fundamental properties of existence. Through our consciousness, we are creating the illusion of time and space. Remote viewing is a practical demonstration of this.

4. What you put out is what you get back: Your dualistic experience of consciousness is the ability to reflect. What you perceive to be on the outside is actually still on the inside, there is no outside. So, everything that you experience is a reflection of you. If you look into a mirror with a frown on your face, the mirror faithfully reflects this back to you. If you get angry at the frowny face, then the mirror reflects back your anger. But if you smile, the mirror cannot do anything but smile back at you. It has no choice, because it is a reflection. What you put out is what you get back, someway, somehow.

5. Everything changes, except for the four fundamentals above: Although when viewed from the perspective of all-that-is, existence is infinite and unchanging, all-that-is viewed from any other perspective is constantly changing. Time is the illusion, change is the constant, now and always.

The basis for this new model is simply derived from the idea that time is an illusion. In addition, this model is coming to us loud and clear from another source too. Although we have a bit more ground to cover before we are ready to be introduced to him.

This model does raise some difficult concepts for us to assimilate, and some really, really tough questions that all of us will have to face up to. Some of those questions are –

- What is the meaning of human life?
- What happens after death?
- What is the cause, meaning, or purpose of suffering?
- Where does God fit into this new model?
- How am I responsible for what I perceive around me?
- How do I make choices in a world where everything is a reflection of self?
- What sort of future do we want to live in?
- And how do we get from here to there?

In embracing this new model of the world, both science and religion will have to swallow some tough medicine. They are both right, and wrong at the same time. This new way of understanding reality opens up a wealth of possibilities for humanity. I appreciate that there are challenges ahead, but all that is required is the intellectual courage to consider these challenges through this model.

Summary

Some of what is included in this chapter sounds rather mystical. *Time is an illusion. All is one. The world exists in you. What you experience of the material world is a reflection of your consciousness*. I think that the apparent mystical nature of these ideas is because in the dim and distant past, the true nature of reality was fully grasped and understood by humanity. Many teachers have attempted to convey this information to us before. And even though the message has been distorted or misunderstood, echoes of it still remain. I appreciate that it can still be hard to understand, because it appears to be so different to how most of our experience seems to work. It is only when strange things like synchronicities enter our consciousness that we stop and wonder.

The curious thing about all of this is that it does not really matter what I say. What you will experience is based on your mind and your beliefs. I can tell you that this is a revolution in thinking, or the overused term 'paradigm shift', and you can just shrug and say, *"So what?"* Then you will experience 'so what'. Equally, you can embrace these ideas and revolutionise your life – the choice really is yours. In fact, some people may say that much of this is not new, and ask, *"Where is the revolution?"* To those people I would say that the revolution is not the revolution; the real revolution comes when you live in accordance with what it means. This revolution does not happen by some force or action on the outside of you, you need to be it by taking charge of your own mind.

I believe that humanity should take its exploration of existence consciously into the realm of consciousness, with our scientific mind-set intact. If we do this, there are no boundaries for us. We can end conflict and misery on the planet; time and space will melt before our very eyes; the distance to the stars will shrink to nothing at all, and death will no longer be the end. Instead, it becomes a transition into something else. People, we stand on the very edge of a cliff. We can leap and fall, or leap and fly; again, the choice *is* yours.

This may also just sound like some alternative philosophy, conveniently using some selective bits of science to support nothing more than wishful thinking. You may choose to think this way, but it is possible to move these ideas from concepts into direct experience, or what you might call 'knowing'. So that is where we are going next.

What have we covered:

- Things-in-space over time do not exist. What does exist are Nows.

- Time is an illusion. Change is constant, not time.
- Existence is *probably* infinite.
- All is one.
- Consciousness is self-reflection.
- What you experience as the material world is contained within your consciousness.

What remains to be explored:

- Can we have more direct experience of this new model?
- How do we live in a world where the world is within us?

PART II

Change Your Life

5. KNOWING

"Show me a sane man and I will cure him." – Carl Jung.

In 1898, Morgan Robertson published a novel called *Futility*. It is the tale of John Rowland, an ex-US Navy officer who has fallen on hard times and become an alcoholic. During the story, Rowland serves as a deckhand on an ocean liner called the *Titan*. The ship is the largest in the world and is considered to be unsinkable. It is eight-hundred feet long and displaces forty-five-thousand tonnes. During April, on a voyage from the UK to America, the ship hits an iceberg on the starboard side, four hundred miles from Newfoundland, and sinks. Its twenty-four life boats prove inadequate for the two-and-a-half-thousand passengers and crew. There are only thirteen survivors, one of whom was Rowland. The sinking happens halfway through the book, and by the end Rowland had successfully managed to turn his life around.

On 31st March 1909, the keel was laid for what was then the largest passenger liner in the world, the *Titanic*. It was eight-hundred-and-eighty-two feet long, displaced forty-six-thousand tonnes, and was considered to be unsinkable. On 14th April 1912, during its maiden voyage from the UK to America, lookout Frederick Fleet spotted an iceberg off the starboard bow. The bridge was alerted, but by then the collision was inevitable. After hitting the iceberg, the *Titanic* sank, four hundred miles off the coast of Newfoundland. The twenty lifeboats were inadequate for the *Titanic's* two-thousand-two-hundred-and-twenty-four passengers and crew; only seven-hundred-and-ten people survived. Robertson never claimed to have any special powers, or that he had even made a prediction, it was all just a strange coincidence.

Synchronicity

One nice summer's day in the early 1980s, a man came to the door to sharpen knives. My parents and siblings were out for the day, and I was in the house by myself. I did not realise until after he had gone that the guy was a small-time conman. I paid him five pounds, and he did nothing at all. Once I knew that I had been duped, I was rather disappointed in myself. In those days, even though I was somewhat confused about religion, I was still a churchgoer. So, that night I prayed for a chance to prove that I was not the complete idiot that I now thought I was. The very next day, someone else came to the door to sharpen knives. I answered the door and turned them away. In the thirty years or so that my family lived in that house, these are the only times that I can remember someone came to sharpen knives. Now, this is simply an anecdote, and there may well have been other times when people came to sharpen knives and for whatever reason I simply do not remember them. Even without the benefit of any scientific, statistical analysis that could have been performed on the chances of such events happening as they did, the whole thing made an impression on me. Not that I thought there was a deity listening to my prayers. Instead, what I noticed was how there was a coincidence between external events and my internal thoughts, and how it all came together so seamlessly.

It was Swiss psychiatrist Carl Jung who coined the term synchronicity in the early 1950s. He postulated that alongside the usual rules of cause and effect as understood by physics, there was also a linkage in meaning between events as well. Jung recounts several illustrative stories in his book *Synchronicity*. This one he draws on from a writer called Wilhelm von Scholz:

"...a mother took a picture of her small son in the Black Forest. She left the film to be developed in Strasbourg. But, owing to the outbreak of war, she was unable to fetch it and gave it up for lost. In 1916, she bought a film in Frankfort in order to take a picture of her daughter, who had

been born in the meantime. When the film was developed, it was found to be doubly exposed: the picture underneath was the photograph she had taken of her son in 1914!"

I expect that if someone had investigated at the time, a causal link in real world events could have been traced. But that is not the point here. The point is primarily about the significance that the events have on the person who experiences them. For Jung, the outside world contained reflections and metaphors of some higher order, a deeper meaning, and a hidden truth. When synchronicities occur, they alert you to that deeper structure, and can bring aspects of 'you', which are unconscious, into your conscious awareness.

I worked with a client called Peter (not his real name), whose whole life was punctuated by synchronous events. He was somewhat baffled about how these strange coincidences cropped up time and time again. One simple example was a few years earlier; he thought it would be great if he could play football with Alan Shearer, an English footballer. A few weeks after thinking that, one of his friends got in touch to say that he was organising a charity football event. Some ex-players would be there and he thought Peter might want to attend. And so, Peter ended up playing football with Alan Shearer. He had many other similar stories too, ones which I am sure many people would have. Then after our initial session he emailed to say that a couple of even stranger things had happened not long after we met. He said he was at work and had forgotten to bring any money for the coffee machine. So instead of having a coffee he had to settle for a glass of water. As he returned to his desk from the office kitchen, he passed the coffee machine, as he did a 40p credit appeared on the machine. He got himself a latte. Strange though that was, it was not the reason that he emailed me. Shortly after the coffee machine episode, the satellite navigation (sat nav) device that he used in his car broke. He thought, *"I better get a new one."* A few days later a new sat nav arrived in the post from the retailer B&Q. The information with it said that Peter had won it in a raffle, but he had no recollection of ever entering the raffle.

During the first session with him, he also told me that from an early age he was convinced he would be either a millionaire or bankrupt by the time he was forty years old. Not long afterwards, he got involved in a business venture to which the word 'penny' carried significance. During the initial stages of setting up the business, he text me to say, *"I just found a penny on the floor, the lady who checked me into my hotel last night was called Penny, and I'm about to go to a meeting in a pub called Penny Farthing on Penny Lane. Do you think this is some kind of message?"* I did not see him for a number of years after that, but a few years ago, he got back in touch to tell me that the business venture had not gone well, and that he had indeed been declared bankrupt. He said that the letter inviting him to the court bankruptcy hearing arrived the day before his fortieth birthday. But he'd had the foresight to move his assets into his wife's name, and as a consequence of being declared bankrupt, all his credit card debt was cancelled, so he ended up better off!

When synchronicities crop up in our lives, we get a gentle prod that reality is not what we had heretofore thought it was. In a world where time and space cease to be fundamental, cause and effect as we previously understood it breaks down. Synchronicities are telling us that the outside responds to the inside, and in a manner where statistical probabilities are defied. And we are being challenged to recognise that we are a part of something larger and deeper than our earthly physical life. This larger deeper aspect has its own structure and sometimes we are gifted a chance to see it.

The spark that lit the fuse to the first World War was the assassination, in Sarajevo on 28 June 1914, of Archduke Franz Ferdinand, heir to the Austro-Hungarian throne. Six members of the Black Hand gang, radical Serb nationalists, planned to assassinate the Archduke that day. As his cortège drove through the city, on its way to a civic reception at the town hall, one of the members of the gang leapt from the crowd and threw a bomb at his car. But it bounced off and instead exploded under the car behind, injuring several people. After attending the civic reception, a rather shaken Archduke decided to cancel the remaining official events planned for the day. Instead, he decided to visit the hospital to see the people injured in the earlier bomb attack. However, his driver was unfamiliar with the layout of Sarajevo and took a wrong turn. As he was reversing to correct his error the car ended up virtually stationary next to another member of the Black Hand gang, Gavrilo Princip. Princip could not believe his luck. He drew his pistol and fired two shots into the car, mortally wounding the Archduke and his wife. The events of that day then echoed around the globe, and had tragic consequences for millions of other people. A small detail about this historic episode for you to ponder over is this: the car that the Archduke and his wife were in that day is housed in a museum in Vienna, its number plate is A 111 118. It does not take too much imagination to rearrange this into 11-11-18, which was the date that the armistice ending World War I was signed.

Synchronicities can be little ways of knowing that consciousness is not created in the brain. And there are more dramatic and direct ways of knowing this too. In 1944, Jung had a Near-Death experience during a heart attack where he floated out of his body, and saw the whole of planet Earth beneath him.

Death's Door

One of the enduring mysteries of life is death. We all know that death awaits us. It has a pressing inevitability about it. Religious belief seeks to reassure us that there is a heavenly after death realm. But modern, secular, scientific thinking scorns the idea of life after death. If you believe that consciousness is produced in the brain, then the death of the physical body means the end of your consciousness. However, throughout human history there have been persistent accounts of people close to death, who have reported vivid conscious experiences. These are rare but they do exist. As I said in *Chapter 2*, there is even one in Plato's *The Republic*, about a soldier called Er, who 'died', spent some time in another realm, and was then sent back.

It seems likely that the general improvement in medicine and resuscitation in the 1960s and 70s led to more people surviving a close brush with death, who are then able to talk about what they experienced. The term Near-Death experience (NDE) was coined by Raymond Moody in his 1975 book *Life After Life*. Moody first came across the idea of NDEs in 1965 whilst studying philosophy, when psychiatry professor George Ritchie told him about his own NDE. This occurred when Ritchie was clinically dead for nine minutes some years earlier. Later, whilst Moody was teaching philosophy, a student approached him with a question about immortality. The student's grandmother had related an experience to him that would today be regarded as an NDE. Moody continued lecturing, and then decided to study medicine. Throughout this time, he collected near-death stories from lecture attendees, patients, and even doctors. Initially, he collected a total of one-hundred-and-fifty of them from people who were either clinically dead at the time they had the experience, or had a close brush with death without actually being clinically dead. He also gathered second-hand stories from relatives of people who had died shortly after relating their own NDE. Moody's book was based on fifty mainly first-hand accounts. The thing he noticed was that all these experiences had similar features, and a similar progression.

Moody's collection of accounts from experiencers set the scene for others to do more structured and scientific research. This research has been conducted by doctors and nurses. This was done by either collecting stories from patients and retrospectively checking their medical records, to ensure that they were indeed dead; or in hospital-based studies where all patients suffering a close brush with death were interviewed afterwards. *The Handbook of Near-Death Experiences*, edited by Janice Holden, Bruce Greyson, and Debbie James states that between 1975 and 2005, fifty-five researchers from across the world published sixty-five research studies involving nearly three-thousand-five-hundred Near-Death experiencers. The studies addressed the experience, its aftereffects, or both. Although these included near-death as a result of accidents, drowning, childbirth, illness, and suicide, the largest number of people studied are cardiac-arrest survivors. In this group, between ten to twenty percent of people have reported NDEs. All this research supported Moody's initial findings. Broadly speaking these are the commonly reported aspects of an NDE:

- *Feelings of peace and joy* – There is often a sense of being free from pain, and or feelings of joy.
- *Out-of-Body experience (OBE)* – This is sometimes foreshadowed by buzzing sounds or clicks, then the experiencer floats above their body and witnesses events happening around them, such as resuscitation attempts.
- *A tunnel or darkness and light* – Not everyone experiences a tunnel as such, but a transition through darkness into intense light is common.

- *A life review* – This is a rapid, panoramic, replaying of the experiencers life, much like watching a movie. Key events are highlighted and the emotional impact of the experiencer's actions upon other people are felt. Sometimes a presence is sensed that guides the review, but if there is any judgement experienced it is self-judgement.
- *Meeting deceased loved ones* – Dead relatives are quite frequently encountered, even ones that the experiencer did not know was dead.
- *Return* – Towards the end of the experience something which symbolises a barrier that they cannot cross is encountered. They sense or are even told that they cannot go any further, and that they must return. Shortly thereafter they find themselves back in their physical body.
- *Being of Light* – Either during the life review or at the point when they must return, a being of light can be experienced. This can be interpreted by the experiencer through a religious filter, as a specific deity, but is commonly simply described as a being of light.

As one might expect, the initial stages of the NDE, such as feelings of peace and out-of-body experiences (OBE) are more frequently related than the later stages, which include a life review, meeting deceased relatives, or a being of light. It also seems that anyone can have an NDE. There is no difference between the sexes, prior expectations, religious beliefs, race, education, social standing, or age, though younger people do seem to experience them slightly more frequently. There are even instances of people who have been blind from birth who have reported vision-like experiences during NDEs.

More NDE studies have been conducted in the West than in the East. Nevertheless, hundreds of cases from India and China do exist, which largely support the findings from Western studies. The notable difference being that a tunnel is often not reported. Though the core NDE stages are fairly consistent throughout the world, sometimes the way that these are interpreted is coloured by pre-existing religious or cultural models of the world. For example, Westerners are more likely to describe the entities encountered as being angels, Jesus, or God, particularly if they are

Christian. Indian experiencers are more likely to describe meeting Yamadutas, assistants of Yama, Hindu God of the dead. Also, in accordance with cultural expectations, Indian experiencers tend to have their life deeds read to them from a book, rather than having a panoramic life review. And instead of being told that it is not their time, or that they have unfinished work on Earth to do, as with Western experiencers, Indian ones are told, rather bureaucratically, that a mistake has been made and they are simply sent back. No researcher to date has produced an explanation as to why only a minority of people have an NDE in near-death situations, other than the ability of their short-term memory to retain the experience.

Pam Reynolds

Cases where information is obtained during an experience, and is then corroborated later do exist. One of the best examples in the NDE literature is the case of Pam Reynolds, reported by cardiologist Michael Sabom in his book *Light & Death*. This case has been the subject of television programmes and is frequently quoted in books on the subject of NDEs. The reason for that, as you will see, is that the environment in which it occurred was highly monitored, and because it provides excellent evidence for the presence of consciousness, where there should be none present at all.

Pam had an aneurism in an artery deep within her brain. This is a weakness in the artery wall which causes the artery to balloon out, pushing on the brain. It also means that there is a constant risk of the artery bursting. If it did, the effect on Pam would be immediately fatal. Pam's only hope was Dr Robert Spetzler. He was pioneering a surgical procedure known as hypothermic cardiac arrest, nicknamed 'standstill'. Pam's body would be cooled to 60°F (16°C), and all of her blood would be drained out of her, which would allow Spetzler to safely remove the aneurism. Though the surgical procedure itself carried a high risk of death, it was Pam's only option. Throughout the operation, Pam's whole body was very highly monitored. She was under general anaesthetic, her eyes were taped shut, and one-hundred decibel clicks were being played in her ears from moulded speakers, to measure brain stem response. There were twenty doctors, nurses, and technicians present as surgery began. Dr. Spetzler opened the scalp on the right-hand side of Pam's head, and then he opened the skull using a pneumatically powered saw. This is where Pam's NDE began with her having an OBE, and thereby witnessing elements of the surgery.

After removing a portion of the skull, Spetzler confirmed that the aneurism was too risky to operate on with any blood in Pam's body. Standstill surgery would indeed be necessary. An incision in the groin was required to remove all the blood in Pam's body. Her heart had to be stopped and her body cooled to prevent brain damage. At this point in the surgery, Pam had no respiration, no heartbeat, no brain activity of any kind, not even from the one-hundred decibel clicks in her ears, and of course, no blood. Nevertheless, her conscious experience continued and deepened. In her own words from Sabom's book.

"There was a sensation like being pulled, but not against your will...The feeling was like going up in an elevator real fast. It's a dark shaft that I went through, and at the very end there was this very little tiny pinprick of light that kept getting bigger and bigger. The light was incredibly bright, like sitting in the middle of a lightbulb.

I noticed that as I began to discern different figures in the light – and they were all covered with light, they were light, and had light permeating all around them... Everyone I saw...fit perfectly into my understanding of what that person looked like at their best during their lives. I recognized a lot of people... They would not permit me to go any further...."

The full account of Pam's case in Sabom's book, or in Leslie Kean's book *Surviving Death* are worth exploring. Pam's surgery took place in 1991 when she was thirty-five years old. She died of heart failure in 2010. Her visual perceptions of the surgery were confirmed by the surgical team. Though there are many other examples of accurate information being reported by experiencers whilst clinically dead, cases like Pam's are rare.

Out-of-Body-Experiences (OBE)

One of the elements of an NDE is the out-of-body-experience. But it is not just through a close brush with death that one can have an OBE. There are many personal stories from people who have had spontaneous or even self-induced OBEs. This type of experience has been documented for hundreds of years, through all cultures, and is in all likelihood a natural human experience. Some writers point to ancient Egyptian ideas of the Ba (personality) and Ka (life spark or spirit), or to biblical accounts from prophets, or shamanistic experiences. All of these support the idea that OBEs are a fundamental component of human existence.

In its basic form, the experiencer has the sense that they have shifted the focus of consciousness away from physical reality. This is sensed by the quality of the experience, which is usually a sharper and more heightened sense of conscious awareness. Often, in the initial stages of the experience, the physical body is viewed directly from the outside. For experiencers, there can be subtle differences in the way that the physical reality appears from this perspective. Colours can be different, and physical reality can be seen as energetic patterns, rather than as solid shapes. The experiencer is convinced they have left the physical body and they feel just great, much like in the NDEs. As the experience deepens, other entities that seem to have independent thoughts and actions can be encountered. In this non-physical realm, thoughts and the experience of reality are instantaneously connected. There are no secrets here, nothing is hidden, which is much like what remote viewers experience too.

Through careful and dedicated work, it is possible to cultivate the ability to have OBEs. According to experiencer and writer Graham Nicholls, this can be assisted by practicing visualisation, relaxation, and by being free of fear. All writers on the subject of OBEs state that there is nothing whatsoever to fear in these experiences. From personal experience, I would say that it is not an easy skill to master. As described in the *Introduction*, I did have a modicum of success with my very first attempt, but it is something that I have struggled to replicate since. Many writers and experiencers talk about the need to place the physical body in a sleep state, whilst keeping the mind awake, then willing or tricking the mind out of the body.

Robert Monroe

There have been many modern writers on the subject of the OBE phenomenon. One who I think warrants closer examination is Robert Monroe. In 1958, he was a successful businessman and owned several radio stations. He was married with two children, one would say he was normal in all respects. Then, in the fall of that year, he started to have spontaneous OBEs. These were precipitated by his experimentation with binaural beats to facilitate learning. Binaural beats are two sounds, one played in each ear, that are of slightly different frequencies. This creates the sense of a third tone in addition to the first two. Initially, he did not make the connection between the binaural beats and the OBEs. Instead, he thought that he was ill or dying, so he sought medical advice about both his physical and psychological state. These examinations indicated that he was in perfect health. So, he began to accept the OBE state as a natural part of his life experience, and he decided to explore. Eventually, as his OBEs deepened, he established a research institute to examine the phenomena more thoroughly. The Monroe Institute runs training courses that can assist people achieve the out-of-body state, or to simply expand their horizons.

Monroe also wrote about his experiences in three books: *Journeys Out of the Body*, *Far Journeys*, and *Ultimate Journey*. In my mind, Monroe stands out for his achievements. He is a modern-day Ferdinand Magellan, mapping not the planet but the consciousness energy systems associated with it: an achievement which is not yet either widely known or appreciated. What Monroe says through his books is of immense significance to our understanding of the human condition. But why should we listen to Robert Monroe, any more than we should listen to the Pope, the Dalai Lama, a leading scientist, or a great philosopher? Well, what Monroe learned through his hundreds of out-of-body-explorations, over a span of thirty-seven years, is consistent with a model of the world where time and space are illusions and everything is a projection of consciousness. His experiences are recent, unhindered by cultural overlays, and free from priestly doctrinal interpretation. But as he said himself, *"What to me are Knowns can produce only beliefs in you unless you have had similar experiences."*

Monroe's understanding of consciousness is expressed in what he called focus levels. These are accessible through the OBE process whilst still having a physical life. However, they are better understood by considering what happens after death. The focus levels beyond biological death start with those entities still resonating closely with the physical. The entities here may not even initially know that they are dead, because their experience is so similar to their prior physical existence. The focus levels then extend out to what Monroe calls belief-system-territories. In these locales, one is drawn into an experience based upon the beliefs that one strongly bought into whilst still having a physical experience. In essence, all devout Christians sharing the same earthly beliefs congregate together, as do people who adhere strongly to other religions and denominations. Beyond the belief-system-territories, Monroe describes what he calls the Reception Centre, where entities who do not have strong beliefs about a specific after-life-experience are drawn. Here they are assisted in the process of acclimatisation to their new circumstances. Beyond that, Monroe says there are levels of non-human consciousness.

Knowing

Having an NDE or an OBE does tend to have a transformative effect on people's lives. Pim van Lommel, a Dutch cardiologist, conducted one of the largest hospital-based studies of NDEs, which included three-hundred-and-forty-four experiencers. He then followed up with this group, and with a control group of non-NDE cardiac-arrest survivors after two and eight years, to measure the long-term effect of the NDE experience. Over time, the number of survivors that he could follow up with from both groups did decline. Nevertheless, his studies showed that the NDE group had a greater acceptance of others, were more empathetic and loving, and had a greater appreciation of the ordinary things in life. They had also reduced their fear of death, compared with how they felt about it before their NDE, and when compared with the control group. These findings are consistent with other similar studies that have reported an increased sense of spirituality, but a reduced interest in organised religion. Another of the transformative effects that an NDE can have on people is to increase their psychic abilities, such as clairvoyance, telepathy, precognition, and the ability to have OBEs. Remote viewer Joe McMoneagle had an NDE during a heart attack prior to joining the STARGATE programme, and another one whilst part of the programme. This may have enhanced his ability to remote view.

This sort of direct spiritual experience moves someone's thinking from an intellectual understanding to an experiential 'knowing'. Knowing for sure, knowing for real that you are, in the words of Robert Monroe, *"More than your physical body."* These are game changers for people who have had these experiences. You are no longer being asked to believe, you just *know*. To quote Dr Michael Sabom from *Light & Death* -

"You can read a book of stories about near-death experiences and walk away as sceptical as you were before you picked it up. But when you look into the eyes of an experiencer, and from four feet away watch the ebb and flow of authentic tears, your scepticism begins to wash away."

It is also highly likely that many shamans, founders of religions, and prophets have had similar experiences. Their efforts to describe their experiences or to teach others about them would not be easy. Think again about Plato's cave in *Chapter 2*. After they died, their followers, lacking the ability to replicate the experiences for themselves, would likely fall back onto ritual or dogma to support their views.

Summary

NDE and OBE experiences are a little bit of a conundrum for the materialist brain-creates-consciousness model of the world. As soon as the heart stops beating, blood flow ceases, and ten to twenty seconds after blood has ceased flowing to the brain, all brain activity stops. This can be measured by monitoring electrical activity across the brain using an electroencephalogram. Also, brain stem reflexes can be tested and found to be absent, as was the case with the one-hundred decibel clicks applied to Pam Reynolds' ears. This is clinical death: no heartbeat, no respiration, no brain activity, and no reflexes. Without medical intervention, within five to six minutes brain damage begins to set in, and as time progresses this clinical death becomes irreversible biological death. In a brain-creates-consciousness model of the world, consciousness during clinical death of the kind experienced by Pam Reynolds is impossible. Several physiological explanations have been proffered to explain NDEs, whilst still retaining the brain-creates-consciousness model, including hallucinations, anoxia or hypoxia (lack of oxygen to the brain), disassociation or depersonalisation, hypercarbia (excessive carbon dioxide in the brain), and endorphins released by a dying brain. All have been refuted by the quality of the experiences reported, and by the medical doctors who have conducted the NDE research. If you want to read more about this, Chris Carter's book *Science and the Near-Death Experience* is a good place to start. The quality of the accounts, the results of hospital-based studies, the testimony of healthcare professionals, and the transformative effects of the experiences, mean that we must take this phenomenon seriously.

It is still difficult to say that life after death has been proven scientifically by these accounts. After all, by definition, the experiencer who has the NDE is not dead. What can be said is the brain-creates-consciousness materialistic model is seriously challenged, if not refuted. However, these experiences are consistent with the new model of the world that I am presenting here, where our experience of the material world is a projection of consciousness, within consciousness. In this model, death is simply a transformation to a new form of conscious experience. What this actually means is that we have been mis-labelling the whole out-of-body aspect of NDEs, and the whole field of OBEs. You are not getting out of your body; you do not have a material body, and spirit or soul. What you are doing is journeying further within your own consciousness, not outside of your body, because your experience of a body is inside your consciousness in the first place.

For me, it is the fact that you can interpret the science the way that I presented it in *Chapter 4*, NDEs, and my own OBE, that together convinces me that consciousness continues beyond what we call death. At the very least we need to start changing our narrative about death. It is something which we should no longer fear. This does not mean that it is something which should be sought either. There is value in this physical experience.

Death is a transition to another form of consciousness, the doorway to another range of experiences. I believe that beyond biological death, we take with us the learnings and the experiences of our earthly persona. Yet, still deeper inside we are not just our personas, we are more than that. But what on earth is going on here, or to put that another way, what is the purpose of this Earth life experience? Well, I am afraid we need to go back to school to answer that one…

What have we covered:

- Sometimes, under certain conditions, consciousness can be experienced independently of the physical body.
- Death is not the end.

What remains to be explored:

- What is the purpose of the physical experience?
- How is the physical different from the non-physical?

6. EARTH LIFE SCHOOL

"Life is not a problem to be solved, but a reality to be experienced." - Søren Kierkegaard.

In the film *Saving Private Ryan*, Tom Hanks plays US Army Ranger Captain John Miller. After leading his troops off Omaha Beach on D-Day, he is sent on a dangerous mission behind enemy lines to find paratrooper Private Ryan, who is one of four brothers. Ryan needs to be safely extricated from the dangers of war, because his other three brothers have already been killed in combat. In *Cast Away*, Hanks plays FedEx employee Chuck Noland, who survives a plane crash over the Pacific, and is washed up on a small deserted island. He survives there for several years before deciding to make a bid for freedom. *In Bridge of Spies*, Hanks plays insurance lawyer James Donovan, who is given the unenviable task of defending a Soviet spy in 1950s America, which then leads him to East Berlin to negotiate with the Russians. And in *Toy Story*, Hanks is the voice of Sheriff Woody, whose position as his owner's favourite toy is challenged by the arrival of new toy, Buzz Lightyear. Although he is a great actor, we still know it is Tom Hanks who is playing each role. But each part that Hanks plays is a different character, a different persona.

Reincarnation

In the last chapter, we saw that NDEs and OBEs give us a glimpse of life after death. But we must remember that we only have accounts from a very small percentage of people about what the non-physical is really like. After all, if four aliens were to visit Earth and went separately to New York, the Sahara Desert, the Amazon rainforest, and Antarctica, they would all leave with very different ideas of what Earth was really like. One thing that we do get hints about is, whoever we really are seems to come back again and again to have another Earth life experience.

The belief in souls reincarnating into different bodies is accepted as part of most Eastern religions, including Hinduism, Sikhism, and Buddhism. A little less well-known is that many of the Greek philosophers believed in it too. As I mentioned earlier, in *The Republic*, Plato tells us a story about a soldier called Er who had an NDE. During the experience, Er also observed souls choosing to return to life on Earth, and drinking a draft of forgetfulness before doing so. The modern mainstream version of the Abrahamic religions of Judaism, Christianity, and Islam do not accept reincarnation as part of their belief system. However, the idea of reincarnation does exist in the Jewish oral traditions of the Kabbala. It did exist in historic Christian sects such as the Cathars, and does exist today in the Alawite Islamic sect. Debate still rages about what early Christians did or did not believe; nevertheless, it does seem to be the case that prior to 325 CE, the idea of reincarnation was held more broadly by Christians too. Reincarnation is also a commonly held belief in Western esoteric thinking, the body of secret knowledge passed down orally and only to initiates. But just because some people did or still do hold a belief in reincarnation does not necessarily make it true. After all, it seems a little difficult to prove.

In 1960, American psychiatrist Ian Stevenson published a paper in the American Society for Psychical Research journal titled "*The Evidence for Survival from Claimed Memories of Former Incarnations*". This was a review of forty-four cases, mainly of children, who claimed to have lived previous lives. Stevenson then set out to study cases himself with the help of other investigators. In 1966, he published the book *Twenty Cases Suggestive of Reincarnation*, which covered cases in children from India,

Sri Lanka, Brazil, Lebanon, and from the Tlingit Indians of Alaska. With financial assistance from a sizable donation to the University of Virginia, Stevenson then dedicated much of his career to studying accounts of past lives in children. Today, his work at the university is being continued by child psychiatrist Jim Tucker. Over the past fifty years, they have collected over two-and-a-half-thousand cases of childhood reincarnation.

The pattern suggested by these cases is that, usually between the ages of two and four, small children start talking about a previous life. They will say things to their parents like, *"You are not my mommy"*, or, *"When I was big like daddy…"* Or even a little boy saying, *"Mummy, when I was a girl…"* Children often show unusual patterns of play, phobias, or strong emotions associated with the life that they believe they lived previously. Where possible, Stevenson meticulously documented cases of birthmarks or birth defects. He found that many of these birthmarks were associated with surgery that the previous personality had undergone, or even with their cause of death, including bullet entry and exit wounds, which Stevenson matched with autopsy records. By following up on the information that the child had given, the existing family or investigators would aim to find out who the previous person had been. And to prove or disprove the accuracy of the information provided by the child. Whenever they could, meetings with family members from the previous life were also arranged. If the previous personality could be satisfactorily identified, and if it could be shown that the child had provided correct, verifiable information, the case was described as being solved. This did not prove that it was a case of reincarnation, but it distinguished those cases from one's in which the previous personality had not been identified. Between the ages of six and eight, past life memories tend to fade, and the child grows up in the way any other child would.

James Leininger

Our Western cultural arrogance tends to make us dismiss cases of reincarnation from places such as India. Because after all, people there believe in reincarnation in the first place, and maybe it is just wishful thinking on the part of the families concerned. As most people in the West do not believe in reincarnation, if a child talks about past life memories, they do not tend to get the kind of sympathetic hearing that allows for a serious investigation. However, Jim Tucker has focused his research on Western cases. One of the best documented cases was thoroughly researched and solved by the family themselves before Tucker reviewed it. This is the case of James Leininger, who was the subject of a Primetime TV programme in 2004. In 2009, James' parents Bruce and Andrea Leininger published the book *Soul Survivor*, with Ken Gross, about their son's past life recollections.

In 2000, when he was just past his second birthday, James started to have dreadful nightmares. The nightmares and the accompanying screaming and thrashing in bed became frequent, occurring several times a week. His mother was always there at his bedside to comfort him, and she assumed initially that it was normal, or maybe related to the family's recent house move. Then, as the nightmares persisted, she began to notice that whilst they were occurring, James was saying: *"Airplane crash! Plane on fire! Little man can't get out!"* From about this time, James became obsessed by aircraft, particularly World War II aircraft. Months passed, and James' nightmares had not abated. Then, one night, whilst his mum was reading him bedtime stories, James lay on his back and kicked his legs in the air, like he did in his nightmares, but this time without the emotion. He said, *"Little man is going like this."* Then, he kicked in the air again and said, *"Ohh! Ohh! Ohh! Can't get out!"* When his mum asked him who could not get out, he said, *"Me"*. Andrea fetched her husband so that he could listen to what James was saying too. Then, they asked James what happened to his plane. *"It crashed on fire"*, he said. His mum asked him why, *"It got shot."*, he replied. And when his dad asked him who shot his plane, two-year-old James made an exasperated face, rolled his eyes, and said, *"The Japanese!"*

Over the next few weeks James' father gathered more information from his young son. James told him that he flew Corsairs, an American World War II fighter, and that he flew from a boat called 'Natoma'. His father did not believe him; partly due to his Christian upbringing, which prohibits the idea of reincarnation, and because if anything, 'Natoma' sounded Japanese, not American. Nevertheless, a quick internet search brought up the name of the US escort carrier that had served in the pacific during World War II, called the *Natoma Bay*. Over the next four years, Bruce

Leininger investigated the increasing amount of information his young son gave him. Initially, he set out to prove that James was wrong about his past-life-memories. But eventually, Bruce became convinced that James is the reincarnation of World War II American pilot James Huston. There is a lot more to this story, which I have not included here, some of it is simply staggering.

From the Mouths of Babes

Based on the analysis of the two-and-a-half-thousand cases that the University of Virginia has gathered over the past fifty years, Tucker makes the following observations:

- Seventy percent of the cases are described as solved.
- Ninety percent of the children in the cases talk about a life as the same gender.
- Seventy-five percent of the children in the cases talk about their mode of death.
- Of these, seventy percent died an unnatural death, which means murder, suicide, or accidents.
- Of the unnatural death cases in the collection, seventy-three percent are boys.

This final statistic actually mirrors the proportion of males, compared to females, who die unnaturally in the general population. Tucker found that the median age of death in the previous life was twenty-eight years old, and that the median time between incarnations is only fifteen to sixteen months. Though in the Leininger case, the time between incarnations was fifty-three years. The number of children talking about life between lives is small, at around ten percent, but the descriptions given bear an uncanny resemblance to NDEs, including out-of-body observations, going to a light, and even choosing re-birth parents.

So, what does this mean? If we accept that these stories from small children are not fabrications, something which, given the investigations and the corroboration, seems to me to be unlikely in all cases, then we are being asked to accept that memories and emotions are accessible from one person to another over time and space. This is possible in the model of the world we are exploring here. If time and space are illusions, if everything is one thing, and if vibration and resonance are key, then these sorts of experiences are entirely feasible.

But in this new model, the word reincarnation is not well-defined. And this is because memories of a previous life that people have are not past in a literal sense. In the model of everything existing now, these are simply experiences that you are accessing about events which are also happening now. It is much like having several television screens on at the same time, all of which are showing different programmes. Most of the time, you are focusing on one of the screens, but from time to time, you watch the highlights which are playing out on another channel. James Leininger and James Huston are not the same person. In our space-time reality, James Huston appears to be a past life of James Leininger, but in reality, both lives are happening now. What is remarkable in this case is that James Leininger is able to connect to James Huston in such a conscious manner. In all likelihood, at some other level of existence, they do share a common experience, much in the way that white light can be divided into all the colours of the rainbow. From the perspective of the white light, all the colours are one; nevertheless, from the perspective of both James', they are different colours of light.

Know Thy Self

So far, this new model is suggesting that time is an illusion; our experience of physical reality is a projection of consciousness, within consciousness; death is a transition, and at the very least, memories and their emotional content are accessible across life-times. A wild ride indeed, and you might be left wondering: if all this is true, then, *"Who am I?"*

For years, whenever I introduced myself, I would say: *"Hi, I'm Ewan, I'm an accountant."* I guess what I really meant was, *"Hi. I'm the personality construct and the physical body which other people will recognise by the name that my parents gave me, which is Ewan."* That always seemed like a bit of a mouthful, and perhaps I should not have been describing myself as simply being my profession. So, I shortened it down for convenience to *"Hi, I'm Ewan."* But is that really who I am? I have twice had the experience of waking up in the morning, with no drugs or alcohol involved, and of lying in bed looking at the ceiling thinking, *"What is this!?"*. What I meant was, *"What is this experience that I am having?"* At the same time, I was not making any connection to the personality construct or the physical body identified by the label of 'Ewan'. 'Reality' returned to my consciousness with the thought of, *"Oh, that's what I'm doing"*. Maybe I should be describing myself by my behaviour after all.

Perhaps you have never even asked yourself the question, *"Who am I?"* But it is often the simple questions that yield the greatest insight. If we do consider this question, and if we are honest with ourselves, the best that we can come up with is, *"I am a personality construct having a physical experience"*. This means we consider ourselves to have had past experiences currently represented by memories. We have beliefs about ourselves, things that we value in life, preferences, skills, and we do certain behaviours, either by habit, instinct, or choice. All these things together we might call our persona. And the Latin root of the word 'persona' means 'mask'. But if we take off the mask, we are left with the idea that we do not really know who we are, not for sure anyway. I encourage you to explore this idea. You consist of layers, much like an onion. Get to know yourself better, examine the components of your personality, and keep on digging deeper, because whoever or whatever you think you are, you are still more than that…

What Does it Mean?

In Douglas Adams' novel, *The Hitchhiker's Guide to the Galaxy*, the answer to the ultimate question of 'life-the-universe-and-everything' is presented by super computer Deep Thought, after millions of years of computation, as forty-two. Deep Thought tells its confused audience that its answer may seem meaningless, simply because its programmers did not really know what the question was. Deep Thought goes on to say that it does not know what the ultimate question is either, but it can help design an even better computer which will do that job. This super computer is, of course, Earth. Many convoluted theories have been suggested about why Adams chose the number forty-two as the meaning of life. He was asked many times too, and this was all that he ever offered: *"It was a joke. It had to be a number, an ordinary, smallish number, and I chose that one... I sat at my desk, stared into the garden, and thought '42 will do'. I typed it out. End of story."*

What he highlighted with the whole 'forty-two' meme is that nobody really knows for sure what the meaning of life is, and what makes us think that there should be any meaning anyway?

How do we make sense of a world where time and space are illusions, where everything is a projection of your own consciousness, and where 'we' seem to have more than one life, simultaneously? It is almost enough to make you ask, *"What's the point of it all?"* Well, actually, you have already been living in a world where time and space do not exist, where everything is a projection of your own consciousness, and where 'you' live more than one life; you just did not know that you were. As I have said before, everything starts with awareness. What we need to do is unlearn what we have been taught which is erroneous, and re-learn who we are, how cause and effect works, and where all this is taking us.

A good place to start *is* with the big question: *"What is life all about?"* If you asked a thousand people this question, you might well get a thousand different answers. All the disciplines that we have touched on so far have their own versions and sub-versions of what the meaning of life is. In the paragraph below, I have set out what I think life is all about. Nevertheless, somewhat inevitably, you will have to decide what the meaning of life is for yourself.

If now is all there is, then we must be able to answer even a big question like *"What is life all about?"* in this now. In the now, you have two things: you are aware, and you are aware of something, which is your experience. Therefore, awareness of the experience must be the point. *Why do we keep on making it more complicated than that!* All the time that you are conscious, you are having an experience; therefore, your experience is the purpose. When you are watching television, doing the ironing, sitting in a traffic jam, eating, sleeping, watching a sunset, having a drink with friends, or working: all of these experiences, every single experience that you have, *is* the purpose. But what does your experience mean?

As Above so Below

There are some features about the non-physical locale which stand out from all the OBE literature. One is that your experience changes immediately in accordance with your thinking. Another feature is like-attracts-like; it is your vibrational frequency that determines which focus level you will experience. And communication between entities seems to occur by some form of thought transference. To quote Robert Monroe, *"As you think so you are. In this environment, no mechanical supplements are found. No cars, boats, airplanes, or rockets are needed for transportation. You think movement, and it is fact. No telephones, radio, television, and other communication aids have value. Communication is instantaneous."* In the non-physical, your perception is enhanced and physical reality is a pale facsimile of the non-physical. For example, vision is reported to be three-hundred-sixty-degree. In his book *The Holographic Universe*, Michael Talbot reports an account from an American WWII veteran who reported an NDE. When he returned to the physical, he temporarily retained his three-hundred-sixty-degree vision, and *"...while running away from a German machine-gun nest... Not only could he see ahead as he ran, but he could see the gunners trying to draw a bead on him from behind."*

From our earthly perspective, our whole narrative is predicated on there being a physical reality, because that is how it seems to be. What we then debate is whether we have a soul or a spirit, and if there is a non-physical reality too, or not? By changing our model of the world, one of the things that we need to unlearn is that 'physical' reality is not physical in the way that we think it is. What we call physical reality is a projection of consciousness within consciousness. The principle difference between physical reality and the non-physical is that here, in the physical, there is a gap between thought and experience. Or to quote Kabbalist Yehuda Berg, *"Kabbalah defines time as the distance between cause and effect."*

The physical world is a slowed down version of how things operate in the non-physical. The other big difference, of course, is that we think that physical reality is real; and by 'real', I mean that it has existence independent of our consciousness, whereas it does not. Physical reality exists *within* our consciousness. The difference lies in the fluidity of the non-physical as compared to how we currently experience the physical, not in the underlying nature or structure of reality. It is different in type, yes, but not different in form, which is that experience is based on thought. Just another way of saying that it is a reflection of mind, or consciousness.

So, if everything is slowed down in the physical, what might be the purpose of doing that? Well, in the physical, *we* slow things down to learn how to do them before we then speed them up. *Tai-chi* can be many things to different people. It can be a mild form of exercise, a meditation of movement, or a regular spiritual discipline. The root of *Tai-chi* is that it represents a way of teaching martial arts moves by performing them in slow-motion.

I believe that this is also, at least in part, what the Western esoteric tradition is referring to with the maxim, *"As above so below"*. This statement is embedded within the symbolism of the Tarot, the Free Masons, the Star of David, and it even appears on the Great Seal of the USA, above the eagle's head. I understand it to mean, the way cause and effect works *there*, is the same as how it works *here.* Our physical reality has the same structure as the non-physical. It is only our attachment to continuity, frame by frame, that makes it seem otherwise. And we are only doing that because we think that physical reality is about things-in-space-over-time, although as we have already discussed, that notion is false.

Earth Life School

In the instances where a life review occurred, or a being of light was met during an NDE, there was no external judgement. If there was any prompting from the 'outside', it was in the form of questions. Such as, *"Are you ready to die?"*; *"What have you done with your life to show me?"* These are examples from Raymond Moody's book *Life After Life*. Moody believes that the questions are used to create an opportunity within the experiencer to reflect on their life so far. From these sorts of questions, and from the experiences of people who have had life reviews, Moody thinks that what is being stressed about life is learning to love other people and acquiring knowledge.

Reading Robert Monroe's work, you get the distinct impression that who we are is not just a human persona having a physical experience. Instead, he suggested that we are some form of 'soul' energy accessing a series of human experiences, so that we can learn and grow. According to Monroe, souls are attracted to the uniqueness of the human experience. They then undergo a descent into human form. In the process, they forget who they are, until through many lives, they ascend, gradually remembering who they really are until they finally emerge from the human cycle profoundly changed by the experience. The impression coming through Monroe's work is that Earth, and the human experience, is like a school, from which one eventually graduates.

One of the things that is interesting about Monroe's observation is that it echoes the work of mythologist Joseph Campbell. Campbell studied myths from all cultures, and through his book *The Hero with a Thousand Faces*, he brought the idea of The Hero's Journey into our consciousness. Broadly, the Hero's journey plays out like this:

- The hero is called. The hero may resist the call, but eventually, the hero departs on their journey.
- During the journey, there are tests and trials, but there is also assistance, often supernatural.
- There is a climax, transformation, the death of the old self, and the birth of the new.
- Finally, the hero returns to serve.

Campbell traced this construct through ancient mythology, although you can see it in modern storytelling too, such as JRR Tolkien's *Lord of the Rings*. It is present in the *Star Wars* films as well, which were directly influenced by Campbell's work. And you can see the same motif played out in the film the *Matrix*. The story of the Hero's Journey can also be told through the Tarot, which actually represents more of a teaching tool rather than simply a fortune telling curio.

Campbell's Hero's Journey runs like a thread through a series of lives, individually and collectively. Forgetting, descending, being tested and challenged, and through that process changing into something new and expanded. Human experience is a school, or rather, a high-class university. Graduation is a prize worthy of the challenge. There are several learning outcomes, which we will explore in the next chapter. Nevertheless, these can be summed up by the word *transformation*. We are engaged in an exploratory, experiential learning exercise, which includes forgetting who we really are, so that we can rediscover who we are from a new perspective.

It is only with this sort of expanded model of the world that it is possible for us to make sense of our human experience. If, as I am saying, everything is a reflection of you, then who in their right mind would choose to have a particularly negative experience that may include pain, suffering, and/or injustice? It is only with an expanded perspective that it is possible to make sense of these aspects of the human condition. Using film as an analogy, if each life is like watching a film, what sort of film would you choose to watch? Comedy, thriller, romance, science fiction, or horror? Personally, I would never choose to watch a horror film, because I watched them as a teenager, and I did not enjoy the experience. But some people do like the drama and the emotional rollercoaster of horror movies. So, if someone I loved asked me to watch one with them, because they really like them, then I would watch a horror movie, so that I could share the experience with the person I love. And if you saw a film where everyone was happy at the start, stayed happy throughout, and faced no challenges at all during the film, what would you think? I for one would leave the cinema thinking that I had just wasted two hours of my life!

If you want to learn about compassion, then you need someone else who is suffering. If you want to experience forgiving, you need someone to do something to you that permits you to forgive. If you want the experience of being a doctor or a nurse, you need someone who is sick. If you want to teach, then you need people who have things to learn. If you want the experience of discovering something new, you need to forget that you already know it. And if you want to experience transformation, then a descent into darkness is actually a good idea.

The God Illusion

"A god is personification of a motivating power or a value system that functions in human life and in the universe." – Joseph Campbell.

Blaise Pascal, a 17th century French mathematician, suggested that every rational person should believe in God, because if they are wrong, they lose nothing, and if they are right, they have an eternity in heaven to gain. The idea of an omnipotent, all-powerful deity is not unique to the monotheistic religions of today. In ancient Egypt, Amun existed within and beyond Nun, the deep limitless ocean from which the Earth arose. Amun was the supreme, invisible, unseen power behind all things; he was self-created and existed before all other gods. Re or Ra was the manifestation of physical power represented by the sun at midday. So, Amun-Ra was the combination of invisible and visible power. In Persian Zoroastrianism, Ahura Mazda was an all-powerful invisible deity. As I said in *Chapter 2*, Zoroastrianism is most likely the monotheistic branch of an early belief system, the polytheistic branch of which is Hinduism. In Hinduism, Brahman is the creative principle behind all that is. The God of the *Bible*, which is in effect the same God for Jews, Christians, and Muslims, is similarly regarded, but chronologically comes along after the gods of the other belief systems that I mentioned before. Buddhism and Daoism are religions without a supreme deity. In Buddhism, one seeks to free one's self from suffering and attain enlightenment. In Daoism, there is an underlying sense of connecting with the way that everything is, and by so doing, everything happens. And from philosophy, Kant said that you cannot really prove or disprove the existence of God.

So, there are plenty of ideas and philosophies about God. Science has pushed right back against the prior province of God, but it has not provided a full and comprehensive alternative picture, or you could argue that it has not done so yet. In the model of the world that I am presenting here, where time is an illusion and everything you experience is a reflection of your consciousness, there is nothing on the outside. There is no need for a creator because everything that exists just exists. If now is all there is, then there cannot be a creator in the first place, because there is no 'first place'. If you like labels and want to retain an idea about God, then the label that fits best is Pantheism. This suggests that God is the universe, and everything in the universe is God. This label is often retrofitted to Spinoza's ideas of oneness, and Pantheists claim Spinoza as one of their own. I think everything is one thing, because I think that is where quantum physics and the science of time takes us. It is also where the evidence that consciousness is not produced by and in the brain takes us too. Within this understanding, I see no need for a creator and no need for a deity. In a sense, we are all aspects and expressions of God; there is no separation, all is One. There is no deity involved in people's lives, nor is there a deity watching His creation unfold from the outside. When people sense a deity listening to their prayers, they are experiencing the material world projected by their own mind, through the filter of the religious idea of a deity. By this understanding, *you are God*, and so is everyone else…

Nevertheless, I appreciate that this is a tough pill to swallow for the millions of people around the world who believe in, and take comfort from, the idea of some form of supreme deity. But by doing so, they are giving up their own creative power to something else that they think is on the outside. The thing is, there is no outside. Man creates the concept of God, and then he projects that idea out onto what he considers to be the outside world. What we have failed to realise is that all the power of creation has always been on the inside all along.

"All the gods, all the heavens, all the hells, are within you…You've got to find the Force inside you." - Joseph Campbell.

Summary

In this chapter, we have been pushing right up against the limits of what we can know and asking ourselves: *"Who am I?"* and *"What does it all mean?"* My journey and the journey of others is suggesting to me that this human experience is like being in a school; Earth Life School. We are here to experience, to interact, to learn, and to love.

I get the sense that we have, at some level, chosen to have a human experience. We come into this life-dream with a persona that evolves and develops as our life unfolds. We have a theme in this life that we are exploring, and challenges to face, so that we can overcome them and thereby experience and grow. Imagine it like this: at your very core, who you are is Tom Hanks. But in this life, you might be Tom Hanks being Captain Miller, saving Private Ryan. So, do not try to be Tom Hanks; just be Captain Miller, and become the best Captain Miller that you can be. In rare instances, as you are being Captain Miller, you might connect with the sense of being Chuck Noland working at FedEx. But in this film, you are not Chuck Noland, you are Captain Miller. And at the same time, although the experience of being Captain Miller feels so real, know that deep down inside, you really *are* Tom Hanks.

So, if we are in school, what are the specific lessons that we need to learn?

What have we covered:

- Who are you?
- Physical reality is structurally the same as non-physical reality.
- You are God and so is everyone else.
- Physical reality is Earth Life School.
- Life is about experience and transformation.

What remains to be explored:

- How do you live life as your current persona?
- What do individual experiences mean?
- What are the lessons that we need to learn whilst in Earth Life School?

7. LESSONS IN LOVE

"Live as if you were to die tomorrow. Learn as if you were to live forever." - Gandhi.

There are many ways to learn something, in education one size does not fit all. As a teacher, you must find a way to communicate with your students so that they learn what they need to learn in a manner that works for them. You can use direct instruction, or metaphorical stories, you can set tasks or exercises, and you can provide feedback. You also need to consider the sequence that information is taught in. Make sure it is not too big-picture, because this could lose your students. And that it is not too detailed, as this might bore them. You can teach students deductively or inductively. Teaching deductively means laying out the big-picture before going into the details. Teaching inductively means that you teach the details and allow your students to make the connection back to the big-picture for themselves.

It seems to me that Earth Life School is an immersive, inductive learning experience. We are given the detail of our lives and we are left to figure out what it all means by ourselves. In my opinion, inductive learning is the most effective way to teach, because it makes students think in a connective and expansive manner. However, too much of it can make your students grumpy, because they *are* having to think more for themselves. So, in the interest of adding a little balance back to our learning experience, I am going to start deductively with the big-picture. I am going to suggest what I think the learning outcomes in Earth Life School really are. In my opinion, through a series of lives, we learn how to take responsibility for our own life; we learn to love ourselves; to cultivate a mentality of abundance; to love others; and to deal with adversity. By achieving these learning outcomes, through your current life, and through other lives that you may be connected to, you can ultimately graduate from Earth Life School.

Responsibility Class

Perhaps the most important class of all for us to graduate from is Responsibility Class. Responsibility is your innate ability to choose how to respond to situations that crop up in your life: your *response-ability*. If your experience is a reflection of your consciousness, then you are responsible for what you experience. What this means is not necessarily that you have chosen your experience, not consciously anyway. Rather, it is that you have the power to choose how you respond to your situation.

To the extent that you do not accept responsibility for where you are in life, then you are powerless to transform it. If you persist in blaming other people for your current life situation, then you are saying to yourself that the situation is outside of your control. By doing so, you will then have the experience of being out of control. Remember, your experience is a reflection of your thinking. If your current life situation was the fault of your parents, your teachers, your partner or ex-partner, if it is God's will, some grand conspiracy, decisions made by large corporations, or simply blind chance, then you are giving up your power to do anything to change your circumstances.

If you choose to accept your responsibility for the situation that you are in, then you are empowering yourself to transform it. To be honest, I find most people are prepared to accept that there are some things about themselves and their lives that they are responsible for; but for some other things it is more difficult. Of course, that is perfectly fine. The way that I encourage people to approach this issue is like this: your current circumstances do not matter, all that matters is how you choose to respond to those circumstances. If you believe that at some 'higher' and very unconscious level, you chose to undergo the experience that you are currently having, then knowing that consciously does not always take away the pain from the current experience. So, whether you really did choose it or not does not make any difference, but choosing to act like there is positive purpose in the experience makes a huge difference. Because despite what is happening or has happened to you, if you accept it and respond positively to it, you will reflect that positive response back into the physical world you experience.

Here are a couple of examples from people I know. One was a British soldier who stood on an improvised explosive device (IED) in Afghanistan. As a result of this, he lost both legs above the knee and his right arm above his elbow. He was right-handed. Since then, he has medalled in the Invictus Games, and he does motivational talks for business, schools, and charities. He says the whole experience was tough, particularly the rehabilitation and learning to walk on prosthetics. But he also says he is now able to do things in his life that he would not have been able to do without going through the experience. The other person I know is someone who had cancer in his tongue. This required surgery to remove half of his tongue and then reconstruct it. The path for anyone through serious illness is tough. He has had moments of doubt, anger, and pain. Frequently, he has asked himself the question, *"Why me?"*. Yet, he has had the courage to confront this disease and share his journey from diagnosis through surgery and rehabilitation. He has listed ten positives of going through the experience, including deepening his relationship with his wife, and helping others who are going through similar experiences. What these people have done is accepted responsibility for their situation, even if they would not have consciously chosen to go through the experience. They reacted positively and have produced a positive effect.

Someone else that I take a lesson from here is Viktor Frankl. Frankl survived seven months as a slave labourer in Auschwitz and other concentration camps during World War II. He was a psychiatrist before the war, and afterwards he wrote the book *Man's Search for Meaning*, about his camp experiences. He spoke about how his life was reduced in the camp, about the cold, the pain of starvation, and the injustice. He wrote about how he was able to transcend even these experiences. To quote Frankl: *"the last of the human freedoms – to choose one's attitude in any given set of circumstances, to choose one's own way"*. Frankl was not saying that he was responsible for being held in a concentration camp. But he was saying that once he was there, he was responsible for choosing how to react to being there. Frankl is a very influential figure in the personal development field. His book still helps people facing adversity today.

Being able to pass Responsibility Class can be a big ask for us, individually and collectively. But if we are going to move forward by ourselves and together, then it is one that we must study hard at and aim to get good grades in. If we fail this class, then we will be left shaking our fists at some invisible force outside of ourselves, when in reality, all we are actually doing is looking in a mirror at some angry person shaking their fists right back at us!

"Life ultimately means taking the responsibility to find the right answer to its problems and to fulfil the tasks which it constantly sets for each individual."- Viktor Frankl.

First Love

One of the most important aspects of our lives that we need to take responsibility for is our own sense of self-worth. After all it is called *self*-belief and *self*-confidence for a reason, because it comes from within. If we think we are not good enough, then we tend not to push ourselves outside our comfort zone. And if things are not going our way in life, we internalise that sense of failure and blame ourselves, or lash out at the people around us. This can become a disempowering, destructive cycle, and can be quite debilitating, preventing us from doing things in life that we want to do.

But think about yourself this way instead: you exist within the infinite vastness of all that exists in the Super-Now. You exist. Therefore, there must be value in looking at existence from your perspective, otherwise you would not exist. But you do! So, there is value in your existence. Know that. Self-confidence and self-belief are about being open to the questions and challenges that life presents to us, not necessarily about having all the answers. For sure, we do not all come into this life with the same skills or abilities. Therefore, do not spend your life comparing yourself negatively to other people. Compare yourself only with the person that you have been before, and the person that you want to become. If there are things about yourself that you do not like, then do something about changing them. If you cannot or do not want to change them, then live with them, because they then become part of the expression of who you are. Love and accept yourself as you are. If you cannot love and accept yourself, then how can you expect anyone else to love and accept you? Imagine if I went on a date and said, *"Hi, I'm Ewan. I think that I'm unlovable and unworthy. But you have to love me!"* If you do love and accept yourself, you do not need anyone else's love anyway. This is actually the best mindset to start a new relationship from. Understand now that you must take responsibility for your own life and that, before we even consider sharing our love with others, we need to love and accept the person that we are now. There are many reasons why people think they are unworthy or unlovable. Usually, it is the contextual frame of their past that leads them to have beliefs about themselves, and negative emotions in the present that hold them back. Whatever the perceived cause, it is still possible to change these in the now and to be able to love the only person that you can guarantee will be in every scene throughout the movie of your life, which is you, of course.

I believe everyone is doing the best they can with the resources that they have. This is the basis of forgiveness. You may well do better and achieve more in the future, but right now, and in the past, you did the best you could with what you had. We all make mistakes in life. I have made too many to even list here. But what is important is to learn from the mistakes that we make. I know that sometimes we do not learn straight away either, and we go on to make the same mistakes again. But it remains possible for you, and for us all collectively, to learn what we have failed to learn before, and to do that right now. After all, we are not in Earth Life School because we have nothing to learn. Just because we made past mistakes does not mean that they need to define us now. So, find the courage to forgive yourself. If you think it necessary to apologise for what you have done in the past, then do so. Even if you cannot do so face to face, at least do it with conviction in your own mind; learn, and move on. Let your future behaviour become testimony to your experience and your ability to learn.

If I search deep down inside myself, I know that at my very core I am positive. And there is nothing special about me, so I would expect that deep down inside, everyone else is positive too. Behaviour that we judge to be negative comes from the disconnection to both our inherent positivity and our unlimited creative power. Our only fault is not realising just how powerful we are. That does not mean that we need to put up with negative behaviours in our society. But we do need to work on our societal structures, so that people can learn about their power in a way that does not bring harm to self or others.

As I said above, we do not all have the same talents, we do not all have the same skills and abilities, and we do not all make the same contribution. But you exist as equally as everyone else does. Imagine existence to be a large mosaic. Each individual tesserae might be a different colour or combination of colours. One might be the eye of an angel, the toe of a frog, or simply a blue piece of sky. Each piece of the mosaic is just as important as every other piece. No one piece is better than another, they are all made from the same material, and the whole scene depicted by the mosaic is incomplete unless every single piece is present.

Abundance Mentality

The reality that I am describing in this book is a multiverse. We are having the experience of living on a small rocky ball, orbiting an average star. But we are not really just living on a small rocky ball orbiting an average star. Every second of every day, we are traversing through billions of static frames of information, which then gives us the *impression* that we have continuity and physicality. But this sense of continuity and physicality is not part of the underlying structure of our reality. What that means is we are not limited by what we think of as the material world. We are not bound by the past, other people, society, government, money, or natural resources. The only limitations that we have in life are the ones that we have imposed upon ourselves. And to be fair, not all limitations need to be regarded negatively anyway. Some are present in our lives so that we can have certain experiences and thereby learn and grow. But the limitations that we face in life that stop us being who we are can be released, by understanding that existence, our existence, is inherently abundant.

If time is an illusion and everything exists now, then we are not constrained by our past. It does not define us and it cannot limit us. In this new model, it is the present that defines the past, not the past that defines the present. All of what we understand to be the past we access in the now. In the next now, we could connect to a very different past; and if we retain the idea of continuity, then we would never even know that the past we had before was different to the one that we experience now.

If you break the continuity, then you might be a little confused, or you might think a miracle had happened. There is a teacher I know who told me that he was out for a walk with friends and was having such a great day, he thought that the only way to make it better would be to have enough money to buy his friends afternoon tea. But unfortunately, he had no money. At the very moment he had this thought, he told me that his *"pocket filled with change"*, and he had just enough money to buy his friends afternoon tea, and no more. In a things-in-space-over-time model, that sort of experience is impossible. The only explanation would be that my friend forgot that he really did have the money, that he had some form of delusion, or even that he lied to me. But in this new abundant model, what happened is that he traversed into a different time-line where everything else was just as it was in the previous one; the only difference was that in this time-line, he did have some money in his pocket. Because he somehow broke the sense of continuity that we all usually hang on to, the experience really did stand out to him as somewhat strange. I have re-told this story many times on training courses. On one course, a senior police firearms officer was attending. We were having a drink after the course, and he said he enjoyed the training, but he did not believe that money could just appear in one's pocket. We then went to the bar together to get a round of drinks. As he was about to pay, he looked down, and there on the floor at his feet was a ten-pound note.

When it comes to other people in our lives, we are sharing an interaction with them. As they take the information in a Now and project it through their consciousness, you are doing the same thing through yours. In this space-time-earth-life experience, we are separate and independently functioning entities, even if we are all one at some other level. The other people who are in your life now are all there to reflect things back to you. And in their reality, you are reflecting things back to them. Then, based on your choices, you traverse into another frame that contains a *version* of the other person that will be reflecting something back to you based upon *your* choices. They will appear to have continuity to the person in the previous frame, but they may not actually be the 'same' person that you interacted with before. It does not really matter if they are or not, what matters is realising that you are not limited by other people around you. They reflect you, and if you consciously or unconsciously choose to be limited by them, then you will have the experience of being limited by them. Although I know that everyone else is a projection of my consciousness, I still interact with them in a way that honours them as separate entities. At some level, they are. You might think that does not sound much different to a things-in-space-over-time model. But the very big difference is that you are not *limited* by others unless *you* choose to be. I assume everyone I encounter is just like me, no better, no worse, and that they are in my life to reflect something back to me.

Act in a manner that connects with the idea of abundance. Live your life knowing that your expression of you within this abundant existence is also abundant. I use the idea of abundance to help guide coaching clients to where they want to go. In the same way, I buy into your ability to achieve, because in this abundant multiverse, the person you want to be already exists now!

Relate

"Once a human being has arrived on earth, communication is the largest single factor determining what kinds of relationships she or he makes with others and what happens to each in the world." – Virginia Satir.

It is important to understand that everyone else in your life has their own unique perspective. They have their own prior experiences, values, beliefs, and preferences. So, you can begin to appreciate that not everyone else thinks and behaves the same way that you do. This is why clear honest communication in relationships with other people is essential. I have a preference for the big picture, contemplating ideas and concepts, but my business partner prefers details. She also represents her world visually and through feelings, whereas I prefer thinking as a way to understand my world. She was brought up in working-class inner-city Manchester, and she played volleyball for England. On the other hand, I grew up in a middle-class family in the suburbs, and performed at my best academically. We have had totally different life experiences, so we need to make sure that we communicate effectively to work together. We do this by making allowances for the fact that our perspectives are different; well, most of the time… Communication encompasses at least as much listening as it does talking. And even talking is not the only way that we communicate either. Much of what we are communicating comes from our physiology and the tone of voice we use.

There are always three parts to any relationship: you, the other person, and the relationship. Because people change over time and because our life circumstances can change too, any relationship will evolve. Allow other people in your life to be who they really are. Give them the space to explore who they are. Avoid wanting to put them into a box, just because that box works for you. By doing so you can then become who you really are too. Build trust with others by aligning what you say with what you do. Reinforce positive associations with other people. This means doing things together that you enjoy doing together, whatever that is. And communicate honestly without judgement. By doing these things you are taking responsibility for your input into the relationship. Become an example to other people by the way you behave in the relationship. Invite them to match your positive choices, without insisting that they do.

As well as loving yourself, loving others is a key learning outcome in Earth Life School. The easiest way to quickly assess your love for others is to ask yourself, how unconditional is your love? Usually, for most people their unconditional love is reserved for their pets and their children, and not for anyone else. How unconditional is your love for your partner? Now, I am not saying to you that it needs to be unconditional, I am just asking you to explore that. As you reflect on this, notice also how easily love expands. You have an unlimited supply of it. As more people come into your life, your love grows to accommodate them.

If you intend to stay in a long-term relationship with someone, then I would recommend that you find the courage to forgive past mistakes. This does not mean that you accept certain behaviours happening again. It simply means that if you want a relationship to continue, then constantly bringing up the past becomes a barrier to moving forward. Forgive, or move on. Remember that other people are there to reflect things back to you. One of these things could be the idea that it is time to move on from this form of relationship with this individual – we are not manacled together for ever.

The Good, the Bad, and the Ugly

"We came to this world to create positive change within ourselves and the world around us. Positive change will encounter resistance, conflict, and obstacles. We must embrace these difficult situations." – Yehuda Berg.

Sometimes, there are challenges to be faced in life. Everything is not always peaches and cream. How can we make sense of what appear to be negative experiences? One of the things to remember is that experience is just experience. You only assess what it means by comparing your current situation with others, and then asking yourself which one you prefer. If all your life had been spent sleeping on hard ground, you would not think that this was unpleasant or unnatural. If you then slept on something which was, by comparison, much softer, then you could choose which one you preferred. Good and bad are words which imply a comparison. All meaning is context dependant, each individual situation does not come with a built-in meaning. You only know what things mean in comparison to other things that you have experienced, or could imagine experiencing. That does not mean that you do not or should not have preferences; you do. Just avoid invalidating a situation based on your immediate judgement. Sometimes, you need to see the whole unfolding of events to help make sense out of what is happening in a particular moment. Here is a story from Robert Hopcke's book, *There Are No Accidents*, which I have paraphrased.

"Stephen had a long-held ambition to become a filmmaker. He got a degree in filmmaking and set out to follow his dream. He applied for several jobs, but no one was hiring filmmakers. A year later, all he had been doing was taking pictures of babies. Then his car caught fire and blew up, almost killing him. Resigned to never becoming a filmmaker, because TV stations always wanted people with experience that he did not have, he decided to sell his movie camera. He had originally bought it

thinking that he would become a filmmaker, but now, he needed a replacement car if he was going to continue as a baby photographer. So, reluctantly, he put his movie camera up for sale in a newspaper. One morning, he received a call from a guy at a TV company who was looking for a spare camera to keep in his car. The man said he would pop round that evening to check out Stephen's camera. When he did, he asked Stephen whether or not he could film live broadcast news. Apparently, that afternoon, another cameraman had been shot, and they needed a short-term replacement while he recovered. This break gave Stephen the experience he needed to get a job with another station a few months later."

Things turned out well for Stephen, but they seem a little tough on the guy who 'took a bullet' for him. Though the ultimate truth of the matter is that we do not know if that guy thought the experience he had was tough or not. We just do not know, and we cannot judge.

So, what does an individual experience mean then? Again, if we examine this question in the moment, who is it who decides what things mean? Well, that would be you. Your consciousness is a reflection of you, so you get to decide what your experience means. In any situation, there is always a choice as to how to interpret the experience. If you fail an exam, you get to choose what you think about that situation. You could decide that your failure was because you did not do any revision; or that you did not allocate your time well enough during the exam; or maybe that you mis-read a question, or that you are actually no good at that subject; or perhaps all of the above. The result is the result, the situation is the situation, but you still get to choose what it means. For sure, we do get other people on the 'outside' who are telling us what an experience should mean. If you failed an exam, your parents, your teachers, or your friends might try to 'help' you interpret what that should mean for you. But when all is said and done, you still get to do the choosing. If you break the law in the country where you live, again, people on the 'outside' are going to try to tell you what that experience means for you. But even if you end up in jail, you still get to choose what that experience means too. If you did not get to choose, then surely everyone who comes out of prison would be reformed by their incarceration.

And still, you may be tempted to ask, *"Why do bad things happen to good people?"* Remember that good and bad are words created by an unconscious comparison. Inside yourself, you judge whether or not something is good or bad by comparing it with other things. Again, your experience does not come with a pre-set built-in meaning. You get to decide what it means. But you do not get to decide what it means for someone else, they have to do that. You might say, *"Why did this super-nice chap have to stand on an IED in Afghanistan?"*; *"Why do children get cancer?"*; *"Why did my partner have to die so young?"* You do not know! How do you know that someone is really 'super-nice'? How do you know that this 'bad thing' will not actually turn out to be the very best thing that ever happened to someone? It is their life, and their experience. They get to judge, and to choose about it for themselves, and you get to choose and judge things about you. Someone else might even go through something which you think is terrible, so that you can learn from it by vicariously watching them, rather than having to go through something similar yourself. If that was the case, then their 'terrible' experience could be regarded as a very loving act indeed. Pause for a moment and look at what Viktor Frankl experienced. Explore the value in the negative experience that he endured and see how he then used it to help others. Notice the transformation of negative to positive, from darkness to light.

The purpose of life is the experience, but there is no built-in meaning, it means to you what you choose it to mean. What then happens is that we reflect back this meaning we have chosen into our 'physical' reality. What I would suggest is that, if we really are in Earth Life School, then learning from our experiences, and imagining that something positive will transpire as a result comes highly recommended. Let me finish this section with a Daoist teaching story.

A long time ago there was an old farmer. One day his very best stallion ran away. His neighbours came round that evening to commiserate with the old man about his bad luck. But he simply said, "Maybe it is bad luck, maybe it isn't." The following day the stallion returned, accompanied by five wild mares. Immediately the farmer's neighbours rushed round to his house to celebrate his good fortune. But the old farmer simply said, "Maybe it is good fortune, maybe it isn't?" The next day, as he was trying to saddle and ride one of the wild mares, the farmer's son fell off, and broke his leg. The old farmer's neighbours turned up to empathise with him about his misfortune. But he just said, "Maybe it is misfortune, maybe it isn't." The following day government officials came to take the young men in the village to fight in the Emperor's army. But seeing that the farmer's son was incapacitated they left him behind. And the neighbours stopped, and thought to themselves about the meaning of good and bad.

Summary

This is your life and your responsibility, whether you believe you have chosen it or not. Learn to love and accept yourself as you are. Change what you can and embrace what you cannot. Connect to the idea of abundance, even if you do not currently feel as if you are fully expressing it. Use what appear to be negative situations as an opportunity to transform them. Explore the unconditionality of your love.

We are all in this Earth Life School for a reason. None of us are perfect, *all* of us have something to learn. In each individual life, we do not start with the same skills or abilities, and we do not all want to have exactly the same experiences. To eventually graduate, we need to meet the school's learning outcomes. But we do not need to learn everything in one go through this persona. Nevertheless, we can work towards ultimate graduation by expressing the full potential of our current persona. The new model I am presenting in this book will enable us to do that much more easily. And I appreciate that it does represent a very different way of thinking. So, how do we live this new model? What processes should we follow? If physical reality is a dream-like projection, how do we live the dream as this persona and not the nightmare?

What have we covered:

- You are responsible for your life.
- Love yourself, and communicate effectively with others.
- Existence is abundant, and so is your reflection of existence.
- Can we learn to love unconditionally?
- Do not rush to judge apparently negative experiences.

What remains to be explored:

- How do we live in a world where physical reality is a projection of consciousness?

8. LIVING THE DREAM

"The measure of who we are is what we do with what we have." - Vince Lombardi.

After posting its worst ever season in 1958, American Football team the Green Bay Packers appointed Vince Lombardi as head coach. In his first year in charge, Lombardi led the Packers to a winning season. Straight away, the fans sensed they were witnessing something special. In the 1960 season, they sold out every single home game, and have done so ever since. Lombardi's team went on to win five Championships in seven years, including the first two Super Bowls. On the way to their second Super Bowl win, they played the Dallas Cowboys at home on 31st December 1967, in the NFL Championship game. This game became known as the Ice Bowl. The temperature on the day was -26°C, with a significant wind chill adding to the freezing conditions. It was so cold that as the referee started the game, his lips froze to his whistle. As the frigid encounter unfolded, the Packers ended up down 17-14 with under five minutes left to play. But they did have the football on their own 32-yard line. Their quarterback Bart Starr then led the team on a 67-yard drive down field to the Dallas 1-yard line. But they then failed twice to get the ball into the end zone for a game winning score. With just two attempts left to secure the win, and with only sixteen seconds left on the clock, quarterback Starr consulted with Lombardi on the side-line, before finally forcing the ball over the line himself. As the game finished, it emerged that several players had developed frost bite, and one spectator had died of exposure. In 1969,

Lombardi became the Head Coach of the Washington Redskins, leading them to their first winning season in fourteen years. Lombardi never coached a team to a losing season, and he had an overall career win to loss ratio of seventy-six percent. His players achieved what they did because of, and for Lombardi. After his own untimely death in 1970, the NFL named the Super Bowl trophy the Vince Lombardi trophy. Coaching is about empowering others to express their potential.

The Consciousness Trinity

It is all well and good to imagine that we have a core soul that is eternal and experiences many lifetimes, but right now, we are living this life through this persona. Therefore, it is essential that we make the most of our lives, right here, right now. We need to maximise the learning and experiential opportunities of our persona in this lifetime. If we really are having an experience in Earth Life School, then it is a good idea to acquaint ourselves with the school equipment. In this model, where time is an illusion and your experience is a reflection of consciousness, within consciousness, your mind is everything. The most important basic construct of the mind is that you have a conscious and an unconscious. In its simplest form, your conscious mind is dealing with everything that you are currently aware of, and your unconscious mind is dealing with everything else. In summary, this is what your unconscious mind is doing for you –

- It stores and organises your memories. In the model we are exploring here, that means it is making connections from the Now that you are currently in to other Nows. We then call this process of making these connections memories.
- It runs your body for you. You do not have to think about pumping your blood or digesting your food, it is all automatic.
- As we discussed in *Chapter 1*, your unconscious mind is in charge of your perception. Again, this runs automatically.
- It maintains habits and instincts. These might be what you define as good habits, like exercising, or bad habits like drinking too

much coffee and eating donuts. Instincts include things like the drive to reproduce and your fight and flight reflex.

- Your unconscious mind is also where you store aspects of your persona such as your preferences, beliefs, and values. You can certainly bring these into your conscious awareness, but they are stored in the unconscious.
- Your unconscious mind naturally represses and then re-presents negative aspects of the persona to the conscious mind. It does this so that you can think about them, learn and then let them go.
- And all your behaviour runs unconsciously. You may well have conscious volition to do things, like raising your arm in the air, but it is your unconscious mind that raises it in the air for you. From the time you were a small baby, you have learned how to gain control over your limbs and move your body. Simply raising your arm in the air involves the movement of at least fifteen muscles; do you know consciously in what order to move them? We do consciously choose to do things, but the doing of them is unconscious.

To complete our trinity of consciousness, we also have a higher conscious mind. The higher conscious mind is that aspect of ourselves that has perception outside of the space-time framework where our earthly human lives play out. But do we *know* that we have a higher conscious mind? Except through out-of-body experiences, Western esoteric thinking, and cases of childhood reincarnation, then the answer is no; we do not know that we have a higher conscious mind, not for sure. This is because all the communication that we perceive is coming through our unconscious mind into conscious awareness. Flashes of inspiration, creative urges, insights, knowings; all of these could be attributed to a sense of higher consciousness, but all of them come to us in awareness through the unconscious mind. I believe that we do have a higher conscious mind, that aspect of self that is guiding us through life to have an exciting, fulfilling, and expansive experience. But again, you will have to come to your own conclusions about this. For me, synchronicities are little reminders of being connected to that sense of higher-consciousness.

But we can still choose to ignore these and not align ourselves with our own higher conscious mind if we want to.

To return to a film analogy for a moment, you can think about the conscious, unconscious, and higher conscious minds like this:

- Your conscious mind sits in the cinema and watches the film. It is absorbed by the drama and associates with the main character, thinking what they think and feeling what they feel. Your conscious mind is the 'experiencer' and the 'chooser'.
- Your unconscious mind hires the actors, the extras, the cameramen, the lighting, sound and special effects technicians, and the costume designers. It creates the cinema and projects the movie. It might even serve you some popcorn, and it does all of this automatically.
- Your higher conscious mind writes the screen play and directs the filming. It does this whilst you watch the film, faithfully editing and re-writing based on what you think, and how you react emotionally to the film as you watch it. But you would never know it was there; your conscious mind just thinks that how the movie unfolds is how the movie unfolds.

To re-use the analogy from *Chapter 6*, your higher conscious mind is Tom Hanks, or some form of super Hanks/Spielberg combination; your conscious mind is Captain Miller, and amongst other things, your unconscious is automatically creating the three-dimensional space-time world that Captain Miller inhabits.

Once you have a big picture appreciation of the structure of your mind, then you can let your trinity of consciousness do the jobs that they are supposed to do. The formula for a happy and productive life as this persona is to then have all three parts of your mind *aligned* with each other, all doing their own jobs, whilst supporting each other.

The Passion Principal

"If you do follow your bliss you put yourself on a kind of track that had been there all the while, waiting for you...When you can see that, you begin to meet people who are in the field of your bliss, and they open the doors for you. I say follow your bliss and don't be afraid, and doors will open where you didn't know they were going to be." – Joseph Campbell.

The first step to aligning your trinity of consciousness is to act upon your passions in life. I believe that doing this brings your physically-focused consciousness into alignment with your higher conscious mind. It also seems to me that when I am acting on the things in life that I am passionate about, I feel more alive and more like I am being me. And if you think about it, you cannot actually be anyone else in life anyway, you can only ever be yourself. For sure, you can use other people as examples of how to be, or indeed how not to be. But you are you, and in your life, you can only ever aim to be the best version of you that you can be.

As I described in the *Introduction*, I had a brief OBE whilst I was still working as an accountant. The meaning I took from this experience was that there were more important things to do with my life than adding up other people's numbers. Because of this experience, I decided to do for my career the thing that I was most interested in. And that was definitely not accountancy, but to be honest, I was not one hundred per cent sure what it was either. Nevertheless, having made the decision, I took action in that direction. Very simply, I explored things that were of interest to me. I read books, emailed authors, watched television programmes, meditated, went to seminars, and I took trainings. I engaged with the idea of aligning my career and my passion, and then doggedly kept on going without knowing consciously where on earth I *was* going. Eventually, nearly seven years later and whilst still working as an accountant, I came across Neuro Linguistic Programming (NLP). Then, before taking that interest any further, I started to see 'NLP' in car number plates. Now, I am sure that 'NLP' was in car number plates before, but at that moment, my conscious mind was able to imagine it as a message. Of course, that does not mean it actually was a message. Nevertheless, I interpreted it to mean, *"Ewan, do the NLP training that you have been thinking about"*. So, I did, and it was only at that point that my conscious mind began to see how I could do something for my career that I was passionate about.

If I am passionate about teaching, then there will be people who want to hear the message that I teach. When I then started doing personal development training, the market was already served by several capable and competent providers. Nevertheless, my business partner and I still believed that we had something to offer, and that there would be a market for us despite the competition. And there was. I see no reason to assume that existence is anything other than infinite and abundant. If it is, or even if it is just really, really big but not quite infinite, I still assume that whatever my passion happens to be, I *will* be able to express it.

Does all of this mean that a 'higher' aspect of my consciousness could see how my life might unfold to satisfy the decision I had made consciously years earlier? Did it then guide me to follow a particular path so that I could have the experiences that I have today? I could have chosen not to act on my passions in life. I could have ignored the occasional synchronicity, and that would have been a whole new set of life experiences for me. I can only really say that acting on my passion has brought me expansive and exciting experiences. These have included challenges I have had to face and overcome, and some that I am still facing today. Overcoming challenges has allowed me to grow and expand. I can also quote others, like mythologist Joseph Campbell, who said that acting on your passion in life is essential. Inevitably, you are going to have to test this process out for yourself by acting on your passions in life, and then seeing where that leads you.

In life, all you can really be is yourself. So, why not do the things that arouse your greatest sense of being alive? I work on the *assumption* that acting on my passions aligns my physically focused consciousness with my higher conscious mind. I believe that it has the capacity to see all the Nows containing me, and that if I act on my passion and trust in the process, then I am aligning myself with that sense of higher consciousness. That way, I will have the most exciting and expansive life that I can. Whether or not you believe that you have a higher conscious mind is not what actually matters. What counts is to be yourself and to follow your passion in life, whilst trusting in the process. That is all.

Shadow Boxing

"When an inner situation is not made conscious, it happens outside as fate." – Carl Jung.

Since we have learned about taking responsibility for our lives without too much negative judgement about what we experience; and now that we understand that acting upon our passions in life aligns our conscious mind with our higher conscious mind; then and only then are we ready to face the darker side of our own nature.

The meaning of the Carl Jung quote above is that if you do not bring your negative patterns, or to use the Jungian term, your shadow, into your awareness, then you will be battling with your demons on the 'outside' instead. One of the jobs of the unconscious mind is to bring into conscious awareness negative aspects of the persona, so that they can be rationalised and released. And the conscious mind needs to know that it must deal with what the unconscious presents to it in this way. This is the second step of aligning your consciousness trinity.

We are humans having a human experience. Because of that, we are subject to human needs and human desires. We need food, water, shelter, sleep, and we have a strong innate desire to reproduce. But we can learn to satisfy these needs without harming ourselves or others. As humans, we are also subject to Pavlovian stimulus responses. Ivan Pavlov was an early 20th century Russian psychologist who codified the idea of stimulus response. If at the peak of an emotional state a stimulus is introduced, then the state and the stimulus get linked neurologically. Such that if you are exposed to the stimulus again, it automatically brings back the state which has become neurologically linked to it. In this new model, I would actually say there is a similarity in resonance between the experiences, this then brings up the 'conditioned' response. But standard psychological terminology will suffice for now. You may have noticed this effect if someone walks past you in a bar wearing the aftershave or perfume your partner or ex-partner wears. You can also experience conditioning when someone says something to you, or looks at you in a certain way, and you automatically react either positively or negatively.

Humans have an innate ability to learn. Small children are like little sponges, soaking up information about their environment. Much of this absorption then becomes unconscious programmes that we run. These programmes can be defined as values, beliefs, or Pavlovian conditioning. The current 21st century context of our earthly lives also means we have been taught erroneous things about ourselves and our capabilities. Most often, this is not in a malicious way; it is simply that at this point in our development, we are experiencing a significant number of negative programmes and patterns.

What we experience is in effect the sum total of our conscious and unconscious choices. Having unconscious choices can, at first glance, seem a little unfair. But remember that your unconscious is just you. Build a sense of rapport between your conscious and unconscious minds. Appreciate that it is the job of your unconscious mind to bring negativity into conscious awareness. When this happens, regard it as an opportunity for positive change and growth. Become more conscious of the unconscious programming that you have given yourself. By doing so, it is possible to release unhelpful beliefs, emotional responses, and habits. Over time, that brings the conscious and the unconscious minds into better alignment. Whenever anything happens in your life that you do not prefer, examine it and explore it. What could be the reason or the purpose of 'creating' this experience? Assume whatever happens in your life is there for a positive reason, even if that reason is to bring something negative about yourself into your awareness, so that you can let it go! I have been punched in the face three times in my life, and I can now see that two of these events were wake-up calls. These experiences were asking me to look at my state so that I could start taking more responsibility for my emotions and my life in general. *Your unconscious mind will get your attention, even if it has to punch you in the face to do it!*

Arthur Schopenhauer, 19th century German philosopher, used the analogy of the conscious mind being like a lame sighted person being carried on the shoulders of a sturdy blind person, which is your unconscious mind. If you do not have both of these aspects of your mind aligned and working together, then you are going to be clattering about through life, bumping into things, causing mayhem, and feeling very grumpy about how unfair it all seems.

We are subject to conditioning, and we have a drive to satisfy certain needs. But that does not mean that we have to become slaves to these needs and desires. Remember, what you are experiencing is a reflection of who you are. Everything starts with awareness, so choose today to live your life with more conscious awareness of the unconscious patterns that you are running. Release negativity and bring alignment between all aspects of your mind. This negativity can often be expressed through beliefs that limit us or as negative emotions, like anger or fear.

"If you bring forth what is within you, what you bring forth will save you. If you do not bring forth what is within you, what you do not bring forth will destroy you." – The Gnostic Gospel of Thomas.

Believe it or Not

"We must not allow other people's limited perceptions to define us." – Virginia Satir.

Beliefs are things that we consider to be true about us or the world around us. What we believe to be true for us is demonstrated through our behaviour. The results we get from our behaviour then tends to reinforce our beliefs. Our newly reinforced beliefs then carry on producing our results. So, if we have empowering beliefs about ourselves, we can have an expansive experience in life; but if we have disempowering beliefs, then we tend to be spiralling downwards.

An illustration of this idea about beliefs affecting our reality is the fact that in pharmacology, the testing of new drugs must be performed double blind. What this means is that some patients receive an inert pill, a placebo, and some receive the trial drug. Neither the patient nor the clinicians know who received the real drug and who received the placebo. All of this is necessary because some people will get better simply as a result of receiving a pill in the first place. Because they believe the pill (even if it really is a placebo) could cure them; it does. So, any new drug being tested must perform better than the control group who are on the placebo, in order to receive a licence as a medicine. The placebo effect can even vary from culture to culture. As Rupert Sheldrake says in his book *The Science Delusion*. *"Placebo responses depend on the meanings that people attribute to diseases and cures."* What this means is the placebo effect is not an innate physical human ability as such. Rather, it is a reflection of what each person believes.

In *The Science Delusion* Sheldrake also discusses the idea of how pre-existing beliefs can affect the outcome of scientific experiments. *"...at Harvard, Robert Rosenthal and his colleagues instructed students to test rats in standard mazes. They ask them to compare two strains of rat produced by generations of selective breeding for good and poor performance in mazes. But they deliberately deceived their students. In fact, the rats came from a standard laboratory strain and were divided at random into two groups labelled 'maze-bright' and 'maze-dull'"*. The students then duly produced experimental results that supported their false beliefs about the rats. There is also a phenomenon in parapsychology studies known as the 'sheep and goat effect'. If you believe in the possibility of psychic abilities, then you are more likely to produce results which are better than chance expectations; you are a sheep. And if you do not believe in the possibility of psychic abilities, then you are more likely to produce results which are *less* likely than chance; and you are a goat. Seeing is not believing: believing is seeing.

In the model where 'physical' reality is a projection of your consciousness, our beliefs have a significant effect on our results in life. Therefore, it is essential to harbour empowering ideas about ourselves, and to let go of disempowering ones. This is something I see my coaching clients and people attending training courses doing week in and week out. Bring your limiting beliefs into consciousness, have a good look at them, then ask yourself: *"Do I want this to be true about me?"*

"We can learn something new anytime we believe we can." – Virginia Satir.

Present Tense

"Do not dwell in the past, do not dream of the future, concentrate the mind on the present moment." – Buddha.

It is not just beliefs that limit people, feeling negative emotions in the now associated with past events can be debilitating for people too. When it comes to feeling emotions, you actually have more choice than you might have heretofore realised. What other people do is what they do, but what you do with what they do is all you. Nevertheless, I do appreciate it does not always feel that easy. But consider this story told about the Buddha, who was teaching one day under a tree. Partway through his talk, a man joined the group and started to be quite abusive to the Buddha. After the talk finished and people drifted away, one of Buddha's students came up to him, and asked him why he had not become angry or irritated by the abusive man. The Buddha said, *"If someone offers you a gift, and if you choose not to accept that gift, who owns the gift?"* The student replied, *"Why, the giver of course."*

You can actually be in any state you want by simply remembering a time when you were previously in that state. Choose a positive state, then remember a specific time in the past when you were in that state. Float back down into your body, see what you saw, hear what you heard, and feel that feeling again. You do have the power to choose your state. It does not always feel like this, because we may have triggers from past events, or limiting beliefs about ourselves. Nevertheless, you still get to choose what your emotional state is. Choose states you want to be in, and explore the things that seem to prevent you from being in those states. And remember that it is perfectly acceptable not to be in a positive state too, this is part of the human Earth Life experience.

We do not just have emotions about the past. It is possible to have negative feelings about the future, and this is what we call anxiety. These feelings come with a range of intensity, but the common theme is, when people feel anxious, they are imagining the future not turning out the way that they want it to. What we call anxiety is, in effect, our body's translation of the idea of imagining a future that we do not prefer into a feeling. Therefore, the solution for anxiety must be to imagine things in life working out the way that you do want them to. If you find this idea too simple, do twenty push-ups, and then imagine your life working out the way that you prefer. What I work on with coaching clients is what stops them being able to imagine the future working out in the way that they prefer. This is often negative emotions or self-limiting beliefs; push-ups are not usually required. It is perfectly acceptable to imagine things not working out the way that you want them to as well. By doing so, you can plan and then take action to avoid unwanted negative outcomes. But as we move forward into taking action, focusing on what we want in life is essential. Before I cross a road, I check both ways to see if any traffic is coming. This is because I am imagining things not working out the way that I want them to, so that I can take steps to avert that. When I actually cross the road, I then imagine getting safely to the other side; I do not cross the road imagining that I will get run over!

Emotion is a multiplier and magnifier of your experience. In parapsychological studies, subjects tend to do better when they feel emotionally connected to the research. When subjects become bored with the tests, their results fall back to chance expectations. Just remember that ultimately, the state you are in *is* your choice. If we return to the film analogy: when you watch a film, you laugh at the funny bits and cry at the sad parts, whilst at the same time, on some level of your being, you know that you are really watching a film.

Living the Dream

"All magic is a power of mind over matter." – Jonathan Black.

Dreams can mean many things. They could just be your mind processing the events of the day. They could be your unconscious mind attempting to bring something into your conscious awareness. If this is the case, then you should interpret the dream metaphorically, not literally. And of course, a dream could be a collection of incomprehensible nonsense, and therefore mean nothing at all. Lucid dreaming is when you are aware that you are dreaming. As you have this realisation, the dream changes before your eyes, directed by your thinking. A few months ago, I dreamt I was about to be involved in an armed robbery, but then I thought, *"that's not me"*. With that thought, my dream began to change into something else entirely. I used the example of dreaming as an analogy before to explain that in this new model, you are the dreamer, the dream landscape, and the others in the dream. It is all you. As you embrace these ideas, and as you move forward in life, do not be surprised if events unfold in a somewhat dreamlike, magical way. Begin to notice synchronicities cropping up in your life more and more often.

The Law of Attraction is very popular in the personal development field these days. Its roots can be traced back to the late 19th Century, and probably back further into Western esoteric thinking. It is predicated on the idea that thoughts create what you experience in the physical world, much like I am describing here. To rationally-minded people, it can seem a little unscientific or superstitious. People talk about 'Cosmic Ordering', or the 'Universe' conspiring to help them achieve their goals. Once you know that your physical reality is a mirror-like projection of your consciousness, then it is no real surprise that people might think that. But fundamentally, the 'Universe' does not really care about you at all. It is just a reflection; a reflection of you. Cultivate a better sense of self-awareness, notice your thinking, your beliefs, emotions, and behaviours. Work on improving yourself and generate positive habits. As you do, you will begin to notice how the physical world changes and aligns to your positive thinking. For sure, you may well get presented with some of the old situations. Use these to test how you react. If you do react in the same way that you used to, then you have not yet changed fully; but if you respond differently, then you have.

Knowing the path and walking the path are two different things. As your behaviour begins to demonstrate that your knowing of this new model is being expressed in your actions, then you can start to transform your physical experience. Because you begin to realise that physical reality is not *like* a dream, it *is* a dream. All we need to do is to wake up in the dream and know that it is a dream to transform it.

Summary

"Knowing others is intelligence; knowing yourself is true wisdom. Mastering others is strength; mastering yourself is true power." – Lao Tzu.

Onto the space-time stage our persona arrives, develops, performs, and exits. We all seem to enter with pre-set abilities, gifts, interests, and challenges. These can and do change throughout our period in the spotlight. No two actors in this play of life are the same. Ultimately, whatever we bring with us onto the stage, and whatever happens to us whilst we are here, it is still up to us, and us alone to weave this all together into our own unique performance. But we are also here to help each other. Assist and guide the people around you. Learn how this new model works, and test your knowledge by teaching it to others. As you help them to express their full potential, others will help you too.

One of the themes that runs through this book boils down to this: you have all the power to create the life that you want to live, now. No one and nothing else can stop you, you are the only one that stops you. It is not your parents, your teachers, your ex-partner, the CIA, the Bilderbergers, or God, it is all you. It is only ever someone else insofar as you have chosen to empower someone else to have power over you. Take that power back. Remember you are creating all of what you are experiencing as the physical world, right now. *You are that powerful.* You are unique, abundant, and eternal. You are currently having a very visceral, hands-on human learning experience as your current persona. Take responsibility for your own life. Align your trinity of consciousness, act upon your passions, and start living your dreams.

And then, for me at least, some questions do still remain. One of these is: *"Why this persona, in this Now?"* Considering this question makes me wonder if our earthly drama is playing out on an even bigger stage too. Could it be? In order for us to discover even more about ourselves, collectively and individually, it is time for us to stand back and look at the whole human journey from yet another perspective…

What have we covered:

- You have a trinity of consciousness. Allow them to do their jobs, and bring them into alignment.
- Existence is abundant, and so is your reflection of existence.
- Act upon your passions in life.

What remains to be explored:

- Why this persona and why this Now?
- Is there a bigger drama playing out that humanity is a part of?

PART III

Change The World

9. WELTGEIST

"The history of the world is none other than the progress of the consciousness of freedom." – Georg Wilhelm Friedrich Hegel.

If now is all there is, and if we are not bound by the past, you may well ask what is the point of looking over our shoulders at what has happened before. After all, we are not going in that direction. The past that we connect to is a contextual frame that enables us to understand the present better. The past is somewhere we can learn from and a place where we can rediscover resources that we are not fully utilising right now. It also tends to inform us about who we think we are; as we explore the past, our understanding of ourselves in the present changes.

The spirit, or essence of our time often gets labelled as the *Zeitgeist*. The *Zeitgeist* is this sense of what the now is, or what it means, and it is not a static thing; it changes as we move forward. If we explore the process of the evolving *Zeitgeist*, then we can know the underlying spirit of the world, or to borrow another German word, we can come to know the *Weltgeist*. As we have seen through *Parts I* and *II*, who you are is maybe not who you thought you were. You are a form of spirit energy exploring the human experience. But what is this whole human experience about, and why are we living in this now?

If we want to make the most of our particular expression of being human at this time, then we need to have a deeper appreciation of where we fit into the whole context of humanity; past, present, and future. When we do explore our own *Zeitgeist* in *Chapter 11*, you will see that today we are facing considerable challenges. If we understand who we have been, who we are now, and who we can be in the future, then facing these challenges becomes much less daunting. And if we can get closer to knowing the *Weltgeist*, we can take yet another step in knowing ourselves at the same time too.

Evolution

Imagine that you are standing on a beach, gazing out across the blue ocean. High above you, a few wispy clouds drift across the sky; the midday sun warms your body and a gentle breeze caresses your skin. The only sound you can hear are the waves crashing on the shoreline, nothing else stirs… Because there is nothing else. There are no birds or mammals, no reptiles or fish; there are not even any insects buzzing around on this perfect day. In fact, if you looked behind you, there would not be any vegetation either. If you are really lucky, in front of you, at your feet, you might see a small worm cast in the wet damp sand. This is Earth, but it is Earth at the start of the Cambrian period, five-hundred-and-forty million years ago. Primitive life did start over three billion years earlier, but it was from the Cambrian forward that life seemed to properly awaken. All creatures, great and small, have roamed the land and swum in the oceans in the intervening years. Life has repeatedly probed and explored the sensory world. Today, there are at least ten different types of eye. Humans and octopi share a long, long, distant ancestor, but since then, we have evolved independently and formed totally different body plans; and yet, we have both separately formed the same eye structure. Flight has evolved independently at least four times. Echolocation is used by bats, some whales, and dolphins. And the platypus uses its bill to detect electrical impulses from its prey. The way that life is expressing itself seems to have a rhythm and rhyme. Lions are the tyrannosaurus rex of today, and wildebeest are their triceratops. Finally, here we stand at the pinnacle, the crowning glory of this evolutionary process. But is that really the way that we should imagine this journey? Do dolphins think that they are the pinnacle? And what is it exactly, that is evolving anyway?

In the past five hundred years, the scientific method has delivered numerous advances in a whole range of different areas. In that time, few pieces of work have struck more thoroughly and directly at other models of the world, and at religious doctrine in particular, than Charles Darwin's work on evolution. In 1831, at twenty-two years of age, Darwin joined *HMS Beagle* on a surveying voyage which took five years to circumnavigate the globe. This allowed him to observe a wide variety of natural flora and fauna from different continents. He then spent a number of years developing his theory, but he did not publish anything substantial on the subject of evolution. Then, in 1858, he received a short essay from fellow naturalist Alfred Russel Wallace, whose paper set out in summary the whole of Darwin's own emerging theory. Prompted to act by Wallace's work, Darwin published his book, *On the Origin of Species by Means of Natural Selection*, in 1859.

Darwin's theory is predicated on the ideas that there is inherited, natural variation within members of the same species, and that organisms will continue to expand their numbers until they are unable to do so. This expansive pressure then results in selfish competition, which enables the individuals who are best suited to the overall environment to thrive. Like any good theory, evolution through natural selection is simple to understand. It is supported by the fossil record, albeit a little sketchy and variable here and there. (Marine animals living in shallow seas are well represented and flying creatures rather less so.) It is also possible to study the morphology of existing animals, map the similarities and differences, and then compare these to the fossil record. It is even informative to study the development of embryos, which eerily display resemblances to their evolutionary forebears. Six-week-old human embryos look like little fish. Finally, the discovery of genetics, DNA, and DNA mutation has secured evolution as a scientific fact. Darwin's theory of life evolving through environmental and competitive pressures is well accepted in people's minds today. Only religious diehards hold onto the literal meaning of the Biblical creation story in *Genesis*. And many people still blur the issue by thinking of evolution as God's 'process' for the creation of man. One reason for this is when viewed with the benefit of hindsight, evolution by natural selection does look directed and purposeful. Whereas the only 'purpose' is, at best, environmental fit and reproductive success. Although that is true, there are a couple of evolutionary nuances too. Sometimes, it appears that mate preference affects the evolution of certain attributes. The peacock's tail is an obvious example. The tail actually appears to be an encumbrance to mere survival needs, yet peahens have a preference for this oversized appendage. In a similar way, human breeders have consciously selected certain natural variations in many species for the purpose of the entirely human need of domestication. This certainly allows for a fit to the environment, but there is precious little which is natural about it. The evolutionary process is also quite flexible, and will co-opt one piece of biological equipment for a purpose other than the one it originally evolved for. Like one of the bones in the middle ear of mammals, which was originally part of the jaw joint in the reptiles that mammals evolved from.

Much research and analysis has been inspired by Darwin's work. We can now say with some confidence that all life started in the sea with bacteria, almost four billion years ago, not that long after the formation of the planet. Some soft-bodied animals and algae were present by the start of the Cambrian period five-hundred-and-forty-million years ago. The land started to be colonised one-hundred-million years later, so that three-hundred-million years ago there were fish, amphibians, insects, plants, reptiles, and trees. And by about two-hundred million years ago, there were mammals and birds too. Flowering plants evolved forty-million years later, and grasses perhaps another forty million years after that. Looking back at the fossil record, we can judge life today to be rich and diverse. But the development of life on Earth has not been a smooth straight line moving ever upwards. It has been punctuated by mass extinction events, at least five in total. The biggest was at the end of the Permian, two-hundred-and-fifty million years ago, when ninety-six percent of life on Earth was extinguished. And the most famous extinction event was at the end of the Cretaceous period, sixty-five million years ago, which finished off the dinosaurs. What the fossil record shows is that events like this allow for new expressions of life to flourish in the voids left by now extinct life forms.

Human evolution is a fascinating subplot in the history of life on Earth. What makes us different is our ability to walk upright and our large brain. Upright walking evolved first about four million years ago, probably due to a cooling and drying climate in Africa. This allowed open grasslands to flourish, as heavy forested areas retreated. Brain size did increase in the intervening period, but only significantly so more recently. One of the ways to measure a species' potential for smartness is to examine its brain size in comparison to its body mass. The ratio this produces is known as the encephalisation quotient (EQ). Human EQ is 7.5, your pet dog has an EQ of 1.2, chimpanzees' EQ is 2.5 (which is the same as ravens), blue whales have an EQ of 1.8, and in dolphins, EQ is 5.3. *Homo erectus*, which modern humans probably evolved from, had an EQ of 4.5. *Homo erectus* lived on Earth for almost two million years, going extinct, by some estimations, just fifty thousand years ago. This means they overlapped with *Homo sapiens*, who are currently judged to have arrived on the world stage three-hundred-thousand years ago.

What is implied by the size of the modern human brain is, that there must have been some considerable evolutionary pressure on our immediate ancestors, which necessitated the development of a significantly larger brain. Right now, we do not know what that was.

Prehistory

A lot of what we know about human prehistory comes from the study of the environment. We find clues in sediments containing pollen, seeds, beetles, and snails. Even more information is hidden in the ice core samples taken from the glaciers of Greenland and Antarctica, convenient snapshots of ancient climates. We can discover human and animal bones, as well as human artefacts such as flints and fertility figurines. We can gaze upon rare early art, like the Lascaux paintings, and dig into what remains of ancient structures. We also have prehistoric stories passed down to us orally as myths. Some of these were eventually recorded by historical characters such as Greek philosopher Plato, or even recorded anonymously on monuments. Plato wrote about the myth of Atlantis, a utopian continent *"Beyond the pillars of Hercules"*, which means west of Gibraltar. There remains a debate about where that story came from. Did Plato invent it to make a point about hubris within a culture leading to its destruction, thereby using a metaphorical construct to deliver a message to contemporary Athenians? Or, as some argue, did he hear it from someone who heard it from someone else, who heard it from Egyptian priests? In his book *Magicians of the Gods*, Graham Hancock makes the case that the story of Atlantis was carved into the very stone of Egyptian temples, and is still visible today. We quickly dismiss old stories as the superstitions of ancient people who do not possess a modern scientific understanding, or a more sophisticated concept of cause and effect in the way that we do now. But do not forget that the city of Troy, in Homer's *Iliad*, was for many years considered to be a myth. Now it is believed to be located in western Turkey on the Aegean coast. Troy had many incarnations over several thousand years, and today, Homer's Troy is associated with Troy VII, where there is evidence of a violent conflict. The dating of this incarnation is consistent with Greek accounts, although Achilles, Paris, Helen, and Hector were never found, and neither was a wooden horse.

Whether Atlantis was real or not is unknown. But what is real is that in prehistory, humanity experienced cycles of climate change. One such period of huge climatic change occurred about twelve-thousand-eight-hundred years ago at the start of the Younger Dryas. At that time, there were thick layers of ice covering Canada, parts of the northern United States, and parts of northern Europe. Then, quite suddenly, there was a significant drop in temperature, perhaps by as much as six degrees. There are competing theories as to the cause of this rapid cooling event. One hypothesis is, there was a comet or asteroid strike on the North American ice sheet, a case supported by Hancock. Such an impact would have thrown material into the air, blocking out the sun in a natural version of a nuclear winter. This impact would also have caused melt water to run off the ice sheets into the Atlantic, thereby shutting off the thermohaline circulation and deepening the frigid conditions in the Northern hemisphere. This was a massive cataclysmic event, and would have been a significant challenge for anyone living at the time; the life-giving sun was banished from the sky and the Earth plunged into the freezer. Then, just over one thousand years later, the Younger Dryas ended with another cataclysmic event. This could have been coronal ejecta from the Sun or an asteroid impacting in the ocean. Whatever the cause, the result this time was rapid global warming. Perhaps as much as seven degrees centigrade in just a few years. As the temperature rose, the ice sheets retreated from northern latitudes, dumping their waters into the sea, which then expanded to claim low-lying coastal areas.

Dated to just after the end of the Younger Dryas, a substantial megalithic complex was built in southern Turkey called Göbekli Tepe. The site has been investigated by a German archaeological team led by Klaus Schmidt. And though it has been surveyed, only five per cent of its total surface has been excavated. Broadly speaking, Göbekli Tepe consists of stone pillars six meters tall and weighing over twenty tons, arranged in circular formations. There are about two hundred such stone pillars in twenty circles. Some of the stones have been carved with animals, some with human hands, and some are megalithic 'T' shapes. The construction of such a monument would have required a substantial number of people working together, maybe as many as five hundred. It pre-dates writing, the wheel, and working with metals. It was built thousands of years before the Giza Pyramids and Stonehenge, thus pushing back in time the concept of large-scale, organised human endeavours. Göbekli Tepe's inception just pre-dates current estimations for the domestication of cereal crops and food animals. Though interestingly some crop domestication is thought to have occurred in the Fertile Crescent not long after Göbekli Tepe was built, and the Fertile Crescent starts only a few miles south of it. Also, for reasons unknown, around ten thousand years ago, the site was deliberately buried. We do not know the purpose of Göbekli Tepe, and we are left making educated guesses about unknown religious or social practices. One of the most intriguing findings from the site is a stone known as the Vulture Stone. It gives astronomical dating evidence for an asteroid strike on the planet, coincident with the start of the Younger Dryas. This was proposed by Hancock in *Magicians of the Gods* and was recently confirmed by scientists at the University of Edinburgh, Scotland.

So, what does this mean? For sure, we know that humanity has been through two periods of major climate-based challenge in the relatively recent past. At the end of the Younger Dryas, sea levels rose significantly and continued to do so for many years. The total sea-level rise from then to now is estimated at three-hundred-and-sixty feet (one-hundred-and-twenty meters). Together with the temperature changes, which themselves directly affect flora and fauna, sea-level rise would have been a major trial for prehistoric man. Hancock also makes compelling assertions about an early human civilisation with a global footprint being badly disrupted or even destroyed through the Younger Dryas. If so, one of the things we can learn is that the eradication of our own assumptive hold on a 'civilised' way of life could only be one asteroid strike or significant climate change away.

This period way back in time is often overlooked, but it is from this ancient background that human history emerges from prehistory. Our ideas about prehistory are still evolving, and the emerging impression is more nuanced than a simple linear progression from limited savages to our current civilised way of living. Prehistory is often characterised as the rise of the simple hunter-gatherer, who starts to domesticate plants and animals, and settles into a farming culture. Then, because of his farming food surpluses, he is able to form hierarchically organised cities and civilisations. But there is evidence of settlements and limited farming going way back into prehistory. And our earliest animal domestication, the dog, occurred at least fifteen-thousand years ago and maybe even earlier.

History

Our history starts where prehistory ends, and the dividing line, if there is one, is writing. As a result, our sense of what happened in our history is clearer than our sense of prehistory. It is not easy to say which civilisation was the first to emerge from this prehistoric period, and how they formed their beliefs. There has been a fair amount of cross-pollination of ideas, certainly in recorded history and therefore also likely before then too. Civilisation, as we define it, started in Mesopotamia (modern Iraq), and boasted the world's oldest cities of Eridu, Uruk, and Ur. As mentioned in *Chapter 2*, the Sumerians of Mesopotamia wrote in cuneiform script, wedge-shaped indentations made on clay tablets. The survival of this robust form of writing is one of the reasons that we consider the Sumerians to be the first civilised society. At virtually the same time as the start of Sumerian culture, Egyptian civilisation begins, dated to about 3,050 BCE, with hieroglyphs being used for writing around that time.

If one talks about ancient Egypt, the Giza Pyramid complex immediately springs to mind. This site includes the three large pyramids, small 'satellite' pyramids, the Sphinx, several temples, causeways, and tombs. Egyptologists date the Great Pyramid (known as Khufu's pyramid) to about 2,560 BCE, in what is known as the Old Kingdom period. Even if this dating is correct, the date for the Sphinx is open to debate. The Sphinx was carved out of the limestone bedrock at Giza, and faces due east in exact alignment with the sunrise at the spring equinox. The monument consists of the body of a lion, and the face of a person wearing a pharaonic headdress. Based on water erosion patterns on the body of the Sphinx, geologist Robert Schoch has suggested a very conservative dating for the structure would be seven thousand years BCE, and it could be as old as ten thousand BCE. Basically, Schoch is saying that the Sphinx was built before the accepted start of Egyptian civilisation, when the Nile valley area was much wetter than it is today. And a potential date for its origin is coincident with the building of Göbekli Tepe. For this to be the case, the head of the Sphinx must have been re-carved during the Old Kingdom to look the way it does today. Certainly, to my untrained artistic eye, the head of the Sphinx, in profile, does look disproportionately small compared to the body. The Great Pyramid was built with enormous precision. It is exactly one third of the way between the North Pole and the equator and almost perfectly aligned north, south, east, and west. The original height of the pyramid was 481.4 feet, and its base perimeter is 3,023.2 feet, a ratio of 6.28, or 2π. This is the relationship that the radius of a circle has to its circumference. Interestingly, it is generally accepted that the value for pi (π) was first established by the Greek mathematician Archimedes some 2,250 years after the Great Pyramid was built. Civilisations also emerged along similar timescales to those in Egypt and Mesopotamia in the Indus valley, which includes parts of modern day Afghanistan, Pakistan, and North Western India; and in China around the Yellow and Yangtze rivers.

As we get closer to the present, the resources that we use to understand the past rapidly increase. Nevertheless, we are still left making interpretations to fill in the gaps. We also have a propensity to understand the past through the lens of the present, and our own pre-existing world view. As you know, one man's terrorist is another man's freedom fighter. Surviving records are patchy in places, and even where they are present, they can be biased or silent about important facts. Ancient historians were often more interested in telling a good story than establishing an objective narrative. The professionalism of historians and the tools that they can employ increased as our sciences improved and as discoveries were made. As I mentioned in *Chapter 3*, Egyptian hieroglyphs were only deciphered in the early nineteenth century after the Rosetta Stone was unearthed. Ground-breaking findings tend to be less frequent today, but new material still does come to light, and can help us to re-shape our understanding of the past. For example, the Gnostic Gospels unearthed in Nag Hammadi, Egypt, in 1945, and the Dead Sea scrolls discovered in Israel a few years after that. These are helping us to get a more balance view of early Christian and Judaic thought.

The great libraries and universities of the world are crammed with books about humanity's various activities during the last five thousand years. All of this study has given us a reasonable idea about ourselves. There have been many commendable expressions of civilisation through the arts and the sciences, from all cultures across the globe. Our development has not always been linear, nor always forwards. It has been said that not much happened between 450 CE and 1450 CE, apart from the rise of Islam, the first use of paper money in China, and the Black Death, of course. But when viewed through a modern human lens, we still like to think that we have made significant progress, as if everything before was destined to reach the comfortable Western lifestyle that so many of us enjoy today. But let us not forget that for much of our 'civilised' history, man has walked in darkness. Large sections of our past do not make for pleasant reading; war, slavery, rape, the forced displacement and genocide of people considered to be 'others'. Millions have suffered and died at the hands of other men.

If we look back at the past, the things that stand out to us, or that we pay attention to, actually tell us about who we are in the present too. Often, the past has been used as an excuse to shape actions and policies in the present. When I was schooled in Britain through the 1970s and 1980s, we were taught about Roman Britain, the Vikings, the Norman Conquest in 1066, and the Industrial Revolution. What was also very apparent to me was that we were just being taught some of the stories from the past that shaped life in Britain. There was a whole host of world history that was left unmentioned. We did not learn about the American Revolution, probably because Britain lost that particular campaign. Nor did we learn about British concentration camps in South Africa during the Boer War, at the turn of the twentieth century. I guess knowing that would have made us all feel less patriotic about being British, and as such, it was not something to be encouraged.

There is a great deal from our history that we will need to heal, because holding on to past hurt will only darken our future. This process of healing will require some courage, and the letting go of previous wrongs will not come without a good dose of learning. Throughout the past, we have been slow to learn the lessons of history. Very similar mistakes are repeated again and again. And yet, at the same time, we have demonstrated through our achievements that we possess an ingenious ability to solve problems. When faced with mortal challenges, we have invariably found the solutions to overcome them. This is a skill that we are going to need to draw on very deeply in the years ahead.

Weltgeist

Time is an illusion and the physical world is a projection of consciousness, within consciousness. Time is not fundamental to existence, it is an experience within existence. But time is a pre-requisite for evolution: if time is an illusion, then so too is evolution. This then means that evolution is not fundamental to existence either, but is instead an experience within existence. Remember that all the evidence for evolution exists in this Now. The geology, the fossils, the DNA, and current morphology, all of it can be carefully studied, and all of it exists in this Now. Evolution is, not unreasonably, imputed from this evidence in the same way that the Big Bang is too. But the frame containing the pre-Cambrian beach we stood on a few pages ago exists now, as does the frame seconds before the Chicxulub asteroid wiped out the dinosaurs sixty-five-million years ago. If you knew how to access the energy frequency of that frame, you could go and watch the asteroid strike the Yucatan peninsula for yourself.

The way that we think about evolution today is reflecting back to us our own selfish, materialist, reductionist ideas. Once we realise that we are not perceiving separate things-in-space-over-time, but a whole interconnected system of resonance and frequency, then our ideas about evolution can begin to evolve too. By doing so, we will realise that life did not evolve on Earth billions of years ago. In fact, it did not evolve at all anywhere, ever: *life just is*. What is evolving, if anything, is the perspective that consciousness is adopting. It is exploring ways to be and how to experience and express itself, time and time again, through many human and non-human perspectives. When you connect to this process, you connect to the *Weltgeist*. Use this connection to learn and to know more about yourself as you do.

The more we explore what our experience is about, the broader and deeper it becomes. We are some form of spirit energy simultaneously exploring many different ways to experience being human; for the purpose of learning, and also simply for the experience. For sure, this new expanded model seems a little bit large to digest to begin with, but if you take it a slice at a time, it will slide down easily enough. You can of course just shrug and say: *"So what?"* You can go back to thinking that life randomly evolved on Earth, and nowhere else, four billion years ago. You can cling to the notion that your conscious experience is produced in your over-large brain for no purpose other than the selfish survival of your genes… It is your choice.

Summary

Based on surviving writing, we can measure the start of recorded history to be about five thousand years ago. Notice how much longer our prehistory was than recorded history. Human prehistory spans the other two-hundred-and-ninety-five-thousand years of our existence on this planet. Our understanding of prehistory, and its evolution into our very early history is not clearly formed yet either. Why did we develop such large brains, and why did we have a propensity for building large stone structures? Also, notice our connection to millions of years of the evolution of life. In a space-time environment, everything that has a beginning has an end. As one expression of being ends, another one begins. But the *Weltgeist* exists outside of space and time, its experience is always changing, and never ends.

Pause and reflect on the journey of exploration that is contained in this Now. Take a fresh look at the past. What patterns and trends do you see?

What are humanity's strengths, and what do we need to learn? Use the exploration of the past to help you understand better who you are today.

The past can mean different things to different people at different times. But what it represents is the accumulation of the lives of millions of people, over thousands of years, and how their lives have interacted together. Philosopher David Hume said of history that *"Mankind are so much the same, in all times and places, that history informs nothing new or strange in this particular. Its chief use is only to discover the constant and universal principles of human nature."* But this is where I would disagree with the very learned 18th century scholar, because how we live is a reflection of our thinking. Our political and social structures reflect how and what we think about ourselves and the world. As our thinking evolves, so too does how we choose to live. The *Weltgeist* lives and evolves through each one of us, and the way that humans think is not static; it too is evolving, and its evolution has a structure. It took a very smart psychology professor called Clare Graves to see that. Maybe, just maybe, seeing humanity through the lens of his work will enable us to focus on the direction toward human salvation...

What have we covered:

- Evolution of life on Earth, prehistory, and history.

What remains to be explored:

- Can we bring the *Weltgeist* fully into our awareness.
- How is human thinking evolving?

10. EVOLVING CONSCIOUSNESS

"Change alone is eternal perpetual, immortal." –
Arthur Schopenhauer

In 1950, the World War II code breaker Alan Turing postulated the Turing test as a way to measure the intelligence of a computer. To pass the test, a computer would need to convince a human, seventy per cent of the time, during a five-minute conversation, by written text only, that it too was a human. Then in 1991, in an effort to encourage the development of Artificial Intelligence (AI), the Loebner Prize was established to use the Turing test to evaluate the best AI computer programme. The first winner of the prize was a programme that convinced real people that it too was human, in part because it was programmed to replicate human typing errors. On 10th February 1996, IBM's Deep Blue computer beat Garry Kasparov at chess. This was the first time a machine had won a game against the reigning world chess champion under tournament rules. But did Deep Blue know that it had won? Probably not; its winning strategy was to perform a massive number of parallel calculations using brute computing power. It would appear that you do not need to be conscious to be a chess champion.

Games, models, and tests are good ways to explore our understanding of many things, including thinking. In psychology, it is important to have a model of what humans are, and how they think in order to work with psychological disorders, to model excellence, develop AI, or simply to understand what it means to be human.

Clare Graves

Anatomically, we are the same as *Homo sapiens* from three-hundred-thousand years ago, but it is not just our anatomy that can develop. How we use our brains is also evolving and changing. Clare Graves was a psychology professor who set out to understand the enigmatic issue of mature human thinking. He wondered if there was some form of self-actualised state, as psychologist Abraham Maslow had suggested, and if so, what was it? Graves conducted an exhaustive nine-year research programme as well as a supplementary twelve-year study, before forming his conclusions about human psychology in 1970. The output from his work is an assertion that the psychology of the human mind has no final state, and is instead in an open-ended process of continuous development. This led to the title of his book, *The Never Ending Quest*, edited by the late Christopher Cowan and Natasha Todorovic. His work is a mammoth achievement, which we have yet to fully vindicate.

Graves started his study by asking his students to write assignments about what they thought it meant to be a mature human. He collated their efforts, and then asked independent judges to assess and to categorise his students' work. He found the judges had little difficulty in initially defining five distinct concepts from the students' submissions. Next, Graves got his students to defend their conception to their peers. He asked them to repeat the assignment, and then to justify any changes in their conception. He set them group exercises, covertly observing them from behind one-way glass. He also set them standard psychological tests to measure amongst other things intelligence, dogmatism, rigidity, autonomy, aggressiveness, honesty, and independence. He then conducted a literature review to complete the study, which by that stage included eight levels of human thinking, with a potentially unlimited number of as yet unexplored ones ahead of us.

In summary, Graves' model is that there are thinking systems within humanity that can be activated by changes in how a person perceives the outside world. The changes follow a predictable hierarchical path, but the growth is expansive, moving towards greater and greater complexity and maturity. Each different way of thinking, or level, has its positive aspects and can also have more negative expressions. Each level solves problems created by the previous way of thinking, and then itself creates new problems that the awakening of the next level overcomes. This conception of human psychology suggests that humanity has the potential to solve all its own problems, because these are in essence self-created. And it is the very pressure of our own failed thinking that drives our forward motion.

Graves labelled his model the *Emergent Cyclical Double-Helix Model of Adult Biopsychosocial Systems*. Perhaps not a particularly memorable label, but it does capture exactly what his conception of humanity is about.

> *Emergent:* New ways of thinking are waiting to be awakened within the human mind. This process is ongoing, but not guaranteed. It does depend on the individual's life conditions, their biological makeup, as well as how open they are to change. For all of us, the process is unlimited; there is no final state. It is also entirely possible for people to move back down to lower levels rather than further forward, depending upon their life conditions.
>
> *Cyclical Double-Helix Model:* The upward progress of human thinking oscillates between being self-expressive, where the power is within, and sacrificial, where the power is on the outside; be that nature, rightful authority, or one's peers.
>
> *Adult:* Graves only studied adults. He considered children to be more fluid and only defined as adults once they settled into a particular pattern.
>
> *Bio:* Graves found the expression of these ways of thinking was not limited to someone's psychological makeup, but it was also expressed through the mix of chemicals in their brain.
>
> *Psycho:* The different levels are best understood by considering the ways of thinking, the motivations, and the behaviour of individuals.
>
> *Social Systems:* And it is not limited to individuals, because how people organise themselves into larger societal structures is reflected through this model too.

There is only enough space in this book to introduce the model that Graves uncovered. I am doing so because I think his work is highly significant, and both underappreciated and underused. It acts as a beacon to mark out the path to follow if we want to continue developing in a positive manner. I also think it highlights the fact that we have a small problem with our large brains, but we will get to that later.

I have summarised each of the levels below based on Graves' research. Each summary describes the level in a pure form. Graves recognised that individuals have different expressions of these ways of thinking, the content can vary, but the theme is the same. He also identified that as an individual entered a new level, the expression was slightly different than when they were nodal, as he called it, and when exiting a particular level. People could also be functioning well or poorly in a level. A final thought to remember is that as progress is made through the levels, we do retain aspects of the 'lower' levels in our thinking too. Nevertheless, when someone is nodal in a level, that will be their primary way of being. Don Beck, who worked with Graves for a number of years, has described each level like a musical note, which we then use to play our own harmonies. As you read through these levels, see which ones resonate the most with your own thinking.

Level One – Automatic

This most basic way of being has been used by humans for a very long time, but there are very few examples of people living in this way today. It is a reactive existence, where the absence of physiological tension is good, and its presence is bad. If you are hungry, you find food; if you are thirsty, you drink. There is little in the way of a subjective understanding of existence. This then means that there is little sense of time, leadership, or organised activity. People live in groups of twelve to fifteen individuals. Here, humans have barely any sense of being alive, but nevertheless they conduct activities to ensure they remain alive. If life conditions enable people to actually connect with a sense of aliveness, they then project this out into the environment, and the second level begins to awaken.

Level Two – Tribalistic

Graves estimates this next level came into being about forty-thousand years ago, as climate change challenged people living at that time. This is also when we see cave art beginning to emerge. In this new way of thinking, everything, animate or inanimate, is imbued with spirit. There is spirit in the mountains, in this particular riverbend, in the trees, in animals, and in you. Because there is only a limited idea of cause and effect, coincidental events are treated as causal. This way of thinking is what leads to superstitions and taboos; humanity inhabits a magical world. The life and practices of the tribe are simply the natural way of things, and the individual is just part of the tribe; the family. Pavlovian conditioning operates without there being much conscious awareness of it. For examples of this way of being, initially think about African and indigenous American tribes, especially prior to contact with Europeans. And then, realise that this way of thinking can still be seen in developed countries today, maybe in the inner city, or in settled groups in rural areas. Family is important here, but if a family structure is weak, children can be drawn into gangs, which then become their tribe. Graves also believed that the majority of people on the planet today still live at this level.

Within the tribe, you are a nobody; and for some, the boredom of this elder-dominated, ritualistic way of life finally forces a swing back to individualistic expression. The rawness of a separate self fighting for its own survival is born.

Level Three – Egocentric

In this level, the separate self awakens; man considers himself to be a powerful entity separate from others and the tribe. *He* wants to take charge of his personal survival. Man wants to explore and manipulate the world: forests are cut down, cities are built, and roads are constructed. The world is perceived as being rough and tough like a jungle. Man is seeking to survive as an individual, and woe betide anyone who stands in this man's way. This is a 'dominate and submit' way of being. Man will stubbornly resist the power of others until overpowered, but will then submit. This is feudalism. It is rugged, self-assertive, and egocentric. But the ego is a fragile thing. If you shame it, then its owner will hate you for doing that.

This level is about looking good and getting respect; uncalculated risk-taking is considered heroic. Graves states, at this level and below, people do not have the ability to feel guilt, no matter what they do. The neurology for feeling guilt has not yet been activated. The thinking is an eye for an eye and a tooth for a tooth.

Graves estimates that this way of thinking has been around for ten thousand years. There are plenty of examples of this way of being from history. Think about Rome, or of Carthaginian general Hannibal, taking his war elephants over the Alps to face it. In a fun sense, this way of thinking is expressed through things like the television show *Jackass*. If you have ever come across someone, maybe at work, who is utterly ruthless, sexually inappropriate, and easily distracted, then it is likely that you are dealing with a level three thinker; be careful…

Success at this level often involves the unconscionable use of others, which makes people angry. Man begins to realise that sacrificing a little bit of self to others might help *him* to get along, and guilt begins to creep in. More than that, the haves and the have-nots both die. Everyone is left wondering what it is all about, and inequality becomes seen as part of a larger plan.

Level Four – Absolutistic

This way of being is virtually the polar opposite of the one before. Hierarchy, rightful authority, and rule-following are the order of the day. Rewards are deferred into the future. The inequities of this earthly life are endured for an everlasting life in the hereafter. There is a strong sense of right and wrong. Humanity's impulsive, pleasure-seeking nature is controlled by discipline, rules, and guilt. Through the rules and suppression of earthly pleasures, one is being tested to see if you are deserving of reward in the future. There is one right way to do things at this level, and they are done religiously. But, as with all these Gravesian levels, it is the way someone thinks, not the content of people's thinking that counts. This is the same way of thinking that has produced monotheistic religion, rule-based hierarchical government, and even communism. People take their authority from their position, and dutiful rule-following is rewarded, not individualistic thinking. At this level, because there is just one way to do things, schisms within organisations are common, and they arise from the rightful authority that you follow; Catholic, Protestant, Sunni, Shia, Lenin, or Trotsky. When Graves assigned seven to fifteen people in this system a problem to solve, they divided themselves into at least two and sometimes up to four groups. Within each group, a pyramidal hierarchical structure formed. A true inner world exists here, though there are many doubts and fears. Graves estimates this level started between four and six thousand years ago. This is a level that is still very common in the world today, and is still the dominant power force in many components of society.

Once again, death can make one begin to question this way of being. Plague still accounted for the pious and the irreligious alike. Whatever the cause, authority starts to be questioned and the desire to defer rewards wanes. Man wants to become independent and to think for himself.

Level Five – Multiplistic

Graves labelled this level multiplistic, because here people think that there are many ways to do something, not just one way dictated by rightful authority. At this level, science is possible, whereas in level four, true science cannot function. An experimental way of thinking decides the best way, rather than the right or wrong way; nothing is sure until proven. Graves estimates this level started about six to seven hundred years ago. This way of thinking and the science it brings with it gave birth to the Industrial Revolution. And it was the failure to solve the problems of existence using 'lower' ways of medieval thinking that was the catalyst for change.

As I said before, we can arbitrarily measure the birth of modern science from the publication of Nicolaus Copernicus' work on the heliocentric universe in 1543, the year of his death. Now, imagine living in that time compared with living in the relative comfort of today. Just to orientate you a little, England of 1543 was the age of the Tudors; this was the year that Henry VIII married the last of his six wives, Catherine Parr. Houses of the time, used by us ordinary folk, were largely made of timber, white-washed wattle, and daub. Glass was expensive and not commonly used. The vast majority of the population worked farming the land. Life expectancy was just thirty-five years, partly due to high infant mortality. There were no flushing toilets and people used leaves or moss instead of toilet paper. To then assert that all the progress made since then has been because of science is a broad stroke, but one that is not too far from the truth.

At this level, effort is made to analyse and comprehend how nature works, not why. Initially, what is being explored is what God designed but did not choose to control. Life then becomes driven by the quest for knowledge and information, rather than being driven by God or nature. Secular thinking begins to dominate. The authority of ones' own tried-and-true experience replaces professed authority. Humanity asserts an independent way of thinking by learning nature's secrets rather than through the naked force of level three. All this is being driven by the desire to make our world better, now.

At this level, competition, an entrepreneurial attitude, efficiency, calculated risk taking, scheming, and manipulation are all valued. Here, the ends justify the means. At the end of the day, 'business is just business': *"it's not personal"*. The system generated by this thinking pretends that self-interest is actually in the best interest of others too. People operating at this level are critical and cynical, often delivering cold quantitative evaluation. All life is a game, and the purpose of the game is to work out how to bend the rules in order to win. Here, people scoff at weakness and other people's lack of drive. A materialistic world view comes from this way of thinking. People at this level like to break things down into parts, but are particularly uncomfortable sensing that the whole is more than the sum of the parts. Emotions are avoided, repressed, or denied. Humanity is happy to map out the world, but not so happy to intensely experience it.

This is a very common way of thinking in the western world, and has been for some time. It dominates the worlds of business, politics, and science. But this is not the end state for man, because there is no end state. More than that, because of its outward focus on the material world, the conscious self, and the disconnection to the spiritual, this way of thinking is driving us down the path of self-destruction.

Through this way of thinking we have made the world abundant, but we have not yet learned how to live with this abundance, or even to live with others who are still in need. Welfare is just for the deserving, and only so long as it does not devalue independence. Eventually, people at this level realise that they have achieved the satisfaction of a good life, but at a price. We may well be respected, but because of our callous use of others, we are not liked. We may think we have solved material problems, but we begin to realise that there is also a need to get along with others if the good life is to continue. And material success does not fill the gaping, spiritual void in humanity's life; so, the need to belong rises once more.

Level Six – Sociocentric

Graves estimates that level six first appeared in the late 19th century. This level is the beginning of a humanistic expression. At this level, we feel the need to be accepted within our community rather than wanting to go it alone. Our focus shifts inside to knowing our inner self, and then outside to others, so that we can be at peace with ourselves and with the world. The peer group to which we belong or want to belong takes precedence. Therefore, we sacrifice self to the authority of the group. Cooperation is more valued than competition. Welfare is distributed equally with reference to need, not merit. There is a re-awakening of religion, but this is not about the rituals of level two or the dogma of level four; it is instead about spirituality. More of the right side of the brain is activated and a subjective view is taken. Decisions are based on feelings, not logic. This is a warm and affectionate level. People show a capacity to allow others the full expression of who they are. It is from this level that Human Rights are born.

At level three, the central theme is aggression; at level four, it is rightful authority; and at level five, it is my own self-interest. But at level six, the central theme becomes people, friends, community, and the intimacy of shared experiences. A level two man will fight if his territory is invaded; at level three, man fights just for the fun of it; at level four, man fights ideologically; at level five, man fights for selfish gain, but at level six, we begin to question whether there is any purpose in fighting at all. At Level six, man's aggressiveness towards others goes, although Graves found that the suicide rate was the highest.

At level six, man is warm and caring, and he tries to let everyone have their own way, without appreciating that you simply cannot do that. Not everyone else on the planet is nice! A level three thinker cannot be changed with love alone; more than anything else, they need discipline and rules. The level six thinkers know what is wrong on the planet, but despite this, there is a general unwillingness to do anything about it. Meditating about inner peace might feel good, but it does not prevent things getting worse and worse. Level six thinkers need to stop talking about what is wrong with the planet and start doing something to change it! If the abundant success of level five means that our level six's good life is not challenged, then there is no impetus to change. People need to become dissatisfied with a lack of results to activate the neurology for level seven thinking.

Level Seven – Systemic

This next transition brings with it a profound change. It did take Graves a little while to make sense of this shift, but what he eventually realised was that the whole spiral from levels one to six was being re-started, only at a higher level, a higher octave. There was resonance in level seven with level one, but it comes with an altogether superior level of thinking. This led Graves to label the first six levels the *Subsistence* levels, and levels seven onwards the *Being* levels. This movement into level seven is about giving, not getting; it's about contributing, not destroying; and it comes with motivation rooted in abundance rather than in a sense of lack. At level seven, humanity's focus is on self and the world. It is important that the world is restored so that *all* life can continue.

Level seven is where true interdependent thinking arises. People are capable of considering that several sets of values are legitimate, depending on the individual and their conditions of existence. My way does not have to be your way. People at this level are comfortable living with differences and apparent paradoxes. Anger and even hostility can be present, but it is used intellectually rather than being emotionally displayed. People have the ability to direct their anger, rather than having the anger directing them. Thinking at this level is less rigid and much less dogmatic than other levels. Compulsive behaviour is not found, and competence is important, together with the autonomy to express it.

A particularly interesting finding of Graves' was that people at this level had a significantly enhanced ability to solve problems. He set groups of people operating at the various levels problems to solve. What he found was that the level seven thinkers came up with more solutions than all the other levels put together. Their solutions were of a better quality, and they arrived at them more quickly. But Graves was not studying intrinsically smarter people. Their intelligence was not higher than people operating at other levels. The average was slightly higher, but only because particularly low intelligence was not present in level seven. Graves put this problem-solving ability down to the absence of fear in level seven thinking, which allows for the greater utilisation of the pre-existing neurology. Level seven thinkers are not afraid of finding food and staying alive, like level one. They are not afraid of being able to access shelter, like level two. They are not afraid of predatory man, like level three. They are not afraid of God or other rightful authority, like level four. They are not afraid of having status or making their own way in the world like level five. And they are not afraid of social disapproval or rejection, like level six. The increased thinking power of this way of being comes from the lack of fear. People thinking this way can find more solutions because they are not afraid to try out new ideas. They still will act with caution in a dangerous situation, and may well still have worries and anxieties, but these do not overly bother them. Threats or coercion do not work with these people because they are not frightened people.

Graves noted that the leading edge of level seven thinking can be seen in physics literature in 1915. In his own data, he started to see this way of being in 1952-53, and overall, it accounted for about seven percent of his subjects. But development does not stop at level seven. Graves started to see a small number of people beginning to enter the eighth way of being in his later studies. In total, he only found six people at level eight, so there is only limited data about this way of being. He labelled this level as the Intuitive Level and detected resonance with level two. What lies as yet unexplored ahead of us are levels nine, ten, eleven, and twelve – and who knows what lies beyond that.

Onwards and Upwards?

This Gravesian way of thinking is used in coaching, because you can get a sense of which level someone's thinking is coming from. It can help you to appreciate a client's strengths and their challenges more effectively. You also get the chance to assess whether or not they are transitioning from one level to another, and if they are, your coaching can support them to do that. Also, if you look at the world as it is now and how it was in the past through these Gravesian filters, everything becomes easier to understand. Today, many parts of the world exist in a tribal way of being, seeking to perpetuate a world they do not understand, whilst fighting others who invade their territory. Some countries are being led by people thinking through level three, and that is not so much of an issue, unless they have nuclear weapons, of course. Organised religion is dogmatically locked in a level four way of being, guided by perceived rightful higher authority, whilst resisting the urge to question. Mainstream science is stubbornly holding onto its level five materialistic reductionist philosophy, unwilling or unable to connect with human experience and the big picture. Human Rights, mindfulness, and a green agenda are on the rise from level six, much to the bemusement of the levels below. But talking is simply not enough, and level six's reluctance to embrace technology is misguided. Through the limited thinking of the first six levels of the Gravesian system, are we creating a planetary environment on the edge of collapse, or one that can act as a springboard for transformation? Notice how the emergence of new ways of being has been accelerating too: as we use more of our neurology, our capacity to use even more is developing rapidly as well. If we maintain this progress, significant changes in the direction and structure of our society are fast approaching…

Finally, back to the small problem with our large brains I alluded to earlier. Why did our neurology evolve this capability to become more complex, when we are only now learning how to use this complexity? Our neurological makeup already contains more expansive ways of thinking and being. What on earth was the evolutionary pressure that laid down these capabilities in the first place three-hundred-thousand years ago? It is as if we evolved a super computer, for some unknown reason, and then simply played *Tetris* on it for thousands of years.

Did we once use all our neurological capability, and then descend to our current state sometime in our prehistory? Is it simply a very happy coincidence, another example of evolution co-opting one piece of biological equipment for a purpose other than the purpose it originally evolved for? Or is there something else entirely which accounts for the large brain of *Homo sapiens* and our more recent ability to use it?

Summary

There are many models of how people think in psychology. Some of these are directly aimed at working with pathology, and are not necessarily aimed at the human experience as a whole. In my opinion, Graves' model is the most comprehensive understanding of how we humans think, and how we like to organise ourselves because of how we think. It is important because Graves did not formulate a conception in his mind and then do testing to prove that he was right. Instead, he set out to explore human thinking, and through that process uncovered this model; no easy task indeed.

If you look at the past through this Gravesian lens, then much of our development becomes easier to understand. Also, if you use it to look at the present, it becomes easier to comprehend too. More than that, this model also points us in the direction of where our thinking should be going in the future. It is because of Graves' model that I can look at today's world and see much to be hopeful about. Because of his work, I can say with confidence that we are on the edge of a transformation in our thinking. We are about to move more thoroughly into levels seven, eight, and beyond. The rate of that change is accelerating too. Through his work, Clare Graves has laid out some of the structure of the human aspect of the *Weltgeist*, and he has done so with such clarity that you can almost smell it. And so, armed with a deeper sense of our past, and emboldened with a comprehensive model of how we think, let us explore the challenges of the present; let us meet our *Zeitgeist*.

What have we covered:

- The evolution of consciousness through psychological ways of being, according to Clare Graves.

What remains to be explored:

- Why is the human brain so large and why are we just learning how to use it?
- What is our *Zeitgeist?*

11. ZEITGEIST

"To truly know the world, look deeply within your own being; to truly know yourself, take real interest in the world." - Rudolf Steiner.

If you could go back in time to any event of your own choosing, where would you go? Would you like to watch a great artist or composer at work? Michelangelo sculpting David, Leonardo da Vinci painting the Mona Lisa, or Mozart composing a concerto? Would you have the stomach to witness a great battle from the past? Hannibal at Cannae, William the Conqueror at Hastings, Napoleon at Austerlitz? Perhaps you might love to hear a great religious leader or philosopher teaching their students: either Buddha, Plato, Jesus, or Muhammad. Maybe you would enjoy watching the first humans leaving Africa, the first performance of a Shakespearian play, or the Wright brothers' first one-hundred-and-twenty feet of powered flight. Great events in the past go a long way to defining the spirit of the time, the *Zeitgeist*. At the time, people can sense the spirit of their age; they are part of it after all. Sometimes, a particular *Zeitgeist* can only be fully understood as we look back on it from the future. Crushing though Hannibal's victory was at Cannae, fourteen years later he faced final defeat at the hands of Roman general Scipio on the plains of Zama.

Remember, we do not perceive the world the way it is, we perceive it the way that we are. As we look at the world around us, we assess it through our own filters, including our own expression of Clare Graves' system. In this chapter, I am presenting the spirit of our times, our *Zeitgeist*, the way that I see it. You may well have a slightly different perspective. As I present my thinking, it would also be a good time for you to reflect on what you think is happening around the world today, right here, right now. Because just by being alive today, you are part of the *Zeitgeist* too.

The Environment

Earth is our home. It is where we all live, but we have not been treating our home very well of late. Since the industrial revolution started, we have been pumping tonnes of pollutants and carbon dioxide (CO_2) into the atmosphere at a prodigious rate. And it is only fairly recently that we have realised that this is a problem. I do appreciate that the idea of climate change is a hot political topic, but before we explore that side of the issue, we need to establish some facts.

The planet's temperature is determined by the energy that we receive from the Sun and the amount then lost back into space. The Earth's atmosphere creates what is known as a greenhouse effect, trapping within it the heat from the Sun. The principal greenhouse gases (GHG) in our atmosphere are water vapor, CO_2, methane (CH_4), nitrous oxide, and ozone. Without these, the planet would be 35°C colder, so the greenhouse effect is generally a good thing. Today we are in an interglacial period, a time where there is relatively little ice coverage in the Northern Hemisphere. Ice-age cycles seem to be dictated by the Earth's orbit around the Sun, its angle of tilt towards it, and by extra-terrestrial impacts. Over the last million years, the planet has cycled between warmer and cooler periods. The relatively warm conditions of today started at the end of the Younger Dryas, almost twelve thousand years ago.

Until the start of the industrial revolution, humanity had minimal impact upon Earth's climate. There are isolated occasions where past human activity can be detected in the environment, such as the brief period of Roman industrialisation. But as we started to use coal and oil as energy sources to power our development, we have been releasing large quantities of CO_2 into the atmosphere. Pre-industrial levels of CO_2 were 280 parts per million by volume (ppmv), whereas today, two-hundred-and-fifty industrial years later, atmospheric CO_2 is now 400 ppmv, which is forty-two per cent higher. We know from laboratory testing that CO_2 is a significant GHG, and we can even correlate the amount of CO_2 and CH_4 in the atmosphere with higher global temperatures going back over the past eight-hundred-thousand years.

In the last one hundred years, global temperature has risen by 0.8° C. So, why has the temperature rise not been even higher? The Earth's climatic system is quite complex and highly interconnected. There are a multitude of contributing factors including ocean currents, methane emitted by food animals, volcanic eruptions, positive and negative feedback loops, and of course, human activity. There does seem to be a slight lag between a rise in CO_2 and an increase in global temperature. Nevertheless, climate scientists estimate that global temperature could rise by between 2.8° C and 5.4° C in the next one hundred years. This is where some of the political controversy arises. This is only a forecast, and as an experienced finance director once told me, *"The only thing you know about a forecast is that it is wrong; because it is a forecast."* But the potential risks of ignoring this particular forecast are huge. In the past, rather than expressing a change in climate in small increments, the Earth has experienced climate change in rather rapid convulsions, before settling into a wholly different, but more or less stable pattern. The effects of rising temperatures are themselves complex and varied, but they are likely to affect rain fall patterns, storm severity, and sea level. Each one of these could make certain parts of the planet uninhabitable. Sea-level could rise by as much as a meter within one hundred years. But if the temperature did rise towards the higher end of the forecast, then melting of the Greenland and the Western Antarctic ice sheets could occur. If these did melt in their entirety, then sea level would rise seven metres for Greenland and eight-and-a-half meters for Western Antarctica.

Humanity has not just been pumping GHGs into the atmosphere either. The rising global population, and with it the rising demand for agricultural land, mainly to graze food animals, has been destroying the natural habitat of many species. This has also led to more deforestation, which in turn has added to the climate change problem. Human-based pollution and its encroachment into previously unspoilt territories is also causing what some people call the Sixth Mass Extinction, as the planet loses more of its biodiversity. Some of the increase in CO_2 has been absorbed by the oceans, resulting in their acidification, which in turn is adding to the loss of biodiversity. Coral, for example, is particularly sensitive to oceanic pH levels. As coral dies, there is likely to be a negative knock-on effect through the rest of the food chain.

For too long, and particularly in the West, humanity has been treating the planet as an unlimited resource to be exploited at will, not believing or wanting to believe that there are any long-term consequences of doing so. Ancient forests have been cut down, mountains stripped for metals and minerals, toxic waste is casually dumped just out of sight, flora is trampled under our feet, and fauna regularly served up on the dining table – all for the pursuit of a 'civilised' way of living. Now, although we are becoming more aware of this, we are still reluctant to do anything about it! Like a morose teenager, we play on our console, continually promising to clean up our bedroom; but we do nothing about it, other than adding more dirty clothes and unwashed pots to our already disgusting abode. One day, there will be a reckoning. Sometime soon, we will realise that it is time to grow up, to take responsibility for this mess, and start cleaning it up ourselves.

Political & Economic Structures

The foundations of our dominant Western society are representational democracy and capitalism. It is fair to say that they have served the West well to bring it to where it is today, but right now, both of these structures are beginning to fail. The very fact that our environment is in the state it is does by itself suggest that both democracy and capitalism are in need of a serious overhaul.

Winston Churchill said of democracy: *"No one pretends that democracy is perfect or all-wise. Indeed, it has been said that democracy is the worst form of Government except for all those other forms that have been tried from time to time."* The aim of democracy is to give the people a say by discussing issues, and then together, by majority, deciding on the best course of action to take. This way, we all accept responsibility for our collective actions. Democracy can be noisy and time consuming, but as the Churchill quote suggests, it is the best thing that we have. There are variants on this theme throughout the world. But generally speaking, the people of a particular country elect politicians who then organise themselves into political parties, and have discussions about laws and taxation in a parliament. This model is largely based on the historic British system, but of course, the roots of democracy go way back to ancient Greece.

As a way of exercising democracy when large numbers of people are involved, politicians have been and still are chosen by the people of a designated area to represent their views. This was an expedient and practical method of organisation in the 17th and 18th centuries, when mass communication was by newspaper and the fastest mode of transport was by horse. However, over the years this system has morphed; instead of being a representative of the people, politicians now represent their own political party. The façade remains; the people are still asked to choose a representative from a small selection of parties. The elected representative then claims that they will represent the people's views. But these are party placemen; the elected politician goes on to represent the party, not the people who elected them. Certainly, in the UK and elsewhere, it remains possible to remove odious politicians or to elect independents. But this is a rare event, as people most often vote in accordance with historic party loyalties, or become so disillusioned by the whole system that they fail to vote at all. The party-political, representative democracy that predominates in the West has in effect disenfranchised the people from the power. Instead, power now rests with the political parties. And again, this has worked well enough for a couple of hundred years. But this party system is susceptible to corruption, and tends to polarise debate. Although sometimes this too is a theatrical, false display of political activity. Our technologies have also evolved faster than our political structures. Mass communication is virtually instantaneous today. The idea of mass decision making has always been possible, and referendums have been used for centuries, but now our technology *could* enable direct, frequent mass participation in the political decision-making process. This would return the power to the people, and make the people more engaged and accountable for the process of organising their lives. This is surely what democracy should be about.

One of the other tools of industrial development is the limited liability company. Corporations are granted separate legal status, and as the name suggest, an investor's liability is limited to the amount of money they invested. Under this structure, the downside risk is known. This then allows the company directors to take calculated gambles. Companies started to appear in the 16th century, and were used as risk-management vehicles to trade with and to explore the 'New World'. One of the most famous of these early companies was Britain's East India Company. During its two-hundred-and-fifty years in 'business', it traded in the East, raised private armies, fought wars, and one way or another, conquered most of India. It even had a company flag. Until finally, under extreme financial pressure, it was folded into the British state.

Another tool of industrial growth is money. Money is an ancient concept; it is used to price and to facilitate transactions, to pay taxes, and as a way to store wealth. Historically, valuable items have been used as money, most commonly silver and gold. The reason for this was that they are relatively difficult to acquire, easy to standardise, fairly easy to carry and store, and very importantly, do not corrode, particularly gold. Today, most of our money is no longer in a physical form and is instead stored in computerised ledgers. The money now issued by governments is fiat money. That is money created by decree, without any supporting, underlying substance. Except for the productive capability of the people represented by the government. The concept of debt then goes hand in hand with money. If I have lots of money, I can lend you some of it in order for you to use it. I can then profit from your endeavours by charging you interest on the loan. Thereby, I can accumulate more wealth simply by virtue of having some pre-existing wealth, a supportive legal structure, and of course, a smart lawyer. The charging of interest has a chequered history. The levying of any charge for money was historically defined as usury. It is prohibited in the *Bible* and the *Koran*, though it is accepted in our society today without a second thought.

With private corporations, a money system, and the start of the industrial revolution, the idea of modern capitalism was born. Market forces, risk-taking, and entrepreneurial flair enabled the harnessing of man's creative powers to bring the material benefits that some of us enjoy today. A wonderful success story, or so we are told. But our vaunted capitalist system is failing, and we are only slowly beginning to realise this. Wealth has been accumulated into the hands of the super-rich. In

January 2017, the charity Oxfam said that eight billionaires owned more wealth than the poorest half of the world's population put together. This is a state of affairs that Oxfam described as *"beyond grotesque"*. In 2017, world debt was estimated by the Institute of International Finance to be $233 trillion, whereas in 2014 World Gross Product, the sum total of the world's activity, was said to be only $78 trillion. Of course, at the end of the day the net debt on the planet is zero. We do not owe anything to Mars or Venus; we owe it to ourselves.

If you did not know it already, these numbers highlight the fact that our capitalist system has created a serious imbalance problem between the haves and the have-nots. Also, the way we have organised our society around material wealth, reflected in money, means that the power has shifted from the people to the politicians, and finally to the white men with all the money. Tax havens, lobbying, and corruption have just become part of the Western capitalist system. It is not easy to get new political parties established without someone else's money. This means that it is not easy to change the system, because those benefiting from the system, maybe not unnaturally, aim to perpetuate it. If all of that was not quite bad enough, our current version of capitalism has now privatised the profits, whilst socialising the downside risks on the people. This was brazenly demonstrated during the 2008 Financial Crisis where, Lehman Brothers aside, insolvent banking and financial institutions, guilty of reckless risk-taking in the pursuit of bonuses and profits, were bailed out by governments. And by the way, that means you and me. The private investors raked in profits for years and years, and when everything went belly-up, the cost of fixing the mess was socialised on the people. This is also what has been happening with climate change. The cost of degrading the planet has never, in a meaningful way, been levied on the private corporations profiting from creating the mess. Once more, the upside has been privatised, and the downside will have to be paid for by everyone else, many of whom have not even been born yet.

The financial system we have today rewards the accumulation of money and wealth. Not necessarily the utilisation of that money, other than lending it to earn interest. And our money supply system does not create money to cover the interest that accrues either. This then generates competition for the existing money, and the lending or the withholding thereof, affects the money supply too. If the money supply increases, money gets devalued, which is called inflation. If the money supply is restricted, no one can do anything, because money is used to price *and* to facilitate transactions. So, economic activity declines and this gets called a recession. Also, high debt levels can lock individuals, or countries into a difficult situation that only bankruptcy, and the accompanying loss of other assets, can free them from. Although it may not be immediately apparent, our current money system is based on scarcity. This means that, even if it is unconscious, we are being driven by a fear of not having enough.

In a true democracy, the people have the power. Politicians sit at the apex of that power and should exercise it for the benefit of the people, not themselves. They are permitted to communicate to the people for the purpose of influencing their opinion. Nevertheless, politicians must be scrupulous enough to just influence and not to manipulate. The difference between influencing and manipulating is that when someone is influencing, they are taking the best interests of the person that they are influencing into account. If someone is manipulating, then they do not take the other person's interests into account: they only consider their own self-interest. The tools are usually the same, such as an impassioned speech laced with emotive rhetorical constructs. Think about John Kennedy's speech about going to the moon, or Martin Luther King's *I Have A Dream* speech. Both of these were positive, uplifting speeches. But you can use language in the same way for a less than positive outcome, as Germany discovered in the 1930's and 1940's.

The requisite skills and methods of leadership, especially political leadership, have been debated for thousands of years; it was a central theme in Plato's *The Republic*. It is a fairly tricky thing to do and to get right. However, the way that I would suggest we measure the effectiveness of leadership is by its results. May I be so bold as to suggest that because of the failure of our democratic and capitalist systems, the leadership of the Western world is also failing. One must remove the filters of partisan preference and look carefully at Western leadership. Over the last seventy years too often it has been incompetent and inept. And sadly, I suspect that even more frequently it has been arrogant, corrupt, manipulative, greedy, and self-serving. Lord Acton, a 19th century British politician, is famous for saying: *"Power tends to corrupt and absolute power corrupts absolutely."* However, I tend to favour the views that author Frank Herbert expressed in his *Chapterhouse: Dune* novel: *"All governments suffer a recurring problem: Power attracts pathological personalities. It is not that power corrupts but that it is magnetic to the corruptible."* Cast your eye over your own political leadership and ask yourself: is this the best we can do? Can we gracefully make space at the top for leaders who are a better reflection of the people that *we* want to be? Can we find leadership that genuinely wants to serve humanity, rather than parasitically feeding off it?

It will depend on your own individual perspective as to how you view our current political and economic structures. Given the backdrop of impending environmental pressure, the disenfranchising of the people, and the undefendable imbalances across the globe, I believe that serious change is required. This change must be focused on the systems, not the people involved in those systems. If we are going to change at all, the way we do so must be as inclusive as possible.

Progress

Whether we like it or not, our times are defined by progress. The rate of change in our development is simply off the scale. Remember it only took us sixty-six years to move from our first powered flight, by the Wright Brothers in 1903, to our first landing on the Moon in 1969. We have sent probes to visit other planets in the solar system and we have robotic devices on the surface of Mars. These achievements, driven by humanity's imagination, ingenuity, and industrious nature, clearly point at our potential. This then is surely an area for considerable optimism. One of the effects of our technological advances to date has been that people are being drawn closer together. We can communicate with large numbers of people over great distances instantaneously. We can travel much more easily and quickly than in the past. Humans today are highly connected through technology, even if we are thoroughly divided by what we think and do. Notice how this trend of increasing connectivity reflects a movement towards expressing, in our physical world, the underlying structure of reality: that everything exists here and now.

Also, we seem to be on the verge of a whole new explosion of scientific growth in genetics, computing, robotics, nanotechnology, and artificial intelligence (AI). The advances in robotics mean that even more of the tasks that humans hate will be taken over by willing, compliant robotic slaves. Nanotechnology, which is about the manipulation of matter at molecular or even atomic scales, could lead to new materials and new methods of manufacture. This in turn could even lead to step change advances in computing, genetics, and AI. Are we on the verge of a virtuous spiral of scientific development? These are exciting areas of human exploration, but ones that quite frankly scare the pants off some people. Is eugenics about to raise its ugly head again? Are we going to create an army of super-soldiers, either by genetically enhancing humans, or through robotics and AI? Are we rapidly approaching the Technological Singularity, where robotic AI takes over the process of upgrading itself so rapidly that it decides it no longer needs humans? Our science fiction books and films are full of apocalyptic imagery of intelligent self-aware robots exterminating dumb squishy humans. I believe that through our science fiction we are exploring some of our deepest fears, so that we can safely consider and then overcome them.

Our scientific and industrial achievements, underpinned with imaginative economic thinking, are things that humanity can be proud of, even if we are about to bring a dose of climate change upon ourselves. The very fact that we are doing so is actually a sign of our progress. And at least, we have developed the scientific expertise that is now telling us what we are doing to the environment. Our ability to make progress, the way we have now, and in the past, is an area for optimism. But we need to make sure that as we move forward, we stay connected with who we really are. By doing so, we can make sure that we stay in balance with our environment and true to ourselves. And I do not believe we can simply invent our way out of our problems without dealing with our underlying issues either.

Spirituality

What does spirituality mean and why is it important? To someone with a materialistic world view, the idea of spirituality is virtually non-existent.

From this dissociated, physicalist perspective, spirituality is simply an imaginary concept that foolish people use to comfort themselves about the crushing inevitability of their own death. To millions of followers of the world's religions, spirituality is the sense of an all-powerful deity, and an afterlife abode for the worthy. How do you currently reconcile in your mind the fact that one day, you will no longer be physically present on Earth?

As we have discussed at length already, I believe consciousness is fundamental to existence – it is what we are. Death is simply a transition from one form of conscious expression into another. The incredibly popular idea of an all-powerful supreme deity is something that cannot really be proved or disproved. But within the new model of the world, no God is required. In fact, a better description is that we are all expressions of the idea of God. Within this model, you do still have genes, and you can have the experience of evolution, but these are not fundamental to existence either.

As I said way back in *Chapter 2*, all the religions of the world had, or still have at their core, a connection to the mystery of existence. It is the realisation that, to quote an ancient Egyptian proverb, *"The kingdom of heaven is within you, and whosoever shall know himself shall find it"*. But all religions also have, to a greater or lesser extent, morphed into hierarchical, male dominated, dogmatic, and book-based priesthoods. In this sense, the people are deprived of direct access to the mystical and supernatural. The spirituality of religion is not present in the now, and is instead deferred to some magical after-death realm. The priesthood are the gatekeepers of the spiritual experience. But the uncomfortable truth for all religions is that our spirituality is ever-present and individually accessible, without the need for a mitigating priesthood. For sure, teachers and guides are useful, but spirit, consciousness, is what you are. As you will recall, many people who have had an NDE or OBE have, through their experience connected more directly with their own spiritual nature. By doing so they tend to become less religious, but more spiritual. To borrow the Zen concept, the world's religions are all like fingers pointing at the Moon. What we see and focus on are the doctrinal differences rather than the core message. We focus on how different our fingers are, instead of looking at the Moon. I do admit, from a cursory glance, it is hard to see that the world's religions are fundamentally saying the same thing. This is because the core message is obscured in 'one-right-way' Gravesian level four thinking.

Given the power vested in the Catholic Church at the time, René Descartes' separation of the spiritual and the material was politically expedient. It enabled the rise of science, which was a good thing. But science's reactionary and dissociated focus on the material world has limited our ability to see our true nature. We have either abrogated our spirituality to a priesthood, or simply denied its existence. Organised, hierarchical religions and secular atheism have removed the people from a direct experience, and connection, to their innate spiritual nature. As a result, we have lost that sense of who we really are, and drifted out of balance. We are not just randomly-created conscious meat-bags perpetuating the existence of our own selfish genes. Nor are we divinely created pawns in a confusing game of 'see-if-you-can-guess-how-to-behave-to-get-to-heaven'. We did rightly use the power of our rational mind to pull ourselves out of the squalor of the Middle Ages. But bereft of a meaningful spirituality, we have largely defined happiness in material terms, or as something that can only ever be achieved as a poorly defined after-life reward for good behaviour. Our satisfaction and happiness in life should be defined by simply being ourselves, and by exploring and expanding into who we truly are. Satisfaction in life comes from the pursuit of *knowing thyself.*

Spirituality is not about lighting incense and meditating, nice though both of those things can be. Spirituality is about knowing that your essence is eternal and perpetual. It is the understanding that you are a soul, and that you are having the experience of a body. You know that the physical expression of the persona is finite, but you know that you are infinite. If you remove all the dogma from religion, you are left with spirituality. But as you can see from the definition above, there is so much dogma to remove from religion that nothing of the old religion is left. Spirituality can be accessed through a religious path, but once you get there, you realise that religion itself is redundant.

Summary

"Pessimism leads to weakness, optimism leads to power." – William James.

Today, humanity is facing a multitude of challenges. Most of them are asking us to fundamentally re-define the idea of what being human really means, both now and in the future.

It seems to me that the principal cause of our impending environmental pickle is our Western materialist reductionist philosophy, as reflected in our society's structures. Our white-male-dominated representative democracy and Western capitalism, expressed through large corporate interests, are holding humanity in an inane death grip. And our true spiritual nature is denied or stifled through dogmatic, male priesthoods. This current state of affairs is simply not good enough; together, we can do much better than this. In order to do so, we need to break free from this dance with death, and change our social and political structures. Otherwise, we all will be going down together. After all, everybody needs food. As King Midas discovered, you will not live very long if everything you touch turns to gold.

There is a lot that we need to do and change, but it is not all doom and gloom for humanity either. Perhaps our problems have not grown big enough for us to start doing anything about them… Well, not yet anyway. But when we do, the good news is that if someone has a problem, they also have the solution; because by defining a problem, you highlight the solution. If you have a problem now, you can solve it now, because you have it now. In the coaching field, when clients are honest with their coach, honest with themselves, and courageous enough to follow instructions, then there is not a problem that cannot be overcome. Sometimes, it is by facing challenges in life that we learn, grow, and change. According to Clare Graves' system, it is the very success of the preceding ways of thinking that creates the problems and the backdrop that provide the stimulus for positive forward momentum.

But wait – before we consider our future and our various choices, there is still something missing from our narrative. As I just said, in a coaching environment, the client needs to be totally honest about their life history and their situation in order to be coached effectively. So, in the interests of full disclosure, there is another topic present within our *Zeitgeist* that we have not yet discussed at all. We really do have to consider this subject before we can fully understand where we are today; once we do, our appreciation of the now will change completely. Only then, fully informed, will we be able to think about moving forward into the future. As clients have often said to me in the past, *"I can't believe that I'm telling you this. I have never told anyone else this before."* The thing is, there are objects flying around our skies that are unidentified. They perform manoeuvres that defy our current materialistic understanding of physics, and they seem to be under intelligent control. Some people call them UFOs…

What have we covered:

- Humanity faces an impending environmental upheaval.
- Our Western-designed political and economic structures are failing.
- We are still making technological progress.

What remains to be explored:

- What are UFOs?
- How do we transition into a more positive future?

12. CLOSING THE FERMI PARADOX

"Our lives begin to end the day we become silent about things that matter." – Martin Luther King.

Enrico Fermi was an Italian experimental and theoretical Physicist. He won a Nobel Prize for Physics in 1938, and led the team that demonstrated the world's first self-sustaining nuclear chain reaction in 1942. That particular experiment was housed in a squash court at the University of Chicago. He later went on to work on the Manhattan Project, which developed the USA's first atomic bomb. In 1950, as part of a lunchtime discussion about life elsewhere in the universe, Fermi asked his colleagues the obvious question: *"Where is everybody?"* It stood to reason that given the enormous size of the universe, or even our own galaxy, and the relative age of our star compared with other stars, surely there should be evidence of extra-terrestrial (ET) life that we can detect 'out-there'. Or even evidence that ETs have been to this planet. But where is the evidence? This question is known as the Fermi Paradox. There are many potential solutions to it, which include the following:

1. Rare Earth: There is no other life in the universe. We are unique, and we have not found evidence of other life because there is not any.

2. Relativity: There is ET life but it cannot traverse the vastness of space to get here or in any other way communicate with us. The limitations of relativity make space travel and communication over long distances very hard.

3. *Self-destruction:* There was ET life, but it killed itself off long ago.

4. *Human Pioneers:* There is ET life, but it has not evolved enough to know that we are here. We are the leaders in the space exploration game.

5. *Passing Ships:* There is ET life, but it is so different to us that we do not know it is there, and it does not know we are here.

6. *Boring Humans:* There is ET life, but it is not interested in us.

7. *Conspiracy:* There is ET life. It is here, someone somewhere knows about it, but they are not telling everyone else.

8. *Watchers:* ET life does exist. They know we are here and they are interested in humanity, but they are keeping themselves hidden from us for reasons unknown.

Of course, there would be no paradox at all if there really was alien life interacting with this planet in a meaningful way, and if we all knew that for sure.

The UFO Phenomenon

I cannot prove alien life is real or that it is visiting Earth, but it is a fact that there are unidentified flying objects (UFOs) in our atmosphere. After ruling out mundane explanations of unusual sightings in the sky, like Mars, Venus, satellites, balloons, aircraft, military prototypes, and the sun reflecting off various objects, there are still some aerial phenomena that cannot be explained. By definition, these are UFOs. And although this is the case, we do not know for sure what UFOs are. Of course, you would be forgiven for not realising there is still an unexplained phenomenon here. By and large, the mainstream media tends to ignore the whole issue, or it treats it in a manner that discourages deeper investigation by the casual observer. The media seem to be taking a lead from government. Most governments do not talk openly about the subject, except to deny that there is anything unexplained. Or if there is, that it might be a threat to national security. Some researchers claim the US government in particular knows a lot more about this subject than it is saying. This idea of a government conspiracy about UFOs and alien life then gets churned around by the mainstream media in an incredulous manner.

This book is largely a presentation of a new model of the world. We are reimagining our earthly existence and discovering how our minds and our thinking create our experience. So, what has this got to do with UFOs? Well, I believe through this new model, we can develop a better understanding of the UFO phenomenon, and ensure we have an expansive and positive future experience with it. At the very least, let us start by being a little bit more grown up about the subject. The time for ridicule about 'little-green-men' is over. Now is the time for some serious examination of this topic.

Over the years, there have been thousands of good quality UFO sightings. In case you have not researched much about this subject before, I have included below a summary of some of the best-known events within the UFO field. Inevitably, because of limited space, I have left much out. You may well want to read further into this subject for yourself, and I would encourage you to do so. Nevertheless, the examples listed here will give you a sense of the various components of the phenomenon.

Roswell

There are reports of UFOs before the July 1947 Roswell incident. These include Biblical accounts interpreted by some as UFOs. There are 19th century reports of strange airships, and from World War II, there are accounts from both allied and axis pilots of strange lights that followed their planes, which American aviators called foo-fighters. According to some researchers, the very genesis of man is inextricably interlinked with the UFO phenomenon. But here we will start with the modern era and the most iconic event of all, the alleged UFO crash near Roswell, New Mexico.

In June 1947, the term flying saucer entered popular imagination as a result of reports by pilot Kenneth Arnold. He saw strange objects in the air whilst flying near Mount Rainier in Washington State, USA. He reported that they *"flew like a saucer would if you skipped it across the water"*. Not long after the Arnold sightings, during a violent thunderstorm something fell from the sky onto a ranch, near Corona, North West of Roswell. The following day rancher Mac Brazel went to check if there had been any storm damage to windmills and fences on the ranch. As he did, he discovered a large debris field that his sheep refused to cross. He took some of the strange material to show the local Sheriff, who in turn asked the military at Roswell airbase to get involved. One of the military personnel who initially arrived at the crash site was Major Jesse Marcel, the intelligence officer at the 509th Bomb Group, stationed near Roswell. At the time, this was the only unit armed with atomic bombs in the world. Marcel collected some of the material he found at the site, and was so excited by what he found that on his way back to base, he went home and showed this recovered material to his wife and son, Jesse Jr.

The following day, 8th July 1947, the 509th Bomb Group's commanding officer, Colonel Blanchard, authorised their information officer to release a press statement announcing that the military had recovered a crashed Flying Saucer. However, within just a few hours, the story was changed, as Brigadier General Roger Ramey told assembled news men at his Fort Worth airbase, that Marcel had made a mistake, and it was only a crashed weather balloon. Marcel was then photographed in front of what clearly seems to be weather balloon debris. Although rumours of crashed UFOs did circulate in the years that followed, the story largely ended there. It lay dormant until 1979, when Marcel broke his silence by speaking to researcher Stanton Friedman.

To quote Marcel, from *Crash at Corona* by Stanton Friedman and Don Berliner: *"When we arrived at the crash site, it was amazing to see the vast amount of area it covered. It was nothing that hit the ground or exploded [on] the ground. It's something that must have exploded above ground, traveling perhaps at a high rate of speed... it scattered over an area of about three quarters of a mile long... several hundred feet wide. It was obvious to me... that it was not a weather balloon, nor was it an airplane or a missile."*

Friedman tracked down and spoke to several army and civilian witnesses, all of whom told the remarkably similar story of a crashed saucer and small non-human bodies being recovered and shipped to Wright-Patterson Air Force Base in Dayton, Ohio. Friedman believes this crash had three debris sites. The initial airborne explosion that created the materials that Marcel handled, a further one where the bulk of the craft was, and yet another one where some form of escape capsules contained the dead crew. Friedman also believes that other UFOs have crashed and been recovered by the US government since 1947 too.

Still facing public pressure to explain the Roswell incident, in 1994 the US government issued a report. This said the material recovered in New Mexico in 1947 was most likely from the previously highly classified *Project Mogul*. This project used microphones attached to high-altitude helium balloons to listen for evidence of Russian atomic tests. However, it seems to me somewhat absurd that Marcel, who had only recently completed training at Radar School, and his commanding officer Blanchard, were unable to properly identify a crashed balloon. Both men were still subsequently promoted in the military: Marcel to lieutenant colonel and Blanchard eventually to four-star general. For some, the whole Roswell incident marks the start of the US government's cover-up about UFOs.

Betty and Barney Hill

Late on the evening of 19th September 1961, Betty and Barney Hill, a newly-married couple from Portsmouth, New Hampshire, were driving home from a short vacation in Canada, when they spotted a light moving in a strange erratic manner across the sky. As they watched, the light stopped in mid-air and started to descend towards them. It continued to follow them for several miles, and then as they rounded a corner, suddenly they encountered a circular disc hovering silently in front of their car, about eighty feet above them. Barney stopped the car and got out. Using his binoculars, he looked more carefully at the craft. It had a double row of windows in the centre, and he could see beings moving inside. He started to feel very uneasy and quickly climbed back into the car, accelerating away to escape. The craft went with them. Betty and Barney then both heard a series of buzzing sounds coming from the trunk, felt some vibrations, got the sense of a roadblock, and an orb resting on the ground. Nevertheless, they kept on driving and finally got back to Portsmouth a little after 5:00 a.m. The strange thing is that by their own reckoning, they should have got back at 3:00 a.m., and they could not account for the missing time.

Over the next few days, they shared details of their encounter with family and friends, and with the US Airforce personnel at their local airbase. They also noticed some strange physical effects. There were several highly polished spots on the trunk of their car. When a compass was placed on them, the compass needle spun around continuously. The leather strap on their binoculars was snapped, the tops of Barney's shoes were heavily scraped, the new dress that Betty had been wearing was torn, and the windup watches that they had both been wearing were irreparably broken.

Over the next few weeks, Betty suffered from nightmares about the events, and as time passed, Barney's physical and mental state deteriorated. He sought professional medical assistance, and it became increasingly apparent that the missing time during their encounter was contributing to his ill-health. This eventually brought both Betty and Barney to the office of psychiatrist Dr Benjamin Simon in December 1963. Dr Simon had worked for a number of years using hypnosis to assist veterans who suffered from what we would call today post-traumatic stress disorder. When used by a medical professional in this way, hypnosis can be a useful tool to help recover repressed memories and thereby assimilate past trauma. The primary purpose of this form of therapy is the resolution of a psychological discomfort that can sometimes also be expressed physically, in Barney Hill's case, as stomach ulcers. Dr Simon worked separately with both of the Hills using hypnosis for several months. He used specific suggestions to ensure any information that either of them recovered was not shared with the other until all of his work had been completed.

Under hypnosis, the Hills revealed they were indeed stopped at a road block that was 'manned' by non-humans. The car was incapacitated, they were placed in some form of trance-like state, and taken on board the nearby craft. Betty was able to walk, but she did resist entering the craft, and this is when her dress was torn. Barney, who was more strongly in a trance state, was dragged and carried into the craft, which is most likely how his shoes got scraped. Both of the Hills underwent a form of medical examination where the skeletal and nervous systems were studied and various samples taken. Dr Simon's opinion about the whole episode was that Barney had overheard Betty's nightmares whilst they slept, unconsciously incorporated this into his memories, and then repressed them. Dr Simon attempted to suggest his hypothesis to the Hill's both in and out of trance. They both denied this was the explanation for the recovered memories. They even insisted the events were real, despite Dr Simon's suggestions to the contrary *whilst* they were in the trance he had induced. Also, Dr Simon's hypothesis does not account for the physical evidence.

The Hill's case is not the first case of alien abduction, nor in fact a particularly isolated one. But it did get well publicised in the 1960s, not at the Hill's instigation, but rather through a breach of confidence when some information was leaked to a newspaper. Later, in 1966, John Fuller published *The Interrupted Journey*, about the Hill's abduction, with theirs and Dr Simon's assistance. The book became a bestseller and was made into a film, *The UFO Incident*, in 1975.

Animal Mutilation

It is not just people who have been targeted either. On 9th September 1967, in Pueblo, Colorado, rancher Harry King found one of the horses that grazed his land, called *Lady*, lying on her side in a clearing with all the flesh removed from the neck up, exposing the skeleton. Closer inspection revealed that the heart, lungs, and thyroid of the animal had been removed, and that this had been done without spilling a drop of blood. The incision to remove the organs and the one around the neck were 'surgical' in nature. They appeared to have been done in a way that cauterised the flesh, like a laser would. But laser surgical tools were not available in 1967. There were no tracks leading to the body, and in fact, the only tracks that appeared to have been made by *Lady* were ones a hundred feet away. Those *"looked like she had jumped around in a circle"*. This was one of the first documented cases of animal mutilation, and by no means the last.

Animal mutilations have been reported across the USA and elsewhere since the 1960s, right up to the present day. Although many animal species have been targeted, cattle are the most common victims. The tissues removed are often tongues, rectums, udders, ears, eyes, and sexual organs, and this is all achieved in a bloodless surgical manner. The reason that animal mutilations are associated with UFOs is that very often, UFOs are spotted in the vicinity prior to the discovery of a corpse. There have even been witness accounts of cattle suspended in mid-air by beams from UFOs. Oddly enough, silent unmarked black helicopters have also been spotted in association with these UFO sightings and cattle mutilations. The official explanations of animal predation, or 'cult' activities, are refuted by the surgical nature of the incisions, as well as the number and geographical spread of the incidents.

Rendelsham Forest

Rendelsham Forest is a wooded area, which in the early 1980s lay between the two US Air Force bases of Bentwaters and Woodbridge in Suffolk, England. The incident here started not long after midnight on 26th December 1980. At that time, US Airman John Burroughs was a security policeman. As part of a routine patrol, he spotted strange red and blue lights in the forest a little way from the base. He was not sure what they were. The best explanation seemed to be a crashed civilian aircraft, but no sounds of a crash had been heard. After a very quick inspection with a colleague, he went back to the base to consult further with his superiors. He discovered that an unknown object had been tracked on radar fifteen minutes earlier, but it had disappeared off the radar screens over the Woodbridge site. Several security personnel then set out into the woods to investigate. But it was Burroughs and Staff Sargent Penniston who made the approach to the site where the lights were coming from. As they entered this small, brightly-lit clearing, there was a silent explosion of light, and both men instinctively hit the ground. As Penniston stood up, he could see a small metallic triangular craft with a light on top, resting on three legs in the clearing. He approached the craft, touched it, and saw it had unusual symbols on it. Shortly afterwards, the craft lifted silently off the ground, out of the forest, and then sped off. At this point, Penniston still retained enough composure to write in his notebook: *"Speed-impossible."* A quick inspection of the site revealed three indentations in the ground where the legs had been, which when joined up made an equilateral triangle.

Late the following evening, the craft returned. This time, deputy base-commander Lieutenant Colonel Charles Halt led a team into the forest. Halt spent several hours with a group of men, initially at the previous evening's landing site, and then later, following strange lights in the forest that at one point hovered over the Woodbridge base. A thin pencil beam of light was projected down to the ground not far from Halt's team, and a similar beam was shone down into the weapons storage area at Woodbridge. Halt recorded at least eighteen minutes of audio on a handheld tape recorder during the night's events, and he considers the craft to have been under intelligent control.

In 1983, the story was leaked to the British newspaper the *News of the World*. Some of the story was factually correct, and some was not. The best access to the truth is through first-hand accounts, which is what the book *Encounter in Rendlesham Forest* by Nick Pope, with John Burroughs and Jim Penniston deals with.

The Belgium Wave

On 29th November 1989, there were a series of UFO sightings around the town of Eupen in eastern Belgium, not far from the German border. In total, one-hundred-and-forty-three sightings were made by at least two-hundred-and-fifty people, including thirteen police officers. The reports were of a triangular craft with bright lights on the underside. The craft was at times observed hovering silently, and it was also seen to send red balls of light down to the ground, which subsequently returned to the craft. Two police officers reported that as they witnessed the craft, it tilted in such a manner that they were able to see its domed superstructure. This had rectangular windows, lit from the inside. Nothing was tracked on radar.

This was not an isolated incident. On 11th December 1989, Colonel Amond, a civil engineer with the Belgium army and his wife witnessed a triangular craft. They stopped their car and got out to observe it better. As they did, a giant spotlight approached to within one hundred meters of them. The craft then made a slow left turn and disappeared into the night at incredible speed. On 26th July 1990, a couple driving in Eastern Belgium also spotted a triangular craft with lights underneath hovering a short distance away. For fun, the husband flashed the headlights of his car on and off. The craft tilted its underside towards them and flashed two white spotlights on and off back at them. It then proceeded to follow them for a short while before accelerating off at great speed.

Further sightings followed over a two-year period. At the behest of the Belgium defence minister, Major General Wilfried De Brouwer was tasked with investigating the whole series of sightings. De Brouwer states that there were two thousand sightings during the so-called Belgium wave. Of these, six-hundred-and-fifty were investigated and five hundred remain unexplained. Three hundred of the sightings were at distances of less than three hundred meters. Although triangular craft were the ones most commonly reported, other shapes were seen too, including a huge craft described as being like an upside-down aircraft carrier. The performance capabilities of these craft were beyond anything known then or now, including US stealth aircraft, which the US authorities denied were operating over Belgium at that time anyway. To quote De Brouwer, from Leslie Kean's book *UFOs: Generals, Pilots, and Government Officials go on the Record*: *"Hundreds of people saw a majestic triangular craft with a span of approximately a hundred and twenty feet and powerful beaming spotlights, moving very slowly without making any significant noise but, in several cases, accelerating to very high speeds."*

Conspiracy

The accusation of cover-up and conspiracy has been levelled at the US government since it changed its story about the Roswell crash way back in 1947. Over the years, the government has officially investigated the UFO phenomenon and published various scholarly studies. The most famous is Project Blue Book, which started in 1952 and was closed in 1969. Project Blue Book concluded there were no UFO reports it investigated which indicated a threat to national security, or that could not be explained in conventional terms. These conclusions run counter to data published in 1955 in Blue Book Special Report 14, which studied over two thousand sightings. It showed that twenty-two percent of sightings could not be explained. This excluded sightings for which there was insufficient data; in fact, when the quality of the sighting was good, it was *more likely* to be classified as unknown. Nevertheless, the thrust of the final Blue Book conclusions, in 1969, is what the official US government line on UFOs is to this day.

The whiff of a deliberate cover-up was again sensed when in 1979, a Freedom of Information Act request turned up a memo from Brigadier General C.H. Bolander recommending the closure of Project Blue Book. In the memo, dated 20th October 1969, he states: "*Termination of Project Blue Book would leave no official federal office to receive reports of UFOs. However, as already stated, reports of UFOs which could affect national security would continue to be handled through the standard Air Force procedures designed for this purpose.*" This seems to suggest that not all UFO reports were considered by Project Blue Book in the first place, and that the collection of reports was to continue secretly after the project officially closed. Since Roswell, there have also been cases of witnesses being sworn to secrecy and/or being intimidated by US government officials. In *Encounter in Rendlesham Forest*, Nick Pope states that the US airmen who witnessed the events on the first evening were subject to repeated interviews, injected with truth-serum sodium thiopental, and hypnotised by intelligence personnel.

The idea of the US government secretly studying UFOs is still very much alive today. In December 2017, the US Department of Defense released footage of a close encounter between a Navy F/A-18 and a UFO. The footage had been studied as part of a twenty-two-million-dollar Advanced Aerospace Threat Identification Programme (AATIP). This was run by military intelligence official Luis Elizondo from within the Pentagon, and was officially closed in 2012. To quote the *New York Times* article that broke the story on 16th December 2017: "[AATIP studied] *aircraft that seemed to move at very high velocities with no visible signs of propulsion, or that hovered with no apparent means of lift.*" Elizondo resigned in protest at the lack of funding made available to study UFOs. In the same article, he is quoted as saying that "[there are] *many accounts from the Navy and other services of unusual aerial systems interfering with military weapon platforms and displaying beyond-next-generation capabilities... there remains a vital need to ascertain capability and intent of these phenomena for the benefit of the armed forces and the nation."* Elizondo is now working with others at the To the Stars Academy of Arts and Science, which aims to raise money to privately study the UFO phenomenon. Another member of this organisation is physicist Harold Puthoff, who as you may recall from *Chapter 3*, studied Remote Viewing for the US military in the 1970s.

It does seem that there are people within the US government who know a whole lot more about UFOs than is publicly admitted. And it is not just researchers who are saying this. Even in 1960, in a statement sent to congress, Vice Admiral Roscoe Hillenkoetter, who was CIA Director from 1947 to 1950, said: *"It is time for the truth to be brought out... Behind the scenes high-ranking Air Force officers are soberly concerned about UFOs. But through official secrecy and ridicule, many citizens are led to believe the unknown flying objects are nonsense."* More recently, John Podesta, who was Bill Clinton's White House Chief of Staff and the chairman of Hillary Clinton's 2016 Presidential campaign, wrote in the foreword to Leslie Kean's 2010 book *UFOs: Generals, Pilots, and Government Officials go on the Record*: *"The time to pull back the curtain on this subject is long overdue."*

The idea of a deep conspiracy within the US government and elsewhere is too much for many people to accept. People struggle to imagine something of this magnitude being kept secret for so long. Personally, I find it more difficult to dismiss the thousands of credible witness accounts. It seems to me that there is a real UFO phenomena, and that there is a degree of cover-up. To be fair, I do have some sympathy with governments in the late 1940s who had to grapple with this issue. World War II, which was a highly traumatic experience for humanity, had just ended; the Cold War had just begun, and we had to come to terms with the idea that through nuclear weapons, we had developed the power to entirely destroy ourselves and the planet – a tough in-tray for any administration. At the same time, it is also entirely possible that governments today do not know a whole lot more about UFOs than the general public does. Or perhaps, they do not know what to do with what they do know.

Closing the Fermi Paradox

Since 1947, there have been thousands of UFO sightings by members of the public, pilots, police officers, and military personnel from across the globe. There have also been thousands of pictures taken of UFOs. James Abbott, author of *The Outsiders Guide to UFOs*, conservatively estimates, based on published studies, mainly from governments, that there are three thousand totally inexplicable sightings every year. That is a lot of unexplained aerial activity occurring around this planet. But is it extra-terrestrial in origin? As Elizondo said, the performance of the craft is *"beyond-next-generation capabilities"*. This is from 9th March 2018 *Washington Post* article about AATIP: *"According to incident reports and interviews with military personnel, these vehicles descended from altitudes higher than 60,000 feet at supersonic speeds, only to suddenly stop and hover as low as 50 feet above the ocean"*.

But it is only on very rare occasions that there have been encounters with physical beings on the ground, like the Betty and Barney Hill case. One such sighting was by police officer Lonnie Zamoura in Socorro, New Mexico, in 1964. Whilst pursuing a speeding motorist, Zamoura heard a roaring sound that changed frequency, and he saw a blue and orange flame in the sky. Thinking that a dynamite shack which he knew was in that vicinity might have exploded, he abandoned his car chase and went to investigate. As he approached in his police cruiser, he saw a shiny metallic egg-shaped object and two small humanoids standing beside it. They seemed startled by his presence. As he drove closer and manoeuvred around a small hill, he lost visual contact with them. Suddenly, the object rose in the air with a roaring sound before speeding off extremely quickly. Though shaken by the incident, Zamoura inspected the site where the craft had been. He found indentations in the ground and smouldering plants that were strangely cold to the touch. Zamoura's case was investigated by Project Blue Book, and was listed as unexplained.

As non-human beings are encountered, and because UFOs appear to be under intelligent control, we tend to think that we are dealing with extra-terrestrials. Other origins for these entities remain possible. One of these is that we are being visited by time travellers from a future Earth. In *Encounter in Rendlesham Forest*, Nick Pope presents some evidence for this. People often ask, if there really are extra-terrestrials, why do they not just land on the White House lawn and announce themselves? The thing is that we do not know for sure whether or not there have been face-to-face meetings between ETs and government officials. What we do know is that there are a fairly large number of UFOs displaying themselves with lights, having the occasional cat-and-mouse game with military jets, and on very rare occasions, there are actual landings.

It seems to me as if 'they' want us to know that they are there, and they are waiting to see how we will react to their presence. Although some pilots have accidently died chasing after UFOs, there are precious few accounts of any hostility being displayed by them. However, there are accounts of nuclear weapons launch and guidance systems being deactivated by UFOs. Are we being given a message here? You will have to make up your own mind about UFOs, but for me, the Fermi Paradox is closed. They are here, and we are being watched.

Summary

Despite all of this, you still might say: *"So what difference does it make, even if there is something real at work here?"*

The chance of any one specific individual seeing a UFO in the next twelve months is less than one in a million, so it is fairly easy for most people to simply ignore the whole issue. Both of my parents were born before 1947, and in all likelihood, they will have lived out their whole lives never having witnessed a UFO, or having their life impacted in any way by these phenomena. It is also possible that my life will run a similar course. I have never seen a UFO or had an encounter, and the phenomena might not play out any more than it already has throughout the rest of my life. At the same time, we do know that something is going on.

As a race, at this time, we are displaying some classic symptoms of split-personality. Our books, films, and TV programmes are packed with ideas regarding space travel, extra-terrestrials, and fantastic technologies. But put this idea into a non-fiction setting and the majority of people start to ridicule it as being impossible. We are dissociating ourselves. We seem happy to imagine these concepts happening to some imaginary human, but not so happy to think they could be real for us. When coaching clients, I will sometimes offer a client the opportunity to consider a path in life by describing it as if it was someone else doing it. This way, they get the chance to consider incorporating that path into their reality, and checking how that feels to them, without it immediately having to be them. Are we doing the same? Are we acting out through our play (books, films, etc.) this expanded space-faring version of ourselves, so that we can check how aligned we are with this idea? If we are, it will soon be time for us to choose to follow that path in reality or to reject it. Play time is almost over, humanity needs to start growing up.

Our governments, who like to present themselves as our protectors and leaders, are body-swerving the biggest story in the history of humanity. In this vacuum created by governmental inaction and denial, we are left to come to our own conclusions about what UFOs represent, and what it means for humanity. I believe the biggest thing this is telling us is that our current model of the world and our understanding of physics is wrong. The whole UFO phenomenon is difficult to understand from a materialistic, things-in-space-over-time model of the world. But in the model where time is an illusion and physical reality is a projection of consciousness, it all begins to make more sense… Anyway, we are not finished with this topic, or should I say, it is not yet finished with us. I would encourage you to take a deep breath. If your world view has not been shattered yet, then by the time you have finished the next chapter it will be…

What have we covered:

- Unidentified Flying Objects do exist.
- There is a wealth of evidence suggesting that UFOs are not of human terrestrial origin.
- There is a degree of government cover-up around the UFO phenomenon.

What remains to be explored:

- Who makes and operates the UFOs?
- What is their purpose for interacting with humans?

13. LOOK INTO MY EYES

"It is said that wisdom lies not in seeing things, but in seeing through things." – Manly P. Hall.

The person who is credited with popularising the term 'hypnosis' was Scottish surgeon James Braid. In 1841, Braid went to see a performance by Swiss mesmerist Charles Lafontaine, in Manchester, England. Although Braid did witness trance states, he was not convinced that they were caused by Lafontaine's mesmerism. Instead, he thought the trance was caused by the fixation of the subject's eyes as they looked up at the lights in the theatre. Inspired by his observation, he went home and experimented on some friends and on his wife. He stood above the seated subject, holding the top of a wine bottle about twenty centimetres from their eyes. He then encouraged them to fix their gaze upon this object for a period of up to three minutes. By that time, the subject's eyelids would close and their respiration deepen. Braid wrote *Neurypnology* in 1843 about his neuro-hypnotic work, and it was from these Victorian origins that hypnosis began. As you can see, the precursor of Braid's work was mesmerism. This is named after Franz Mesmer, a German medical doctor who, just prior to the French Revolution, created a large following in Paris, France, with his practice of 'magnetising'. Mesmer's 'animal magnetism' involved making 'passes' with his hands over the body of his patients, without touching them. He believed that there was a magnetic energetic flow within and between people that could be utilised in healing. However, due to an outcry at his unorthodox techniques, French King Louis XVI ordered a scientific commission to study his work. This was led by Benjamin Franklin, the American ambassador to France, and amongst others included chemist Antoine Lavoisier and Dr Joseph-Ignace Guillotin. The scientists did not study Mesmer directly; instead, they examined the practice of one of his disciples. They concluded that no magnetic fluid was detected, and any healing reported was purely down to the patient's imagination. That alone should have been worthy of further study! Nevertheless, mesmerism had thus been 'proven' to be bunk. As a result, it and the later techniques of hypnosis have been treated with a degree of suspicion ever since. Of course, mesmerism was not the beginning of trance induction either. The trance state is a natural aspect of the human condition and it is, in all likelihood, as old as we are. In the East, there is a long tradition of meditation, which one can argue is self-hypnosis. And in both East and West, stretching all the way back into antiquity, there is eye-gazing, or to give it its proper name, Fascination.

The Abduction Phenomenon

The idea that there are UFOs flying at will around our skies is a big story, but not one that is accepted within society yet. Place some form of extra-terrestrial entities in these craft, and most people start to shake their heads in disbelief. Now, suggest the entities are visiting people in their own homes, abducting them, taking them onto spacecraft, and performing medical procedures on them, and everyone will think you have finally lost the plot! But the fact remains that abduction of people by non-humans has been part of the whole UFO phenomenon throughout the modern era. The first documented, although not broadly publicised case is that of Antônio Vilas-Boas, a Brazilian rancher's son who described being taken on board a UFO in 1957. There are also cases of people being abducted in the 1940s that only came to light during later investigations. But it was with the Betty and Barney Hill case that this aspect of the whole UFO phenomenon began to emerge into collective consciousness. This is probably why their psychiatrist, Dr Simon, had such a tough time attempting to fit it into his pre-existing model of the world.

I do appreciate many people find abduction by ETs hard to believe, but I think that in order for us to get to the bottom of the whole UFO phenomenon, it is essential for us to consider this controversial aspect of it. Simply pretending it is not happening does not fit with the evidence, and ignoring it because it sounds outlandish is just lazy thinking. Having the courage to honestly explore the abduction phenomenon might just take us closer to understanding contact from a non-human perspective, and through that process we may be able to learn more about ourselves too.

The abduction phenomenon is a topic that is difficult to study in an objective and scientific manner. In this sense, it is much like out-of-body experiences. People can talk about their abduction experience and doctors or scientists can see if it fits into known psychiatric conditions, or can be associated with known brain processes. But this phenomenon is difficult to assess from a materialistic model. All its aspects challenge our pre-existing ideas about physical reality and our place within it. Also, unlike an out-of-body-experience, abductions are not something that you can induce by yourself and then study, since they are, by definition, perpetrated by others. On top of this, not all of the memories of the experience are immediately available in consciousness, and some are only brought into awareness using hypnosis. The use of hypnosis is considered controversial by some people, and even abduction researchers argue about the methodology that should be applied.

Any practitioner of talking therapy needs to understand that there is a fine line between elicitation and installation. It is all too easy to presuppose something has happened when in fact it did not occur. This can even arise by the way one asks a question. If someone says that they are in a dark room, and if the therapist then asks: *"Is there anybody else there?"* That is already presupposing the idea that someone else *could* be there. A better response would be: *"Describe the room to me."* Also, any 'recovered memory' does not, by itself, mean that it is objectively true. It could quite easily be a construction of the subject's unconscious mind, and if it was, it should then only be understood metaphorically. That being said, the recovery of repressed memory is most often done in association with already existing conscious memories of UFO sightings, missing time, or some other apparently anomalous happenings. In the abduction field, it is common for people to remember the start and the end of the abduction, but not the middle. Sometimes, the study of the abduction phenomenon is primarily undertaken to relieve the patient of psychological or physiological discomfort, as in the Hill case. On other occasions, the approach is more investigation-led; a direct attempt to uncover information about the abduction phenomenon. As a result of all of this, the 'recovered-information' and its meaning should be treated with caution. This is also a dynamic field; we are still learning more about the abduction phenomenon, and as we do, it seems to be evolving too. The last word on this topic is yet to be had.

Over the past fifty years, thousands of cases have been studied by various different people. But it was the work of New York artist Budd Hopkins that helped to establish the consistent patterns within it. He wrote *Missing Time* in 1981, based on several accounts from the hundreds he studied. He also introduced Temple University History Professor and veteran UFO researcher David Jacobs, and Harvard psychiatrist John Mack to the topic. In a similar way to Hopkins, Jacobs adopted an investigatory approach to the hundreds of cases he studied, whilst Mack's clinical background and interest in eastern philosophy guided his approach. One of the main reasons to seriously consider all of this work is that the basic components of the phenomenon do not vary, no matter who studied it, but the interpretation of what it means does. One can see this simply from the title of books on the subject. Jacobs wrote *The Threat* in 1998, and Mack wrote *Passport to the Cosmos* in 1999.

The late John Mack had strong academic and clinical credentials, and he was not a UFO believer as such at the outset of his studies. He went on to work with over two-hundred experiencers over nine years. He wrote his first book on the subject, *Abduction*, in 1994. He found that aside from the trauma of their abduction and the psychological need to integrate these experiences into their lives, his patients were normally functioning adults, who were free of diagnosable psychiatric conditions. They were ordinary people who nevertheless had extra-ordinary experiences. Mack was impressed by the consistency of the accounts between people who had never met one another and who lived hundreds of miles apart. This consistency was right down to the minutest of details, including the use by ETs of a certain instrument. One patient described this to Mack in an open configuration, whilst a totally unrelated patient described it in a closed configuration. Mack also found that the emotion that his patients displayed whilst recounting their experiences added weight to the idea that what they had been through was very real to them indeed. He did use a modified version of hypnotic regression to bring repressed memories into consciousness, but eighty percent of what his patients recounted was already in their awareness. In *Passport to the Cosmos*, Mack describes common features of an abduction experience like this.

"A person of virtually any age (though the concentration appears to be in young adulthood) is in bed at home, in a car, or out of doors, when his or her consciousness is disturbed by a bright light, a humming sound, strange bodily vibrations or paralysis, the close-up sighting of an odd craft, or the appearance of one or more humanoid or even human-appearing strange beings in their environment. Experiencing varying degrees of anxiety, depending on the status of their relationship to the phenomenon, the experiencers describe being taken, usually against their will, to be floated through walls, doors, or windows into a curved enclosure that appears to contain computerlike and other technical equipment. There may be several rooms in the craft, or whatever it is, and more strange beings are seen busily moving around doing tasks the experiencers do not really understand."

Is the abduction phenomenon physically real, or is it happening in someone's imagination, or in some other non-physically real environment? There is physical evidence in the form of scars, lesions, and scoop marks on experiencers' bodies, which point towards a degree of physicality. In the Betty and Barney Hill case, there was physical evidence in the form of unusual marks on their car, the scraping of Barney's shoes, and Betty's torn dress. Sometimes, other witnesses report UFO sightings that are coincident with an abduction experience. These aside, Mack's view was that the bulk of the experiences were happening in some form of non-physical locale. He highlighted the similarities between what his patients described and what people who have had NDEs and OBEs describe. For example, experiencers often report the presence of strong vibrational energies, *"like an electric current running through you"*. This is what some out-of-body experiencers describe as their experience begins, and it is exactly what I experienced whilst attempting to induce and OBE. Overall, I believe the abductions are happening in what we think of as physical reality, and that the ETs are able to induce a 'phase-shift' in someone's consciousness, that means the experiences happen in a non-physical reality too. At the same time, I also think that the distinction is immaterial. The abductions are a real experience for the people they happen to, again in the same way NDEs and OBEs are.

Hybridisation

Who are these beings? And why are they abducting people and performing various medical procedures on them? To begin with, researchers assumed that the ETs were simply doing field studies to find out about Earth and its inhabitants. By thinking in that way, they were interpreting the phenomenon through a wholly earthbound, human lens. They imagined the ETs to be doing what humans would do whilst studying endangered animals: drugging them, checking their health, tagging them, and then monitoring them over time. But as more information immerged about what the ETs were doing, the pattern of behaviour started to be understood differently.

The physical characteristics of the entities do vary; nevertheless, the most commonly encountered are the Greys. These are described as being short, well under five feet, greyish white in colour, and physically frail, with a large cranium, no hair, a slit for a mouth, not much of a nose, and no ears. They have very large almond-shaped eyes, black in colour, usually without the sense of a pupil as such, and they slant upwards, almost wrapping-around the head. This 'classic' alien type has entered the public imagination and the media. It has done so from the encounter and abduction literature, not the other way around. The Greys appear to be intellectually and technologically advanced, but emotionally stunted. They come across to experiencers as cold and unfeeling. There are also other entities who are very similar to the Greys, but who are just a bit taller and seem to take on a more senior, leadership-type role.

Most commonly, what the ETs do when they abduct people is perform medical examinations. They set or remove implants which are frequently inserted through the ear or nose. Severe and otherwise inexplicable nose bleeds in young children have been reported coincident with abduction events that included implant insertions. Sperm is removed from men, most usually in a mechanically-forced ejaculation. Women report the removal of eggs and the insertion of what are assumed to be embryos. This assumption is based on them experiencing a pregnancy, only to have the experience of a 'foetus' being removed during an abduction event a couple of months later. There are accounts of women seeing foetuses developing in fluid-filled containers, being presented with strange looking babies, and encouraged to hold them in a nurturing manner. There are even accounts of men and women being shown small children who look like a Human-Grey hybrid.

As you might well imagine, these are terrifying experiences for abductees. They have their 'normal' lives shattered by an intrusion, often in their own homes, that they are powerless to stop, and something they feel they have in no way consented to. They are confronted with strange-looking beings who float them out of their surroundings and perform invasive and often painful procedures on them. Mack reports that the biggest aspect that abductees need to integrate into their psyche is the very paradigm-shattering nature of the experience. Nevertheless, in most cases this is what they are able to do, and many of them utilise the experience to undergo a positive spiritual transformation. Finally coming to the realisation that they, and indeed all of us, are connected to and part of something altogether larger and more expansive than we have heretofore realised.

The late Budd Hopkins' take on the experience is as follows, from his 1987 book *Intruders* -

"These men and women are neither devoured nor saved. They are borrowed, involuntarily. They are used physically and then returned, frightened but not deliberately harmed. And the aliens are described neither as all-powerful, lordly presences, nor as satanic monsters, but instead as complex, controlling, physically frail beings who apparently need something for their very survival that they are forced to search for among their various abductees."

As Hopkins says, the ETs are not all-knowing and all-powerful. In the cases he studied, there are at least two occasions when sperm removal was performed on men who'd had vasectomies. The ETs did not seem too impressed about this fact when they realised it later on. There are also cases of people being returned to the wrong bed, or not having their clothing put back on properly. Abductees are repeatedly told they will not remember their experiences, but nevertheless, these sometimes slowly resurface, or are recoverable under hypnosis.

Jacobs writes extensively about the creation of various types of Human-Grey hybrids. He believes there is a range of hybrids with varying degrees of Grey features, all the way to hybrids who appear to look human, which he calls 'hubrids'. Whilst honestly admitting that he does not know for sure the purpose of this hybridisation project, he is concerned that it represents a clandestine alien takeover of the planet. From his 2015 book *Walking Among Us*:

"But the fact that naive hubrids are moving into society surreptitiously and most likely in huge numbers signifies a covert invasion. Unlike normal immigrants, they are not here because they want to be; they are here only to fulfil the aliens' goals."

In stark contrast to Jacobs' views, the biggest finding for Mack was that the phenomenon directly challenges the dominant materialistic world view. To quote Mack from *Abduction*:

"Above all, more than any other research I have undertaken, this work has led me to challenge the prevailing worldview or consensus reality which I had grown up believing and had always applied in my clinical/scientific endeavours. According to this view - called variously the Western, Newtonian/Cartesian, or materialistic/dualistic scientific paradigm - reality is fundamentally grounded in the material world or in what can be perceived by the physical senses. In this view intelligence is largely a phenomenon of the brain of human beings or other advanced species. If, on the contrary, intelligence is experienced as residing in the larger cosmos, this perception is an example of "subjectivity" or a projection of our mental processes."

Look Into My Eyes

One of the most striking features about the ETs is their eyes. Abductees frequently describe being compelled to look into the ETs' eyes, and as they do, trance-like states are induced, communication is shared, pain is relieved, and fear is reduced. Sometimes, people report that the very 'otherness' of the eyes is frightening and disturbing, whilst others say the ETs' eyes are the gateway to a deep, all-consuming sense of connection and oneness.

As I mentioned at the start of this chapter, there is a trance technique that pre-dates mesmerism called fascination. It involves instructing someone to stare directly into your eyes, whilst you either look through theirs, or fixate your gaze between and slightly above their eyebrows. Fascination is not widely practiced by hypnotists today, but historical accounts say that it enables trance to develop quickly, and that thoughts can then be transferred mind-to-mind. In the form of mesmerism that I was taught, one begins the session with a short period of eye gazing. Also, the very first time that I was mesmerised, I experienced a degree of mind-to-mind transfer with the practitioner.

Eye gazing is also used as a meditation that two people can do together. Meditation is most often thought of as an Eastern religious practice. But it is a worthwhile activity for anyone to pursue, and need not be considered as religious or even spiritual. Some of the benefits of meditation are emotional resilience, improved cognition, and an enhanced ability to focus attention; or to put that another way, an enhanced ability to live in the now. Scientific studies indicate that the brain structures associated with these functions, and others, are thickened and thereby upgraded by long-term meditative practice. I commonly recommend meditation to my coaching clients, and it has even been used by the US Marines to help alleviate combat stress. There are many methods that one can follow to meditate, and it is most often thought of as a very solitary activity. However, eye gazing is a meditative practice that you can do with a partner. Sit comfortably opposite each other, set a common intention to connect more deeply, and then just gaze into their eyes, one, the other, or both. Five to ten minutes should be long enough to start with. Once you get past the initial awkwardness, an altered state can develop and other experiences can follow. Simply by focusing on a single thing, in this case someone else's eye, a trance state can develop. Some scientific studies indicate that parts of the participants' brains begin to synchronise during this activity. The cause, effect, or purpose of this brain-activity-matching is not completely understood. Nevertheless, the fact that we humans have a long-standing historical precedent for one of the most striking components of the abduction phenomenon is worthy of further study.

Perhaps the idea of telepathy we see so often in the UFO phenomenon, and in parapsychology could be down to the idea of resonance. It is not that information is being transferred as such, it is more that the frequencies of minds are in lock-step together. Both people have the same thoughts because they are both resonating at the same frequency. They are entrained together such that one can change their thinking, thereby their resonance, and the other person will follow, because they are entrained. This then 'causes' them to have the thoughts of the other. The experience might then feel like a telepathic transfer, especially as we tend to think from a model of separate things. In the coaching and hypnosis work that I do, the idea of rapport is important. One can establish rapport with someone else by subtly matching and mirroring various aspects of their physiology, language, state, and thinking. By pacing someone else in this way, one can lead them to match your own changes in physiology and state. What this then means is coaching clients will be more accepting of looking at their life from a new perspective, and can be encouraged into positive states more easily too.

The Princeton Engineering Anomalies Research (PEAR) laboratory was established in 1979 by Robert Jahn to study the effects of human consciousness on electronic systems. Prior to this, there had been many anecdotal reports of people influencing electronics, and given the rise of computing, this was considered to be a valid area of research. Over a number of years, Jahn and his team performed a huge number of experiments to see if people could, by volition, affect quantum-based random number generators (RNG). The PEAR research findings included the following: when a group of people were engaged in a shared emotional experience, the RNG in the room started to produce non-random patterns; whereas when a similar size group were engaged in a non-cohesive activity, the RNG was still random. They also found that couples with a deep emotional bond produced much more significant results when attempting to influence RNGs together, than they did separately, or when non-bonded couples completed the same experiments. Resonance, frequency, and emotional connection are key, and focused attention reduces randomness.

Channelling

As well as the purely physical aspect of the abduction, information is often communicated too. The communication is invariably telepathic, and it includes what appear to be warnings about humans destroying the planet through our exploitive and aggressive behaviours. Some of the abductees interpret this communication to be about what the beings have done to their own planet, and of course it could be both.

As well as receiving information telepathically, through their abduction experience some of Mack's patients developed the ability to channel. To quote from *Abduction*:

"At this point in the session Peter's voice changed to a kind of monotonous droning and he shifted to speaking from the alien perspective. "We," he said, "want to study the chemical reactions of the brain, and how people will react in order to know when it is time to be present... For as we measure the impulses... we will know at what level the shock will come in, so we will be better able to control it so we will be in tune with the [human] beings as they go through this shock process, as they go through the unfolding of seeing us for the first time..."

After the regression we spoke of the channelling of the voice that had come through during the session... it feels like an extension of his own energy which allows the "alien energy" to come through him. This can occur, he said, when he can "surrender my mind, surrender my ego". He does not altogether trust the information that he receives in this way, but does feel that "it's coming from a higher consciousness, from a spiritual plane". It was occurring in present time he said. "It's live broadcasting.""

This idea of being able to connect through to another dimension of reality and channel information from other entities has been around virtually as long as humans have. Though it is not possible in a materialistic, brain creates consciousness model, it is possible in the time is an illusion and physical reality is a reflective projection of consciousness model. But as with hypnotic regression, it does not thereby mean the information that is 'downloaded' in this manner is objectively true. As I mentioned above, what I think is happening is a locking of frequency between the mind of the channel and the mind of the source, in such a way that both entities have the same thoughts, because their 'vibrational frequency' is aligned. Therefore, there is no 'transmission' of material as such; it is like two tuning forks vibrating at the same frequency, emitting the same tone. But this still does not mean the information is accurate either. The communication is still interpreted through the human-mind filters of the channel. Also, as described in the example from *Abduction* above, the channel needs to surrender their ego. So, even if the content is coming from a higher dimension or frequency, it may not come through entirely free of earthly human contamination.

The idea of channelling is most commonly associated with Trance Mediums, who aim to connect with deceased loved ones. This is a field that has a history of frauds and charlatans, and also innumerable cases where useful and valid information has come through. I have always treated channelling with a degree of caution, because it is difficult to assess the source of the information. But channelled content does crop up again and again in the personal development, OBE, reincarnation, and UFO literature. What you often notice, as in the example above, is a change in the tone of the voice and the speaking style of the channel when information is being conveyed. Fairly well-known examples of this form of information transmission, are Jane Roberts' channelling of the Seth Material, and Esther Hicks, who 'interprets' information from Abraham, the name used to represent a group of entities. When I attended a training at the Monroe Institute, I heard a recording of Rosalind McKnight channelling the consciousness of an entity called Patrick, who although dead, had not made the final step in his transition. The whole experience was facilitated by other beings who also talked through McKnight. Robert Monroe was directed by these entities to communicate directly with the 'lost soul' Patrick, so that he could complete his transition. It seems that earthbound humans, who have a lower vibrational frequency, can 'reach' these lost souls more easily. There is a transcript of the Patrick interaction in Rosalind McKnight's book *Cosmic Journeys*. From the reincarnation literature, in *Many Lives Many Masters*, psychiatrist Brian Weiss describes communication from entities called Masters. They communicated through his patient who was exploring past lives during hypnotic regressions. The channelled content usually happened during the transition between lifetimes, and the information relayed was sage advice about the human-life learning experience.

In the UFO genre, there are also several people who claim to channel information. I have generally steered around channelled content because of the issue of source validation. So, six years ago, when my son asked me to listen to Darryl Anka's channelling of an extra-terrestrial entity called Bashar (not his real name, one just chosen for us to use), I adopted my usual sceptical stance. Anka, through his channelling of Bashar, presents largely personal development, self-improvement, and ET-related content. Assessing this material as a personal development trainer of twelve years standing myself, I am impressed by the quality, consistency, speed, and humour of the channelled content. Anka has been exclusively channelling this entity for over thirty years. The process started after he witnessed a UFO, and then not long after that he attended a course on channelling. Since 2012, I have listened to over one hundred hours of his material, and I have been to two of his events to see him deliver live. Anka freely admits himself that he does not know for sure if the content is really coming from an extra-terrestrial, or if it is just the product of his own unconscious mind.

Prior to listening to this content, I was already familiar with the ideas of time being an illusion, from my exposure to remote viewing, and the work of physicist Julian Barbour. I was also comfortable with the idea of reality being a projection; this theme is taught in the branch of NLP that I teach, it formed part of psychiatrist Carl Jung's thinking, and it is present in esoteric teachings. Nevertheless, the Bashar material unambiguously states that time is an illusion and physical reality is a projection of consciousness. The Five Laws of the new paradigm that I mentioned at the end of *Chapter 4* comes directly from Anka's Bashar channellings.

1. *You exist*

2. *All is one*

3. *Everything is here and now*

4. *What you put out is what you get back*

5. *Everything changes, except for the other four laws*

I cannot prove that channelling is real, I cannot prove that ETs are real either. All I can do is assess what people have said, and then corroborate that with various other sources. The areas in which I have the greatest expertise, and experience, are personal development, coaching, and training. From this perspective Anka's channelled content is very sound indeed. I am therefore minded to consider that the information that he brings through about ETs is also true. Again, as with many of the concepts included in this book, you will have to assess this channelled content yourself. I would encourage you to listen to some of it and make up your own mind about its veracity.

Bashar says there are many ET races who are taking a keen interest in humanity at this time. The Greys are a form of evolved/devolved human from a parallel version of Earth. This race destroyed their own version of Earth by following a developmental path, not too dissimilar to the one that we are currently pursuing. They are highly technologically advanced, but they have lost the ability to reproduce. They are using our DNA to create hybrids in order to perpetuate their own civilisation. By return they are offering to help us to avoid blindly walking down the self-same path of planetary destruction as they did.

This is a quote from an abductee that appears in Hopkins' book *Intruders*; from this you can see that we are getting a similar message.

"The society was dying, that children were being born and living to a certain age, perhaps preadolescence, and then dying [there was] *a desperate need to survive, to continue their race. It is a culture without touching, feeling, nurturing... basically intellectual. Something has gone wrong genetically. Whatever their bodies are now, they have evolved from something else. My impression is that they wanted to somehow share their history and achievements and their present difficulties in survival. But I don't know what they are looking for."*

Also, in an echo of the channelling from Mack's book *Abduction* above, Bashar says that more open contact has not yet occurred, because we humans are not developed enough to be able to cope with face-to-face contact. We need to increase our 'energetic vibration' by acting more in alignment with our passions in life. The ETs are waiting for us to develop – future contact is up to us, not them.

Summary

More than ever, when we confront things as different as UFOs and abductions, we need to consider them through the lens of the new model of the world that I am presenting here. As you will recall:

- We are not who we think we are in the first place. We are a form of soul energy having a human life, for the learning inherent in the experience.
- We do not perceive the world the way it is, we perceive the world the way that we are.
- At some level, likely quite unconscious, we chose our experiences in this life, individually and collectively.
- We also get to choose what our experience means; it does not come with a built-in meaning. Therefore, it is not what happens in our lives, it is how we respond to what happens that is important.
- The collapsing of space and time, in this model, does not prevent expressions of non-human life being able to interact with Earth, right here, right now.

The Gravesian model of the development of human thinking demonstrates that we are evolving without external assistance already. The direction of this evolution is away from our violent, limited, fearful past, towards an inclusive, expansive expression of our innate humanness. This is a direction of movement that we ought to be encouraging, regardless of ET influence or contact. If we can face the UFO enigma from this emerging way of thinking, with confidence and self-assurance, then we can have an expansive positive experience with it. However, if we cling to our fearful them-and-us thinking, then we will have a limited and fear-based experience.

Everyone who is in your life, human or otherwise, is there for a reason; they are reflecting something back to you. I once went to a coaching seminar as a delegate. There was another delegate there who I did not speak to, but whom I judged, from a distance, and not in a good way. I even said to myself, *"I hope she never comes on one of my seminars."*

And as sure as night follows day, on the very next NLP seminar I ran, this woman was there, offering me the chance to let go of my negative judgements. In a similar way, the UFO phenomenon is appearing in our reality now, in the manner it is, for a reason. What do you want that reason to be? Remember, it is how *we* respond to what happens that counts.

UFOs and ETs are not the only things that we need to start considering from this new model. We need to take a long hard look at ourselves in the mirror, because it is time for us to consciously choose the trajectory that we want to have for our version of this human journey.

What have we covered:

- ETs seem to be abducting people for the purpose of creating hybrids.
- Is hybridisation a threat or an opportunity for humanity?
- Is telepathy associated with mind resonance?

What remains to be explored:

- What do we want our future to be?
- And can our ability to focus our thinking and behaviour take us towards what we want?

14. THE AGE OF TRANSFORMATION

"A traveller arrived at a remote village that was suffering from extreme drought. In their desperation the villagers had called in a Taoist sage, renowned as a wonder-worker, to magically bring the rain. The rainmaker came to the village, looked around carefully and talked to the inhabitants. Then he built himself a little shack just outside the village and remained inside for three days and nights. After this time he emerged, took down his shack, and started to leave. As he did so it began to rain. The visitor was amazed and ran after the departing sage. Catching up with him, he demanded: "How did you bring the rain?" The sage replied, "Don't be silly. I didn't make it rain. I simply came to the village and saw that the inhabitants were out of harmony with Tao. This made me feel out of harmony with Tao, so I built myself a little shack and sat in contemplation until I had restored my harmony with the way things are. Having done that, I am now leaving." "So why has the drought ended?" asked the traveller. The sage replied: "When I am in harmony with Tao, everything around me comes into harmony with Tao. When there is harmony the rains come naturally." – From Tim Freke's book *Taoist Wisdom.*

A Coaching Approach

The process of coaching is simple enough. You are assisting someone to move from where they are now, to where they want to go. This process includes understanding the circumstances that your client is currently in, and knowing how they got to where they are now. Together you honestly explore where the client wants to go, and by doing so you uncover what their purpose or motivation is for going there. As the coach, you put yourself into the client's shoes and imagine being them. This allows you to help the client bring aspects of their 'shadow' into consciousness, so that together, you can uncover any deep-seated, root cause of their current situation. Only then, based on a broad holistic understanding of them and their life, can you explore blockages in their thinking, and or in their model of the world. All of this helps the client to see more easily where they need to go in the future, and what are the steps they need to take next. But the coach does not tell the client what to do, that is up to them. You can of course offer clients scenarios to consider, and then pace them forward into that future. By doing so they can imagine what that might be like, before they choose a direction to set off in.

You might be surprised to discover that not everyone who undertakes coaching actually wants to change. Some clients are in denial about their problem: you cannot help anyone overcome a problem that they do not think they have. For some clients, the size of the change they need to make is too much: often, the pain of things staying the same needs to be greater than the pain of change, before some people will move forward. Other clients have what is known as secondary gain: they get a benefit from their problem and will not change unless the same sort of benefit can be derived without the problem. I certainly do not force change on other people: a client's life is their life, and their responsibility.

A coach can stand back and provide careful objective analysis and feedback. They can press motivational buttons, offer support, and encouragement. But you, the client, are the one that must act. And make no mistake, now is the time for action.

As I look at humanity today I see imminent existential threats, and at the same time, a huge opportunity for positive change and growth. If we are to choose transformation over death, then we need to make some significant and immediate changes. Of course you may not think things are bad enough yet. Indeed, you may not think my assessment of humanity today is accurate either. Or *your* life may be relatively comfortable, so why rock the boat? As I have already said, we are all fundamentally eternal.

But this version of the human story is finite, because it is played out in space and time. People, our window of opportunity to easily traverse into a positive future is rapidly closing.

The Problem with Humanity

We have already reviewed humanity's past and present, but before we decide what to do in the future, we must be clear about what the root cause of humanity's problem is. The very foundation of this book is that our current woes lie in our thinking, expressed through our existing materialistic model of the world, backed up by our limited sense of spirituality, as espoused by our dogmatic religions. Or to use Clare Graves' model, the level five scientific materialism; together with the one-right-way of level four; all backed up with a bit of egotistical three; and some tribalistic territorial infighting of level two thrown in for good measure. These ways of being are not wrong or bad *per se*, it is just that we are expressing them in a restrictive, and potentially self-destructive manner. The solution is to both change our expression of these ways of thinking, and to move more thoroughly into higher levels. Step up into the humanistic level six thinking, so that we can reconnect; then, by letting go of fear, we can move into the interdependent, results-based, problem-solving thinking of level seven. The idea that time is an illusion and that physical reality is a projection of consciousness, is aligned with what comes next, which is levels eight and beyond. Level eight resonates with the tribalistic thinking of level two, but instead of seeing everything as being imbued with spirit, you see that everything is consciousness. Or more precisely, you see that *everything is your consciousness*.

If we want to continue moving forward, and to explore more of what is next for humanity, then we need to embrace this new way of thinking. We need to appreciate that the outside world is a reflection of our conscious and unconscious thinking, and the larger, ever-changing *Weltgeist*, as well as its status within its development. *Everything that you perceive around you is a reflection*. The environment, democracy, politicians, capitalism, money, technology, UFOs, ETs, *all of it*. By failing to see that the external physical world is actually a projection of our own consciousness, we blind ourselves to the source of our own innate power. Instead, we have projected it out into the material world. We have then tried, vainly, to dominate that world. We need to reconnect with the process and purpose of human life, and bring our own state of being back into balance. If we do so, we will bring our externally projected world back into balance too. You cannot change this 'external' world by fighting with it as if it was something other than you. But by changing your thinking and demonstrating that change through your behaviour, you change the 'external' world that you experience. In its biggest picture sense, that is the essence of our problem.

"Yesterday I was clever, so I wanted to change the world. Today I am wise, so I am changing myself." – Rumi.

Unity

"We must learn to live together as brothers or perish together as fools." – Martin Luther King.

Once you appreciate the world is a reflection of your own thinking, then it becomes easier to appreciate that the projection we need to work on first is our collective lack of unity. We have divided our human family by gender, sexuality, race, religion, language, geographical location, age, left, right, class, and wealth. You name it, we have subdivided and separated ourselves by it. Very quickly, this then makes us define other humans as being different and 'other' than us. In the past, it has not then taken too much encouragement from our 'leaders' to get us to start fighting, killing, raping, enslaving, and variously dominating each other. So what is the solution? *Stop doing that!* There is nothing about 'others' that you need fear. They reflect you, and at some other level, they *are* you. There really are no 'others'. People it is that simple. Start to see everyone across the globe as just another expression of you. Did someone famous once say: *"Thou shalt love thy neighbour as thyself"*? If your neighbour is really just a reflection of you, then this statement represents a deep truth that we hear, but then totally ignore. *"I will love this neighbour and this neighbour, but I will not love this one."* You must love them *all*. The neighbour that you hate so much is just another expression of you, like white light divided into a whole spectrum of different colours. From a spiritual perspective, it is all just one and the same thing. Even if we consider this issue purely in materialistic terms, human genetic variability is very low. It is even much less varied than the DNA in chimpanzee and gorilla populations. The differences that we like to focus on so much in terms of skin colour and facial shape are only controlled by a handful of our genes. Under the surface, we really are all one family.

There are many toxic expressions of disunity, and one that we must still face up to today is nationalism. There are one-hundred-and-ninety-five separate countries in the world. These are good for sports competitions, for fighting wars, and as tax havens. They are great for subdividing and separating people, and for little else. Take Britain as an example. The British are a nation of immigrants, masquerading as one cohesive, separately identifiable, unique race, with our own set of values. London, the capital city, was founded about two-thousand years ago by Italians (Romans). The very name 'England' comes from immigrants from Northern Germany and Southern Denmark, who started to come into Britain after the Italians left, in about 450 CE. These immigrants were called Angles, Saxons, and Jutes. The three-lions logo on the England football and cricket teams' shirts, comes from Plantagenet English King, Richard the Lionheart. But of course, he was actually French. He was a descendant of William the Conqueror and could not even speak English. As Richard lay mortally wounded, he asked for his heart to be buried in Rouen, Normandy. His statue stands outside the British parliament, a name derived from the French for 'to speak'. The English language is a mix of Latin, German, Scandinavian, and French, which is one of the reasons why it is so hard to learn.

Before the start of the Second World War, the First World War was called the Great War, the war to end all wars. What we needed to learn from this violent conflict was not about the sacrifice of others to protect our way of life, but instead, we needed to learn about letting go of the idea of nationalism. A tough lesson, for sure, and after we did not quite get the point the first time, we then had to repeat the whole thing again, but in a bigger way, twenty years later. Have we learnt this lesson yet? Despite all its current woes, the birth of the European Union was actually an important step in that learning process. Yet, we still cling heroically to our limited and divisive ideas of nationalism. Dwight Eisenhower was Supreme Allied Commander in Europe during World War II, and then President of

America from 1953 to 1961. On this subject he said: *"Every gun that is made, every warship launched, every rocket fired signifies, in the final sense, a theft from those who hunger and are not fed, those who are cold and not clothed."* Destroying cities through war and then rebuilding them could not be a greater waste of time, effort, resources, and lives.

As our climate changes more and more, in the years ahead it will cause the migration of people whose living space has become inundated with sea water, or has been turned into an uninhabitable desert. This will be a challenge for our current 'them-and-us' thinking. Because if we fail to reach out to those in need, we must not be surprised that when we are in need, others will not reach out to us either.

How do we deal with this issue of disunity? We must start to see common humanity in all people. Let go of your own prejudices. Follow the leadership of people who seek unity, and resist the dog whistle calls of those who want to make you hate or dislike others, for whatever reason. There is not a means of division that this does not relate to. This process of re-connection will require us to change some of our current aggressive behaviours. We will have to find other ways to resolve our disagreements.

In the past, so much of our thinking has been driven by the idea that, 'you' and 'them', are separate from, 'me' and 'us', that we have even extended this to our interactions with the planet. It is even considered to be something which is 'other' than we are. Today's urbanised living has removed people from their day-to-day connection with nature. As a result, it has not been very difficult for us to consider ourselves to be separate from nature, and to treat it as a 'thing' ripe for exploitation. Perhaps at some point in our history we did consider ourselves to be stewards of the planet. But today, as other authors have said, we seem to regard ourselves as the chief executive officer of planet Earth, not its steward. And who says that we have to be the steward anyway, you may well ask. Think about it this way: Earth is our home. In your home, you are the steward – end of story, there is no debate required. In your home, you are responsible for the upkeep and maintenance; who else is going to do it for you? Is it in keeping with the neighbourhood, or is it an eyesore? We do not have the luxury of trashing our home and then moving somewhere else, when it becomes uninhabitable. Even if we did, we would surely just trash that place too, unless we change our ideas about who we are. We evolved from the very earth itself, this planet is also our mother. Our re-connection to the idea of being a human family then needs to continue outwards to include the sense of oneness with nature too.

In order for us to re-connect as one big human family, and to accept that we are part of nature, we must learn from, and then let go of the past. We need to find the courage to forgive the wrongs of the past perpetrated on us individually and collectively. However, forgiveness is not about allowing the past behaviours that we are forgiving to continue in the future. The forgiveness that we offer is unconditional, but it comes from a place of self-assurance. We forgive those that caused us hurt from the past, and we now value ourselves highly enough to say that we *will not* allow others to treat us like that again! Our forgiveness also needs to include ourselves. Now and in the past, everyone is doing the best they can with what they have, and that means you too. Forgive yourself for past mistakes, learn, and change your behaviour. Now, become the person that in the future you will be proud to have been. As we extend out our hand of forgiveness to all others, we must help them to learn and allow them the space to change. We cannot actually insist they do so, but step by step, as we connect to the idea of human unity, we *will* transform this planet.

Future Reflections

"Prediction is very difficult, especially if it is about the future." – Niels Bohr.

Another expression of humanity's current problem is we do not have a unifying vision of the future. Together, we need to forge an exciting vision that we can all feel part of and buy into, so that we are motivated to take action in the present. There are some competing ideas around already, of course.

New Age, Prehistoric man

This is the idea that man needs to return to a simpler way of living. We forego our material, scientific advances, and live in harmony with nature and the planet, in the same sort of way that we imagine we did in our prehistory. We only take from the planet what we need, and return what we have used back to the earth. Man is back in harmony with the planet; balance is restored. Love and sex are freely shared, our spiritual nature is re-accessed through hallucinogens. Renewable energy is our principal power source, and people are largely vegetarian. In many ways, this was how indigenous cultures were living before contact with Europeans. To me, this future way of being seems to come from a hankering after that simpler and less stressful way of life. It places the blame for problems on our technology and our progress. Therefore, the solution must be to ditch the progress and the technology.

I do not deny this way of living was effective. Man did live much like this for thousands upon thousands of years. And for me, that is the point. We have already thoroughly explored this way of living. Where does trying to forget everything that we know now, and then starting again really take us? In this regard, we are looking at the past through rose-tinted glasses. Was it really as wonderful then as we like to think it was? We may well have been in greater harmony with nature, but there is still evidence for human on human violence in prehistory. And after all, man decided to make progress for a reason. I think that we still have more unutilised potential in our oversized brain, and it would be more exciting to explore that. If we did reset the civilisation button, surely our true nature would simply rise again, and walk us back down the path to where we are now anyway.

There may be elements of this way of being, like the closer connection to nature and more renewable energy, that we can incorporate into our future. Also, there are huge benefits in going vegetarian or even vegan, in terms of better land usage, which in turn helps to reduce CO_2 and CH_4 emissions. Eating meat uses more than twice as much land as a vegetarian diet does. Even hallucinogens are useful to help people connect more effectively to their spiritual nature. But you can do this without plant-based assistance too. So, even if there are indeed appealing elements to this way of being, I just do not believe this vision is exciting enough for our modern minds. We need to move forward and take our technology with us. We have to be bold enough to imagine a new future, rather than re-inventing a safe, but slightly dull past that we have done before for thousands and thousands of years already.

Materialism

If we just carry on as we are, giving primacy to materialism, then there is just one logical outcome: total planetary destruction through nuclear war, pollution, and or climate change, resulting in human extinction.

Everything that has a beginning has an end. From a materialistic perspective, humanity will die, either by our own actions or by some random, non-human factor. When your brain creates consciousness; time is a fundamental concept; and the physical world is on the outside of you; you will die eventually, and that will be that. In this conception, we could have a partial destruction of the planet, and a brief return to something like prehistoric living, as a way to transition to our final death state. Do you know how to make a computer, a car, or a power station? If the people who know how to do these things, and if the means of doing them are no longer around, then hunting, gathering, and scavenging in the ruins of a lost civilisation is all we will be doing in the future.

You may think that my characterisation of a materialistic future is a little harsh. Perhaps so, but it is inherently devoid of a greater sense of humanity's place within existence. The *Weltgeist* will just make space for something else instead. Disconnected, dissociated thinking will just project itself back at us in the form of total destruction.

Transhumanism

A variant on this materialistic theme is Transhumanism. In this scenario, man uses his technology to continually improve and upgrade himself, physically and mentally. This would be through genetic engineering and/or computerised implants. Here, man consciously enters a posthuman, mechanised world. Another potential route is that man precipitates the Technological Singularity, as AI starts to continuously upgrade its self, thus rendering man obsolete. Or perhaps eventually, man learns how to upload his consciousness into this artificial super-intelligence and becomes immortal. Who needs emotions anyway?

What this conception of a human future fails to realise is that we are already immortal. A transhumanist philosophical approach seems to be based on a fear of death, and it is searching for material ways of avoiding it. Again, there are bits of this approach that we can learn from and utilise, such as genetic engineering to eradicate inherited diseases, and the harnessing of AI in a symbiotic manner with human consciousness. But I do not plan to upload my consciousness into a robot any time soon. I am quite happy for it to transition through death and to then explore what comes next, rather than being a version of this personality stuck inside a robot forever.

Religious Nirvana

Most religions promise an afterlife where you are reunited with your loved ones, where you live in comfort and peace for all eternity, and in the presence of your chosen deity. Sounds like fun, and for a short while, it might be. But what do you do after you have been doing that for a few hundred years? Would that become a bit dull too? Of course, unbelievers like myself will be cast into a fiery pit for all eternity instead. Now, that does not sound like fun, no matter how long you were there for. In the NDE literature, frightening NDEs do exist, but they are rare, and seem to be reflecting back to someone their own fear-based belief system. Also, NDEs where a beautiful, Nirvana-like locale was experienced happen regardless of one's pre-existing religious beliefs. Whether there is a heaven or not does not really matter. If there is, it seems like we will all experience it at some point. Although, to be honest, it might take our robotic transhumanist friends a little longer to get there. Religious Nirvana does not take us any further forward in understanding what humans on *Earth* should be imagining their future to be.

Religious Armageddon

Some religions hold on to the idea that there will be a second coming, a final judgement, and the destruction of the Earth. Some people even seem to be willing this to happen and are rapturously looking forward to it. Certainly, there could be a destruction of the Earth in the future – after all, we have the means to do that now. This concept of Armageddon seems to be driven by the idea that I am right and you are wrong, and I am wanting my deity to come back and destroy you for being wrong, as well as saving me for being right. Well, I am happy if some people want to think this way, providing we do not let them anywhere near the big red nuclear buttons, or allow them any other form of political power. It is alright by me if someone wants to die a glorious sanctified death, just so long as they do not take everyone else with them.

Space Invaders

As I mentioned in the previous chapter, some people think ETs represent a clear and present danger to humanity. Personally, I do not think the evidence supports that. But I do not know the totality of what is out there in the deep obsidian darkness of space. There must be the likelihood of there being good, bad, and indifferent ETs within existence. And let us be honest, we are not always a bundle of laughs ourselves, as exploring Europeans proved to indigenous people all around the planet. But the clincher for me is your thinking. If you are fearful, paranoid, and feel powerless, then you may well get that idea reflected back at you, by being dominated by earthbound humans. If so, then you can surely get that reflected back at you from space too. So, the solution is to connect with our own innate power, build self-assurance, and let go of fear. I do not think that ETs will be coming to save us either. Sitting back and waiting for other people to solve your problems does not work here on Earth, so what makes us think it will work with ETs? Based upon what we saw in the last chapter, it is entirely possible that there is some form of trade and mutual assistance available in our future interactions with non-humans. Let us meet ETs with confidence and curiosity, and without any expectations.

Restore Balance, Connect, and Expand

So, what sort of future vision can we all share that will be worthy of humanity's true potential? Whatever we imagine in the future, it must be expressed with a greater sense of unity. The subdivision of peoples must end. This does not have to mean that your individuality ends; in a world where people are not judged for who they are, there is in fact a greater freedom to express individuality.

The future that we should focus on is one where we restore balance, and then expand out our horizons into space. Balance is about all people living well according to their needs, not simply according to their wants. Balance is where we restore harmony with nature and integrate our technology in a sympathetic manner with our surroundings. Once we have started this process of taking responsibility for our home planet, then we can begin to explore more of the solar system and beyond. The very fact that there are UFOs in our own skies is telling us that space exploration is possible. And it is not just outer-space that we can explore. I would encourage people to explore more of who they are, by exploring the inner-space of their mind too.

Can you imagine a unified human race, at one with nature, harnessing technology, and the power of our own minds, to thoroughly explore the solar system and beyond? Is that a future which is worth facing up to the challenges of today for? It does require us to make some serious changes in how we live now. But I am not asking you to point fingers at individuals, it is the systems and processes that need to change. The change that I am advocating needs to come from a place of inclusivity, not judgement.

Politics and Money

The word 'democracy' comes from two Greek words: *demos*, meaning 'common people', and *kratos*, which is the divine personification of strength. We need to appreciate that the people already have the power. What we need to change is how the people choose to express that power. Today, our Western democracy is suffocating. We need to find the will and the means to breathe life back into this dying system. Support political leadership that wants to unite and nourish humanity. I suspect that truth, reconciliation, and, forgiveness will be required through this process. Judgement and recrimination may well be tempting, but it is not a very positive path to follow.

We also need to find mechanisms that allow people to exchange goods and services more freely, and encourages the sharing of wealth, rather than the hoarding of it. To do so, we need to connect with the idea of our inherent abundance, rather than fear based scarcity.

Energy and Technology

Our ingenuity and intelligence are one of our greatest assets. We need to retain our technological advances and be self-assured enough to push on to achieve even more. There are a multitude of exciting technological developments already in the pipeline. We should continue to develop these whilst making sure that we harness it, rather than allowing *it* to harness us. And with this new model of the world, there will be a whole new way of looking at energy and technology too. One of our most pressing needs is to discover an energy source that does not create pollution or GHGs. I am not saying that I know what this is, but if we do not find one, then wind-powered prehistoric living is all that we will be doing in the future. Without a viable energy source, we cannot explore beyond the planet's surface either. There is no wind in space.

Spirituality and the Self

We need to completely redefine our ideas about spirituality. Divided, dogmatic, male dominated, rule-based priesthoods are of the past, not the future. Start thinking for yourself instead of simply accepting the beliefs that your parents adopted from their parents. Your direct connection to spirit is your birth-right, it is what you are. Explore ways of knowing this for yourself. If you do not think that redefining religion is possible, then explore a little history, review times when Europe was more firmly under the heel of the Catholic Church, and compare then to now. Maybe there was a reason why the only notable European development between 450 and 1450 CE was the Black Death. We can change anything as soon as we decide that we can.

Be of tomorrow today, be not of yesterday tomorrow. Align your trinity of consciousness and deal with your own shadow. This includes releasing your fears. Fear of being good enough, of having enough, of doing enough. *You are enough.* Let go of your fear of authority, your fear of other people or other entities, and your fear of fitting in. Focus on what you want in life. Act upon your passions, and come to know yourself more deeply. As you do, you will see infinity in yourself, rather than in the 'external' world. Become an example to others of how people live in unity together and with nature. I know you can.

According to quantum physics, the future exists as a wave of potentiality. There are many, many possible futures. Therefore, you cannot predict the future, because there is no *the* future. There are many possible valid futures, and they exist now. If you want to experience something specific in the future, then you need to work on it in the now, by being, in the now, what you want to be in the future.

The Age of Transformation

"We are called to be the architects of the future, not its victims." - Buckminster Fuller.

As we decide to follow the commandment to *know thyself*, layer by layer, we build up a sense of the depth and complexity that is inherent within our true nature. We have a persona that is unique and multifaceted. Beyond that, we are some form of spirit energy that is connected to other simultaneous incarnations, in a manner we barely understand. The purpose of our earthly lives seems to be learning, growth, and experience. We can call this process Earth Life School. Intertwined with this concept, there is a sense of a deeper pattern of evolving consciousness, the *Weltgeist*. We are an aspect of this, it is us and we are it. It represents more than just the physical persona of us, and that means we are not just, or only human.

Within this new model, change is eternal and perpetual. Nothing stays as it is. But notice that in this conception, we also get to choose what things mean. For your future experiences, you can choose to follow any of the visions that I mentioned above, or some other one of your own making.

And it also does not matter what other people choose either – you are not bound by them, so do not worry or fret over other people's choices, simply be an example for them.

When I look back through the contextual frame of our collective past, it seems to me that the *Weltgeist* has been exploring thousands of years of darkness. But today, there are important signs that this is changing. Remote viewing, NDEs, parapsychological studies, OBEs, and reincarnation are all emerging into our consciousness today for a reason. Clare Graves' model and the opportunity to connect with intelligence beyond Earth are also clear signs of a directional shift in the *Weltgeist*. The *Weltgeist* courses through you too; maybe you can feel this change inside your being – I can. What I think is happening is the *Weltgeist* is offering us an opportunity to decisively change direction, and move towards the light. But we are the ones who need to hear this call and choose to walk that path. Together, we can choose to define the spirit of these times as the Age of Transformation. We can decide now that we will end the exploration of darkness, and that from this point on, we consciously choose to journey back towards the light. Understand that if you do choose this path, there is much work to do changing ourselves and how we organise human life on Earth. But do not let the size of the challenge stop you from doing it. Think instead of the prize of redefining and transforming human life on Earth, because that *is* a prize worthy of any amount of hard work.

As we move forward into the light, more of what has been hidden by darkness will be revealed. The keeping of secrets is incompatible with the light. Be this secret cabals of white men conspiring to control the world: *gentlemen, you are welcome in a new world, but your scheming and focus on division you must leave behind.* Secret societies professing to know ancient knowledge: *tell us what you know and do so plainly; allow everyone to benefit from your insights and wisdom*. Government officials who know more about UFOs than they are saying: *the people can now deal with what you know, so share your information and let us face this curiosity with self-assurance, together*. The light will chase all the shadows away, so be prepared to face up to your own darker nature too. We all may need to clean out our own personal closets: be prepared to do that work.

This book itself is constructed of patches of light and dark. If the words were all white on a white background or all black on a black background, then you would not be able to perceive the message. It is because it is presented to you in black and white that it means anything at all. And it is not the message that is important either, it is what you do with the message that counts. So that means it is over to you now. It is time for action.

Choose light over darkness, if that is what you prefer. We all now have an opportunity to walk from the shadows into the light. Connect, integrate, expand… Be an example to others. Who you are is demonstrated by your behaviour, so transform the world, not just by your words, but by your deeds.

BIBLIOGRAPHY

Abbot, J. T., 2017. *The Outsider's Guide to UFOs.* Bloomington: Archway Publishing.

Adamson, P., 2015. *Philosophy in the Islamic World: A Very Short Introduction.* New York: Oxford University Press.

Alexander, E., 2012. *Proof of Heaven: A Neurosurgeon's Journey into the Afterlife.* London: Dr Eben Alexander.

Anka, D. & Ewing, L., 1990. *Bashar: Blueprint for Change.* Seattle: New Solutions Publishing.

Anka, D. & Meyers, S., 1997. *Quest For Truth: One Hundred Insights That Could Change Your Life.* Nobul Press: Iowa City.

Annas, J., 2000. *Ancient Philosophy: A Very Short Introduction.* New York: Oxford University Press.

Anon., 1965. *Upanishads.* London: Pengiun.

Arnheim, M., 2015. *The God Book.* Exeter: Imprint Academic .

Arnold, J. H., 2000. *History: A Very Short Introduction.* New York: Oxford University Press.

Atkinson, W. W., 2006. *Thought Vibration or The Law of Attraction in the Thought World.* s.l.:BN Publishing.

Atwater, F. H., 2001. *Captain of My Ship, Master of My Soul: Living with Guidance.* Charlottesville: Hampton Roads Publishing Company, Inc.

Ayer, A. J., 1980. *Hume: A Very Short Introduction.* Oxford: Oxford University Press.

Barbour, J., 1999. *The End of Time: The Next Revolution in Our Understanding of the Universe.* London: Phoenix.

Bauval, R. & Hancock, G., 1996. *Keeper of Genesis.* London: Penguin Random House UK.

Beck, D. E. & Cowan, C. C., 1996. *Spiral Dynamics: Mastering Values, Leadership and Change.* Carlton: Blackwell Publishing.

Behrend, G., 2006. *Your Invisible Power.* s.l.:BN Publishing.

Benton, M. J., 2008. *The History of Life: A Very Short Introduction.* New York: Oxford University Press.

Berg, Y., 2001. *The Power of Kabbalah.* London: Mackays of Chathham,Ltd.

Black, J., 2008. *The Secret History of the World.* London: Quercus.

Bohm, D., 1980. *Wholeness and the Implicate Order.* London, New York: Routledge Classics.

Braid, J., 1843. *Nueurypnology.* London: John Churchill.

Braid, J., 1960. *Braid on Hypnotism.* In: New York: The Julian Press, Inc.

Brandenburg, J., 2015. *Death On Mars: The Discovery of a Planetary Nuclear Massacre.* Kempton: Adventures Unlimited Press.

Brooks, M., 2009. *13 Things That Don't Make Sense: The Most Intriguing Scientific Mysteries of Our Times.* London: Profile Books.

Bruce, R. & Mercer, B., 2005. *Mastering Astral Projection: 90-day Guide to Out-Of-Body Experience.* Minnesota: Llewellyn.

Buhlman, W., 1997. *Adventures Beyond the Body: How to Experience Out-Of-Body Travel.* London: Robert Hale Limited.

Bush, N. E., 2012. *Dancing Past the Dark: Distressing Near-Death Experiences.* Cleveland: Parson's Porch Books.

Butler-Bowdon, T., 2013. *50 Philosophy Classics: Thinking, Being, Acting, Seeing.* London, Boston: Nicholas Brealey Publishing.

Byrd, C., 2017. *The Boy Who Knew Too Much: An Astounding True Story of a Young Boy's Past Life Memories.* New York: Hay House.

Byrne, R., 2006. *The Secret.* London: Simon & Schuster UK Ltd.

Byrne, R., 2010. *The Secret: The Power.* London: Simon & Schuster UK Ltd.

Byrne, R., 2012. *The Secret: The Magic.* London: Simon & Schuster UK Ltd.

Byrne, R., 2013. *The Secret: Hero.* London: Simon & Schuster UK Ltd.

Campbell, J., 1949. *The Hero With A Thousand Faces.* Third ed. Novato, California: New World Library.

Campbell, J. & Moyers, B., 1988. *The Power of Myth.* New York: Broadway Books.

Carter, C., 2007. *Science and Psychic Phenomena: The Fall of the House of Skeptics.* Rochester, Toronto: Inner Traditions.

Carter, C., 2010. *Science and the Near-Death Experience: How Consciousness Survives Death.* Rochester, Toronto: Inner Traditions.

Case, P. F., 1947. *The Tarot: A Key to the Wisdom of the Ages.* Los Angeles: Builders of Adytum.

Caudill, M., 2012. *Impossible Realities: The Science Behind Energy Healing, Telepathy, Reincarnation, Precognition and Other Black Swan Phenomena.* Charlottesville: Hampton Roads.

Chalmers, D. J., 1996. *The Conscious Mind: In Search of a Fundamental Theory.* New York: Oxford University Press.

Charlesworth, B. &. D., 2003. *Evolution: A Very Short Introduction.* New York: Oxford University Press.

Collier, R., 2013. *The Secret of the Ages.* s.l.:Merchant Books.

Corso, P. J. w. B. W. J., 1997. *The Day After Roswell.* New York: Pocket Books.

Craig, E., 2002. *Philosophy: A Very Short Introduction.* New York: Oxford University Press.

Csikszentmihalyi, M., 2002. *Flow: The Classic Work On How to Acheive Happiness.* Second ed. New York: Rider.

Dawkins, R., 2004. *The Ancestor's Tale: A Pilgrimage to the Dawn of Life.* London: Phoenix.

DeLonge, T. & Levenda, P., 2016. *Volume 1 Gods, Man, & War: An Official Sekret Machines Investigation of the UFO phenomenon.* Encinitas, CA: To The Stars Inc.

Dennet, D. C., 1991. *Consciousness Explained.* London: Penguin Books.

DiCarlo, R. E., 1996. *Towards A New World View.* Erie, PA: Epic Publishing.

Dumont, T. Q., n.d. *Mental Therapies or Just How To Heal Oneself and Others.* Whitefish: Kessinger Publishing.

Dyer, W. W. & Garnes, D., 2015. *Memories of Heaven.* New York: Hay House.

Frankl, V. E., 2004. *Man's Search For Meaning: The Classic Tribute to Hope From the Holocaust.* Fifth ed. London, Sydney, Auckland, Johannesburg: Rider.

Freke, T., 1999. *Taoist Wisdom.* New Alresford: Godsfield Press.

Freke, T. & Gandy, P., 1999. *The Jesus Mysteries: Was the 'Original Jesus' a Pagan God?.* London: Harper Collins Publishers.

Friedman, S. T., 1990. *Top Secret/Magic: Operation Majestic-12 and the United States Government's UFO Cover-Up.* Philadelphia: Da Capo Press.

Friedman, S. T. & Berliner, D., 1992. *Crash At Corona: The US Military Retrieval and Cover-Up of a UFO.* New York: Marlowe & Company.

Friedman, S. T. & Marden, K., 2007. *The True Story of the World's First Documented Alien Abduction Captured! The Betty and Barney Hill UFO Experience.* Pompton Plains: New Page Books.

G.Fuller, J., 1965. *The Interrupted Journey: Two Lost Hours "Aboard a Flying Saucer".* New York: The Dial Press.

Gallwey, W. T., 1975. *The Inner Gamer of Tennis.* London: Pan Books.

Gauld, A., 1982. *Mediumship and Survival: A Century of Investigations.* London: Paladin Granada Publishing.

Good, T., 1996. *Beyond Top Secret: The Worldwide UFO Security Threat.* London: Sidgewick & Jackson.

Good, T., 2013. *Earth: An Alien Enterprise, The Shocking Truth Behind The Greatest Cover-Up In Human History.* New York, London: Pegasus Books.

Gosden, C., 2018. *Prehistory: A Very Short Introduction.* Second ed. New York: Oxford University Press.

Graves, C. W., 2005. *The Never Ending Quest.* Santa Barbara: Eclet Publishing.

Haanel, C. F., 2013. *The Master Key System in Twenty Four Parts.* s.l.:Merchant Books.

Handcock, G., 2015. *Magicians of the Gods: The Forgotten Wisdom of the Earth's Lost Civilisation.* London: Coronet.

Hawkins, D. R., 2012. *Power vs Force.* London: Hay House.

Hellyer, P. T., 2014. *The Money Mafia: A World in Crisis.* Walterville: Trine Day LLC.

Holden, J. M., Greyson, B. & James, D., 2009. *The Handbook of Near-Death Experiences: Thirty Years of Investigation.* Santa Barbra, Denver, Oxford: ABC CLIO.

Hopcke, R. H., 1997. *There Are No Accidents: Synchronicity and the Stories of Our Lives.* New York: New York.

Hopkins, B., 1981. *Missing Time.* New York: Ballantine Books.

Hopkins, B., 1987. *Intruders: The Incredible Visitations at Copley Woods.* New York: Random House.

Howard, J., 1982. *Darwin: A Very Short Introduction.* New York: Oxford University Press.

Howe, L. M., 1989. *An Alien Harvest: Further Evidence Linking Animal Mutilations and Human Abductions to Alien Life Forms.* s.l.:Linda Moulton Howe.

Jacobs, D. M., 1998. *The Threat: Revealing the Secret Alien Agenda.* New York: Simon and Schuster.

Jacobs, D. M., 2015. *Walking Among Us: The Alien Plan to Control Humanity.* San Francisco: Disinformation Books.

Jahn, R. G. & Dunne, B. J., 1987. *Margins of Reality: The Role of Consciousness in the Physical World.* Princeton: ICRL Press.

Jahn, R. G. & Dunne, B. J., 2011. *Consciousness and the Source of Reality: The PEAR Odyssey.* Princeton: ICRL Press.

Janaway, C., 1994. *Schopenhauer: A Very Short Introduction.* New York: Oxford University Press.

Jung, C., 1955. *Synchronicity.* London, New York: Routledge Taylor & Francis Group.

Jung, C., 1957. *The Undiscovered Self.* London, New York: Routledge Classics.

Kaku, M., 2005. *Parallel Worlds: The Science of Alternative Universe and Our Future In the Cosmos.* London: Penguin Books.

Kapadia, S. A., 2013. *The Teachings of Zoroasters & The Philosophy of the Parsi Religion.* Milton Keynes: Aziloth Books.

Kean, L., 2010. *UFOs: Generals, Pilots and Government Officials Go on the Record.* New York: Three Rivers Press.

Kean, L., 2017. *Surviving Death: A Journalist Investigates Evidence for an Afterlife.* New York: Crown Archtype.

Keown, D., 2013. *Buddhism: A Very Short Introduction.* New York: Oxford University Press.

Knott, K., 1998. *Hinduism: A Very Short Introduction.* Second ed. New York : Oxford University Press.

Koch, C., 2012. *Consciousness: Confessions of a Romantic Reductionist.* London: The MIT Press.

Koike, T., 2015. Neural Substrates of Shared Attention as Social Memory: A Hyperscanning Functional Magnetic Resonance Imaging Study. *Elsevier.*

Kuhn, T. S., 1962. *The Structure of Scientific Revolutions.* Third ed. Chicago, London: The University of Chicago Press.

Lachman, G., 2006. *Into the Interior: Discovering Swedenborg.* London: The Swedenborg Society.

Lanza, R. & Berman, B., 2009. *Biocentrism: How life and Consciousness are the Keys to Understanding the True Nature of the Universe.* Dallas: Benbella Books, Inc.

Lanza, R. & Berman, B., 2016. *Beyond Biocentrism: Rethinking Time, Space, Consciousness and the Illusion of Death.* Dallas: BenBella Books, Inc.

Leininger, B., Leininger, A. & Gross, K., 2017. *Soul Survivor: The Reincarnation of a World War II Fighter Pilot.* New York: Hay House.

Levene, L., 2013. *I Think, Therefore I Am: All the Philosophy You Need To Know.* London: Michael O'Mara Books Limited.

Lommel, P. V., 2010. *Consciousness Beyond Life: The Secret of the Near-Death Experience.* New York: Harper One.

Macgregor, T. & Macgregor, R., 2010. *The 7 Secrets of Synchronicity: Your Guide to Finding Meaning in Signs Big and Small.* Carlsbad: Hay House.

Mack, J. E., 1994. *Abduction: Human Encounters with Aliens.* New York: Charles Scribner's Sons.

Mack, J. E., 2008. *Passport to the Cosmos: Commemorative Edition.* Guildford: White Crow.

Magee, B., 1998. *The Story of Philosophy.* London: Penguin Random House.

Malkin, V., 2018. *Dangerous Illusions.* s.l.:Arcadia.

Mapson, K., 2017. *Pandeism: An Anthology.* Washington, Winchester: iff Books.

Marcel, J. & Marcel, L., 2009. *The Roswell Legacy: The Untold Story of the First Military Officer At the 1947 Crash Site.* Pompton Plains: New Page Books.

Marrs, J., 1997. *Alien Agenda.* New York, London, Toronto, Sydney: Harper.

Maslin, M., 2014. *Climate Change.* Third ed. New York: Oxford University Press.

Masri, Z., 2017. *Reality Unveiled: The Hidden Keys of Existence That Will Transform Your Life (And The World).* Great Britain: Awakened Media LLC.

McKnight, R. A., 1999. *Cosmic Journeys: My Out-Of-Body with Robert A. Monroe.* Charlottesville: Hampton Roads Publishing Company, Inc.

Mcmoneagle, J., 1993. *Mind Trek: Exploring Consciousness, Time, and Space Through Remote Viewing.* Charlottesville: Hampton Roads Publishing Company, Inc.

Mcmoneagle, J., 2000. *Remote Viewing Secrets: A Handbook.* Charlottesville: Hampton Roads Publishing Company Inc.

Miller, J., 2003. *Daoism: A Short Introduction.* Oxford: Oneworld.

Moen, B., 2005. *Afterlife Knowledge Guidebook.* Charlottesville: Hampton Roads Publishing Company, Inc.

Monroe, R. A., 1972. *Journeys Out of the Body.* London: Souvenir Press Ltd.

Monroe, R. A., 1985. *Far Journeys.* New York: Broadway Books.

Monroe, R. A., 1994. *Ultimate Journey.* New York: Broadway Books.

Moody, R. A., 1975. *Life After Death: The Investigation of a Phenomenon-Survival of Bodily Death.* London: Rider.

Muller, R. A., 2016. *Now: The Physics of Time.* New York, London: W. W. Norton & Company.

Mumford, S., 2012. *Metaphysics: A Very Short Introduction.* New York: Oxford University Press.

Mumford, S. & Anjum, R. L., 2013. *Causation: A Very Short Introduction.* New York: Oxford University Press.

Nagel, T., 1987. *What Does it all Mean? A Very Short Introduction to Philosophy.* New York: Oxford University Press.

New Scientist, 2015. *15 Ideas You Need to Understand: Human Origins, Theory of Everything, Artificial Intelligence, Relativity, Secrets of Sleep and Many More.* London: Reed Business Information Ltd.

New Scientist, 2015. *The Human Brain: Decoding Consciousness, Ultimate Guide To Memory, The Mind-Body Connection, Intelligence Explained, How to Fine-Tune Your Brain, Sleep & Dreaming.* London: Reed Business International Ltd.

New Scientist, 2016. *The Quantum World: Your Ultimate Guide To Reality's True Strangeness.* London: Reed Business International Ltd.

Nicholls, G., 2011. *Avenues of the Human Spirit.* s.l.:John Hunt Publishing Ltd.

Nicholls, G., 2017. *Navigating the Out-Of-Body Experience.* Woodbury: Llewellyn Publications.

Okasha, S., 2002. *Philosophy of Science: A Very Short Introduction.* New York: Oxford University Press.

O'Regan, J. K., 2011. *Why Red Doesn't Sound Like a Bell: Understanding the Feel of Consciousness.* New York: Oxford University Press.

Osborne, C., 2004. *Presocratic Philosophy.* New York: Oxford University Press.

Pagels, E., 1979. *The Gnostic Gospels.* London: Phoenix.

Pagels, E., 2003. *Beyond Belief: The Secret Gospel of Thomas.* London: Pan Books.

Paret, M. & Atkinson, W. W., 2011. *Hypnotic Fascination.* s.l.:NLP International Ltd.

Parina, 2014. AWARE - AWAreness During REsuscitation- A Prospective study. *Elsevier.*

Peake, A., 2011. *The Out-Of-Body Experience: The History and Science of Astral Travel.* London: Watkins Publishing.

Peake, A., 2012. *The Labyrinth of Time.* London: Arcturus.

Perry, P. & Long, J. J., 2010. *Evidence of the Afterlife: Science of Near-Death Experiences.* New York: Harper One.

Philip, P. W. a. N., 2007. *Mythology.* London, New York, Munich, Melbourne, Delhi: Jonathan Metcalf.

Pinchbeck, D., 2017. *How Soon Is Now.* London: Watkins.

Plato, 2015. *The Republic.* s.l.:McAllister Editions.

Pope, N., Burroughs, J. & Penniston, J., 2014. *Encounter in Rendlesham Forest: The Inside Story of the World's Best-Documented UFO Incident.* London: Thistle Publishing.

Radin, D., 2006. *Entangled Minds: Extrasensory Experiences in a Quantum Reality.* New York: Paraview Pocket Books.

Radin, D. D., 1997. *The Conscious Universe.* New York: Harper One.

Radin, D. D., 2013. *Supernormal.* New York: Deepak Chopra Books.

Radner, M. & Radner, D., 1996. *Animal Consciousness.* New York: Prometheus Books.

Ring, K., 1982. *Life At Death: A Scientific Investigation of the Near-Death Experience.* New York: Quill.

Roberts, J., 1972. *Seth Speaks: The Eternal Validity of the Soul.* San Rafael: Amber-Allen Publishing.

Ruthven, M., 2012. *Islam: A Very Short Introduction.* New York: Oxford University Press.

Sabom, M., 1998. *Light & Death: One Doctor's Fascinating Account of Near-Death Experiences.* Grand Rapids: Zondervan Publishing House.

Sabom, M. B., 1982. *Recollections of Death: A Medical Investigation.* New York: Harper & Row, Publishers.

Satir, V., 1967. *Conjoint Family Therapy.* Palo Alto: Science and Behaviour Books, Inc.

Satir, V., 1988. *The New Peoplemaking.* Mountain View : Science and Behaviour Books, Inc.

Satori, P., 2014. *The Wisdom of Near-Death Experiences: How Understanding NDEs Can Help Us Live More Fully.* London: Watkins Publishing.

Schwartz, S. A., 2017. *Opening to the Infinite.* Washington: Nemoseen Media.

Scruton, R., 1982. *Kant: A Very Short Introduction.* New York: Oxford University Press.

Scruton, R., 1986. *Spinoza: A Very Short Introduction.* New York: Oxford University Press.

Shaw, G. J., 2014. *The Egyptian Myths: A Guide to the Ancient Gods and Legends.* London: Thames & Hudson.

Sheldrake, R., 2012. *The Science Delusion: Freeing The Spirit of Enquiry.* London: Coronet.

Silverstein, A. J., 2010. *Islamic History: A Very Short Introduction.* New York: Oxford University Press.

Singer, P., 1983. *Hegel: A Very Short Introduction.* New York: Oxford University Press.

Smith, P. H., 2005. *Reading the Enemies Mind: Inside Stargate-America's Psychic Espionage Program.* New York: A Tom Doherty Associates Book.

Solomon, N., 1996. *Judaism: A Very Short Introduction.* New York: Oxford University Press.

Stevens, A., 1994. *Jung: A Very Short Introduction.* New York: Oxford University Press.

Stevenson, I., 1974. *Twenty Cases Suggestive of Reincarnation.* Charlottesville, London: University of Virginia Press.

Stewart, I., 2017. *Infinity: A Very Short Introduction.* New York: Oxford University Press.

Streatfield, D., 2006. *Brainwash: The Secret History of Mind Control.* London: Hodder.

Subramaniam, S. & Subramaniam, A., 2017. *Adiyogi: The Source of Yoga.* Noida: Harper Element.

Suprise, D. K., 2012. *Synchronicity: The Art of Coincidence, Choice and Unblocking Your Mind.* Pompton Plains: New Page Books.

Swann, I., 1999. *Penetration: The Question of Extraterrestrial and Human Telepathy.* Great Britain: Ingo Swann.

Talbot, M., 1991. *The Holographic Universe.* London: Clays Ltd.

Tanner, M., 1994. *Nietzsche: A Very Short Introduction.* New York: Oxford University Press.

Targ, R., 2012. *The Reality of ESP: A physicist's Proof of Psychic Abilities.* Wheaton, Chennai: Quest Books.

Targ, R. & Puthoff, H. E., 1977. *Mind-Reach: Scientists Look at Psychic Abilities.* Charlottesville: Hampton Roads Publishing Company, Inc.

Tart, C. T., 2009. *The End of Materialism.* Oakland: Noetic Books.

Tertre, N. D., 2016. *How to Talk To An Alien.* Wayne: New Page Books.

Tolle, E., 1999. *The Power of Now: A Guide to Spiritual Enlightenment.* London: Yellow Kite.

Troward, T., 1904. *Edinburgh Lectures & Dore Lectures on Mental Science.* California: Scotts Valley.

Troward, T., 2012. *The Hidden Power and Other Papers On Mental Science.* Cranston: Angelnook Publishing Inc.

Tucker, J. B., 2005. *Life Before Life: A Scientific Investigation of Children's Memories of Previous Lives.* London: Platkus.

Tucker, J. B., 2013. *Return To Life: Extraordinary Cases of Children Who Remember Past Lives.* New York: St. Martin's Griffin.

Warburton, N., 2011. *A Little History of Philosophy.* New Haven and London: Yale University Press.

Waterhouse, J. W., 2006. *Zoroastrianism.* San Diego: The Book Tree.

Watts, A., 1975. *Tao: The Watercourse Way.* s.l.:Random House.

Weeks, M., 2014. *Philosophy In Minutes.* London: Quercus.

Weiss, B., 1988. *Many Lives, Many Masters: The True story of a prominent psychiatrist, his young patient and the past-life therapy that changed both their lives.* London: Platkus.

Westerhoff, J., 2011. *Reality: A Very Short Introduction.* New York: Oxford University Press.

Wilber, K., 2000. *A Theory of Everything: An Integral Vision for Buisness, Politics, Science and Spirituality.* Dublin: Gateway.

Wolf, F. A., 1981. *Taking the Quantum Leap: The New Physics for Nonscientists.* New York,: Harper & Row Publishers.

Wolf, F. A., 1988. *Parallel Universes: The Search for Other Worlds.* New York: Simon & Schuster Paperbacks.

Wood, B., 2005. *Human Evolution: A Very Short Introduction.* New York: Oxford University Press.

Woodhead, L., 2004. *Christianity: A Very Short Introduction.* New York: Oxford University Press.

Zeman, A., 2002. *Consciousness: A User's Guide.* New Haven and London: Yale University Press.

Zukav, G., 1979. *The Dancing Wu Li Masters: An Overview of the New Physics.* London: Rider.

Printed in Poland
by Amazon Fulfillment
Poland Sp. z o.o., Wrocław